walking
after
midnight

ONE WOMAN'S JOURNEY THROUGH
MURDER, JUSTICE & FORGIVENESS

KATY HUTCHISON

New Harbinger Publications, Inc.

Publisher's Note

Copyright © 2006 by Katy Hutchison

First published in Canada by Raincoast Books

New Harbinger Publications, Inc.
5674 Shattuck Avenue
Oakland, CA 94609
www.newharbinger.com

Jacket image by David De Lossy/Getty Images;
Author photo by Destrubé Photography, Victoria, BC;
Jacket design by Amy Shoup;
Text design by Michele Waters-Kermes;
Acquired by Tesilya Hanauer

Library of Congress Cataloging-in-Publication Data

Hutchison, Katy.
  Walking after midnight : one woman's journey through murder, justice, and for-giveness / Katy Hutchison.
    p. cm.
  ISBN-13: 978-1-57224-503-7
  ISBN-10: 1-57224-503-4
  1. Hutchison, Katy. 2. Aldridge, Ryan. 3. McIntosh, Bob. 4. Murder victims' fami-lies—United States—Case studies. 5. Forgiveness—Case studies. 6. Restorative justice—United States—Case studies. I. Title.
HV6248.H795A3 2006
362.88—dc22
[B]
                                          2006022227

08 07 06

10 9 8 7 6 5 4 3 2 1   First printing

to Bob
for living life 110 percent

contents

foreword

Katy Hutchison has created an excellent primer for handling loss with intelligence and dignity. She gives us a life lived through the eyes of a woman who has experienced the devastation of murder, the anguish of grief, and the redemptive power of reconciliation. *Walking after Midnight* is a book where forgiveness emerges because of the beauty of the author's character, the devotion she provides her family, and her instinctual understanding that "an eye for an eye leaves everyone blind." *Walking after Midnight* is remarkable because of the lack of self-consciousness Katy has as she reaches and pushes toward a life of goodness.

I have taught forgiveness to thousands of people around the world and rarely see such a strong grasp of the truth that my unkindness is not that different from your unkindness. All over the world, people defend their hostility, acts of violence, or simple nastiness because of the bad deeds done to them. I would suggest that our species' willingness to excuse our own terrible behavior because others have done us wrong is the primary reason this world continues to offer so much horror and hostility.

Katy will have none of that.

Even though she is devastated by the loss of Bob, her husband, she treats the young man who murdered him as if he is a valuable human being. She acknowledges that the young man merits punishment for his crime but also is a person who deserves love and a chance to redeem himself. To Katy that is a normal response; for the rest of us, hopefully it can be learned.

Katy actually helps this young man on his journey to healing and a life lived with purpose. The young man's life matters to her, and this magnanimity of character leads Katy to a ministry that provides a fitting testimony to Bob's life. I call this finding your positive intention and teach this to people in forgiveness classes. Katy shows us by her life how the rubber of kindness meets the road. It is called forgiveness, reconciliation, and a desire to leave the world as whole as one can. Her story provides a face and narrative that can serve as an antidote for the endless cycles of violence that consume too many lives and too many countries.

—Frederic Luskin, Ph.D., author of *Forgive for Good*, director of the Stanford University Forgiveness Projects, and codirector of the Garden of Forgiveness at Ground Zero Project

preface

My father had an endearing habit. Before he left a room, he would look around to see if anything needed doing. Was there a dirty dish to take to the kitchen, a jacket to hang up, a book to return to a shelf, or a repair to be done? It did not matter to him who was responsible for what needed doing; he simply took pleasure in tidying up and fixing things.

Perhaps it was this behavior in my father that instilled in me a sense of responsibility for cleaning up after myself and those around me—and pride in my ability to do so. I believe we all need to roll up our sleeves and get down to it, whether we are taking care of small day-to-day messes or managing the aftermath of the extraordinarily difficult events in our lives.

Something horrific happened to me in 1997. An unimaginable event brought my life to a halt and then started it off again on an entirely new course. This book, quite simply, is about the job of cleaning up the mess and repairing the harm caused by this event. It is not an easy story, but it's important. It explores bravery, resiliency, and unconditional love, and it reveals the amazing, unexpected things that can happen when we trust our hearts to tap into those inner resources.

The story is also about forgiveness. I decided very early on that I was not going to define myself, my family, or the person who caused the harm by the act that connected us. Using the principles of restorative justice, we sat face-to-face and explored what led up to, caused, and ultimately followed the event. The courage it took to face the situation head-on was rewarded with a renewed sense of safety, community, and hope.

Choosing an unconventional approach of working together rather than as adversaries allowed us to push past the boundaries set by society's expectations of the justice system. Our experience was about humanity and healing rather than shame and punishment.

I never would have imagined that such profound tragedy would take me on a journey laden with life-altering gifts. But it did. I am grateful for the opportunity to share my story.

acknowledgments

Thank you to New Harbinger Publications for bringing my story to the United States. My appreciation to Michelle Benjamin, my Canadian publisher, for finding my unopened letter and then taking a chance, and to the team at Raincoast Books for making the writing of this book a reality. And to my editor, Audrey McClellan, for telling me at the start that napkins have no feelings, and for sticking with me until I got it right.

To my mother, Betty, for her unconditional love; and to David for his quiet wisdom, Heather for asking all the right questions, Greg for his enthusiasm, Jenny for believing in me from day one, and George for keeping me nourished on the road.

To Bob's family for their grace and support as I found my way.

To John, Barbara, Terry, Judi, and Robin for welcoming my family into your family.

To my best-friend-in-the-whole-world Shauna for being a sounding board and my handler, and for sharing so generously in every way, especially in giving me a home-away-from-home. To Colin for putting up with an extra wife, Cody for giving up her bed, and Tate for the constant reality checks.

To Nicola for forty years of friendship, Marilynne for being so real and fun, Robert for the Sinatra, and Lana and Madi for being forever pals.

To Gordie and Shauna for finding your own way. To Louis Eisman for teaching me how to work hard and listen to my heart, and to Sal for "general contracting" the temple of grace.

To my friends in Squamish, especially Pete and Gill, for building a proud legacy to honor Bob. To Shelley, Dave, Brooke, Tara, Morgan, and Bonn for being old friends and new friends. To Mary and Bob for "getting it." To Richard and Lois for moving past the loss, and to Doug for finding me a good lawyer.

To Ryan for bravely coming along on this exceptional journey, and to his family for their encouragement.

To Reta Clark, Brian Hall-Stephenson, Sue Connell, and Julie Czerwinski for encouraging me to stand up and speak out and to the thousands of young people across the country who have opened up their hearts and minds to my story. To the Corrections staff and volunteers who made it possible for Ryan and me to work together.

To the restorative justice community, and especially Dave and Sandi, for lighting the way and keeping the candle burning.

To gns for the wonderful learning environment my children look forward to being a part of every day.

To Adam and Carlie for expanding their family to include us.

To Linda-Loo for taking such good care of us all.

To my grandmother, writer Catherine Anthony Clark, for planting a seed. To my father, who continues to teach me years after his death.

To Halle for sitting patiently at my side each day as I wrote.

To my son Sam for the constant reminder that "Life is Large" and for still letting me hug him.

To my daughter Emma for her innate sense of justice and exceptional creativity.

And my sincere gratitude to Michael, my beloved husband, thank you for the wings and directions home. You have expertly steered the boat as we navigated uncharted waters. I love you with all my heart—forever, and a day.

auld lang syne

Should auld acquaintance be forgot
and never brought to mind?
Should auld acquaintance be forgot
and days of auld lang syne?

When I open the front door around 11:00 P.M. on New Year's Eve, 1997, I do not expect to find a police officer on the step. It is a struggle to sort out the incongruity of the scene. I recognize the officer, not from the police station, but from the local hospital where she works as a clerk. She handles admissions and takes your information when you go in for lab tests. I remember her name is Brenda. She must be a volunteer auxiliary officer, I decide. Brenda is trying hard to maintain her composure. I think instead she might faint.

Pushing past Brenda is Gordie. Less than an hour before, he had been sitting at our dinner table, enjoying a delicious meal. The candles are still burning on the table; dessert dishes are waiting to be cleared. A collection of favorite jazz tunes is playing in the background.

I began preparing the bouillabaisse early in the day. Wanting to get rid of the fishy wrappings before our guests arrived, I cut up the mounds of fresh sole and scrubbed the mussels. As usual, my husband, Bob, called from his office to give some input on dinner. I smiled to myself, knowing he would breeze through the door after the messy prep work was done and finish things off. Bob's famous bouillabaisse...

Eleven years earlier, the first time I was to meet Bob's sister Donna, Bob had suggested that he make his famous bouillabaisse for the occasion. Happy that I did not have to test my culinary skills on her, I was also delighted to think that my husband-to-be knew his way around a kitchen. Was there anything this man couldn't do? However, when I saw no sign of groceries, or even a shopping list, on the afternoon of the dinner, I ventured to ask Bob how his preparations were coming along. It was only then that he casually mentioned he had never actually made bouillabaisse and perhaps I could find a recipe for him. Frantically looking at my watch, I grabbed my well-used copy of *The Joy of Cooking* and fled in exasperation to the market. Bob took off in the opposite direction to the beach for a run.

By dinnertime it had all come together. While chatting to his sister, Bob stood over the stove, wineglass in hand, stirring and adjusting the seasonings. I recall watching in amazement, thinking about how I had sacrificed some basic preparations for the evening, like showering and running the vacuum over the brown shag carpeting in our rental suite, to help Bob save face. I wondered what other gourmet delicacies he would be renowned for.

More than a decade of celebrations with family and friends has passed since then, and one of our customs is that Gordie Griffiths, his wife, Shauna, and now their two-year-old daughter, Delaney, too, come up from Vancouver to Squamish for a New Year's sleepover. This year they arrived in the early afternoon, and while Delaney played with our four-year-old twins,

Emma and Sam, in the family room, Shauna and I put on the kettle and began puttering in the kitchen. Gordie got the kids going with his crazy antics as he waited for Bob to wrap up his half day at the office.

I am sure not much law gets practiced on the morning of December 31, but there are some time-honored traditions that are always observed. Once the secretaries have been sent home, Bob and his partner, Doug, go for a run on the Alice Lake trails. Bob cherishes both the business relationship and the friendship he has with Doug. They complement one another well. Bob's impulsive and bigger-than-life character is offset by Doug's thoughtful, grounded, and meticulous nature. They like to wrap up the year together on the running trails that they have shared for many years.

As soon as Bob walks through the door, he heads straight for the stove, stopping to welcome Shauna with a hug on his way. He pulls me close and kisses me as he grabs the wooden spoon from my hand. "How's my bouillabaisse?" he inquires. While there seems to be some tension over the order in which ingredients have been added, it is quickly lost to the anticipation of the festivities that lie ahead.

Gordie is like a big puppy dog, patiently waiting for Bob's attention. He amuses himself by reading a book about animal poop aloud to the kids. Each page produces uproarious laughter and pleas for an encore. Bob leaps into the room to join the fun. The kids squeal with laughter.

Shauna and I exchange a knowing glance and wait for the routine that invariably follows. First, Bob will discover some obscure food item is missing from the evening's menu. Then Gordie will suggest that they run to the grocery store to pick it up. It is really an elaborate cover-up for their annual New Year's trek to the pub. No matter how well organized Shauna and I are, they always think of something that is missing, and off they go.

We have been friends for ten years, since 1987. In the early days, keeping Bob and Gordie under control was a challenge. Shauna and I hauled them out of more than one pub, putting an end to numerous hilarious and potentially embarrassing situations. Each time we were adamant that we would no longer tolerate their bad behavior, but our scolding had no effect, and in spite of the punishing hangovers they suffered, they were always ready for more.

Since Bob and I moved to Squamish eight years ago, he and Gordie have seen less of one another. Distance, children, and the demands of their careers make it more difficult to get together. New Year's Eve has become their regular opportunity to play catch-up.

Those first celebrations were wild. One year the two of them got into the martinis and then into my closet and were in full drag by four o'clock. After begging us to do their hair and makeup, they disappeared across the street to a neighbor's party. Gordie distinguished himself by goosing an older gentleman dressed in a kilt. Shauna and I went over and brought them back home, finally tucking them into bed around 9:00 P.M. after several attempted escapes, including a partially naked slide down the banister that nearly took it off its posts.

Another year, exhausted from chasing three babies around the house, Shauna and I could not keep our eyes open until midnight and went to bed just after the kids. Bob and Gordie amused themselves for several hours by filming themselves dancing together to country music. Because the video camera was perched on the corner of the kitchen counter, they had to dance on their knees in order to be visible in the lens.

And last year, 1996, there was almost a disaster. As the women cleaned up after dinner, the men went to the garage to listen to Bob's collection of vinyl records. A friend they had duct-taped to a barstool toppled down the driveway. Luckily they'd thought to put a bicycle helmet on him. They soothed his sore back by spending several hours in the hot tub with a bottle of Rémy Martin.

This year has a mellower feel. While Bob and Gordie do go in search of the missing grocery item, they are back within an hour. They are happy to play with the kids while Shauna and I set the table. As we lay out the plates, I notice a beautiful new TAG Heuer watch on her wrist. She calls Gordie over and he proudly holds out his arm to model the matching men's version. They have bought the watches to celebrate the other significance of this December 31—it is the tenth anniversary of their engagement. Bob and I still wear the TAG Heuers we exchanged on our first wedding anniversary. The four of us stand together, contemplating the wonder of passing time and strengthening bonds so perfectly represented by the watches.

One by one, the three children are settled into bed. The last to be tucked in is Sam. He always hates to miss out on anything. Bob patiently inches him closer to the stairs, and when he finally begins to climb them, Bob calls out, "I love you, Sam." The contented smile that follows his words fills the room.

The flavors of the bouillabaisse have melded beautifully. We dish it up, accompanied by big chunks of French bread and a mesclun salad. As we seat ourselves around the table, it feels as though we have already said all that needs to be said. Just sitting together, watching familiar faces in the flicker of the candlelight, is enough. The promise of a new year stretches before us. We quietly reflect on the years left behind and the good memories we will carry forward with us.

Our neighbors, Shelley and Dave, join us for dessert. They bring along their two youngest children. While their two older sisters are out with their teenaged friends, the young ones are excited to get to stay up with the adults to ring in the New Year. They happily curl up by the fire in the family room with a movie while we make room for two more chairs around the dining table. Wine is poured, a cheese platter appears. The intimacy of the earlier part of the evening lightens. We relax into easy laughter and festive anticipation as midnight draws near.

Shelley and Dave are a valued part of our life. They live behind us on another cul-de-sac. A small, forested trail connects the two streets. Their older girls have babysat for us since Emma and Sam were just months old. Shelley is a dear friend and my role model as a mother. She possesses a natural sense of nurturing and goes about all she does with grace. Managing a home with four children, she is also involved in Dave's business and active in our community.

As we settle around the table, Dave mentions that Jamie is having a party. Jamie is the teenaged son of another close friend in Squamish, Richard Cudmore. We met Richard and his first wife, Sue, when we moved to Squamish and soon found ourselves included in their close circle of friends. Richard has another important role in our lives. He is our family doctor. He stitched up my hand after a dog bite and watched our children being born. When Richard remarried in November, Bob was a member of the wedding party, proudly wearing his kilt for the joyous celebration.

Richard and his new bride, Lois, have gone to Mexico for a vacation over Christmas. Jamie, Richard's son, usually lives with his father, but has been spending the holiday with his mother at her condominium in Squamish. Evidently, he has returned to his father's home and has invited some friends over to celebrate the New Year.

Hearing this, Bob goes to the phone to call Jamie to make sure everything is under control. The young person who answers cannot locate Jamie. Assuming he has just gone to get something from his car or the carport, Bob waits a few minutes and then calls back. This time someone different answers, and this person cannot find Jamie either. Bob hangs up the phone. His face has lost its expression of relaxed joy. Pacing around the kitchen, he announces that he is not comfortable with the prospect of Jamie inviting a number of people over without Richard there to supervise.

Gordie is upstairs, looking in on Delaney, when Bob tells Dave he wants to go check out Jamie's party. The Cudmores' home is a short walk away—at the opposite end of our cul-de-sac and down a steep hill along a narrow trail. Dave is not keen on the idea, since he has just arrived and has barely had time to sit down. But Bob insists and calls to Gordie to grab his jacket.

Gordie is game for another excursion, even though he does not know where they're going or why. The three of them put on their jackets, Bob cracks open a beer for the road, and they head out our front door into the snow.

Minutes later Dave reappears, expecting to find Gordie and Bob with us. He tells Shelley, Shauna, and me that the Cudmores' place is full of kids and he assumed the other two had thought better of getting involved and returned home. Since they have not come back, we send Dave to the Cudmores' to find them. Rolling our eyes, we joke that these men are playing out some type of Three Stooges skit, and by the time they find one another they will end up missing the countdown to midnight.

But now a police officer is standing on my doorstep, and Gordie shoots into the house like a pinball that has broken free of its game. He is not the same person who left a few minutes earlier, enjoying the casual camaraderie of his friends. As he comes through the door, the warm dinner smells and intimate laughter are sucked out into the December air. I am disturbed by the fact that he is alone. I am accustomed to him sticking with Bob. They are a duo. Now there is something terribly wrong with the act. Bob isn't there, and Brenda is at the door in full police uniform.

Gordie struggles to get a coherent sentence out. "Bob has been hurt, you need to come."

My first thought is that since I have been drinking wine throughout the evening, I cannot drive. Clearly that is not even a consideration, since Brenda, the reluctant officer, appears to be our driver. This is not looking good.

I feel like I'm in slow motion and fast-forward all at the same time. I agonize over what shoes to put on. I'm wearing the new red-and-black-plaid wool skirt I bought when Bob and the twins and I were shopping in Vancouver on Boxing Day. But the elegant black high heels I have chosen for our dinner party are not the right shoes to wear out the door with the police. Bob gave me some red suede hiking boots for Christmas. They'll work with the skirt, I decide. They'll be safe, too, and that seems important just now. I sense I'm going to need my feet firmly planted to face what is coming.

Shauna and Shelley sit in stunned silence in the kitchen. They assure me they will watch over the twins, who are fast asleep upstairs with Delaney. As I leave them, I look for something safe to think about. I wonder if they will soak the pots from dinner. The bouillabaisse kettle will be messy to deal with later.

As the police car winds through the maze of streets that leads out of our subdivision toward the highway, I try to focus. The blood is rushing in my temples and my mind is jumping back and forth between drastically different scenarios. I imagine first that Bob has slipped on the ice, breaking an arm. Then I leap to the awful possibility that he has dropped dead of a heart attack. Either is entirely possible. I want to throw up.

Gordie has become strangely quiet in the back of the police car; I sense that he is struggling to retain his composure. He keeps leaning forward between the front seats as if he wants to say something, but then can't get the words out.

It seems to be taking all of Brenda's energy and attention to keep the police car moving quickly in the right direction. As I have feared, we are heading toward the local hospital. She pulls up in front of the low building and I am out of the passenger seat before the car has come to a full stop.

Usually the smell of a hospital chokes me as soon as I walk through its door, but tonight it seems oddly familiar. Only weeks before, I had been discharged from the same facility. Once again, autumn had got the better of me, as it has done since the twins were small. One year it was strep, the next bronchitis, and this year it was pneumonia that finally earned me the reward of several nights in a narrow hospital bed for IV fluids, medication, and some much-needed rest. Bob has no idea how much work it is to get through the day with the twins. Their energy is relentless. It consumes me. I wonder if this pattern of collapsing will continue to be an annual event. Something I can look forward to. That is a pathetic revelation. I make myself stop resenting Bob, just in case things are serious.

Pushing through the double swinging doors into the trauma room, I recognize the doctor on call. Ken is one of Bob's running companions. Most Sunday mornings, he will join the men for their weekly trek through the network of trails around Alice Lake, often ending up back at our house for coffee. But now he is holding the defibrillator paddles in his hands, preparing to jump-start Bob's heart. Our eyes lock for a second. The blood drains from Ken's face when he sees me. Only now does he realize the trauma patient he is working on is Bob. Up to this point, his focus has been on continuing the chest compressions that began in the ambulance. The gurney is positioned in such a way that Ken has not been able to recognize Bob's face.

The two paramedics who were in the ambulance with Bob watch for a moment and then gently push me out through the doors toward the nurses' station. I can still see them through the doorway; they stand away from the doctor and nurses, watching and pacing back and forth.

At the counter, the nursing supervisor hovers and is oddly calm. I realize that Ken, the paramedics, and this nurse are all desperately clinging to everything they have been trained to do in unthinkable situations. But I also know that at some point their shift will end and they will get to go home. I am not at work. My shift is never going to end. At this moment, I have to be in control. Whatever is happening here, it is going to need my full attention and energy.

I don't want to make the nurse uncomfortable by asking her too many questions. I try to be calm. I do ask her if she thinks Bob is going to be okay. She assures me he will be just fine. We both know that is not true. But the pretending lets me feel some control for the moment. Can I use the phone? Thinking perhaps I could use some more support, I call two friends at their respective New Year's parties. Do they mind coming up to the hospital? Bob isn't well. Of course, they are on their way.

The paramedics keep looking over at me through the doorway from the trauma room. Whatever they are watching is making them speak anxiously and quietly to one another. I try to ignore them, try not to second-guess the situation. I control what I still can, my body, my breathing, stockpiling the reflex to breathe in and out; it is unconscious now, but it may not be later. A constant urge to relieve myself becomes a welcome distraction. It allows me to periodically check my face in the bathroom mirror. Even under the pale fluorescent light, I can see each time that I am still there. No visible damage yet. The nurse assures me that voiding frequently is a totally normal reaction. Normal is good. She seems pleased to be able to offer reassurance in what is becoming an increasingly stressful situation. Neither of us wants to acknowledge what we both know is happening.

I am vaguely aware of Gordie's presence at the end of the hospital corridor. He is agitated and frightened but is keeping himself away from me and from the trauma room. I hope there is someone to support him. Right now it cannot be me.

And then Ken appears through the swinging doors of the trauma room. The sound of his voice yanks me out of my suspended state. His face is ashen and his movements awkward. The words jerk out of him like a child's sobs. "I don't know what happened. Bob is dead."

Ken's crying fades beneath another noise. It takes a second before I realize it is coming from me. It is not a sound I have heard before, or one I knew any human was capable of making. My knees give way. I am doubled over on the floor and the noise keeps coming. I don't want it to be like this.

People begin to appear from all directions. My neighbors arrive first. They immediately left their party when I called just minutes ago. Anne is a psych nurse, and Ray is the captain of the North Vancouver Fire Department. They have spent their careers witnessing scenes like this. I am hoping they will be able to handle the chaos and support me as well.

Somebody must have called our home, because Shelley is the next to arrive. It is Shelley who takes control. The emergency ward is filling with the typical aftermath of an evening of celebration. Many of the patients in the waiting area are drunk and become curious about the obvious seriousness of the activity in the trauma room. Shelley gains access to a small doctors' lounge where I and the friends who have come to support me can have some privacy. In the same way Shelley and I have always moved effortlessly around one another's kitchens, we now set to work building a safe cocoon in which we can cope.

We begin making phone calls. There is too much commotion going on out in the hallway to think that word is not already spreading. I need certain people to hear it from me. I sense that the telling of it may help me believe that Bob is dead. Apologetically, I wake Bob's partner, Doug, with my first call. I feel even more helpless when I have no answers to his questions.

My sister Jenny and I spent over an hour on the telephone earlier that day as I was preparing dinner. Revealing the painful reality that her marriage of almost thirty years was over, Jenny told me she and her husband were going to explain the situation to their two adult children over brunch on New Year's Day. As horrible as it was to hear her say the words, her honesty was a welcome relief, since I had long suspected she and her husband were having problems. Now I am calling her to come and be with me. "Bob is dead. I need you here. I have no idea what has happened. The police are with me at the hospital." I hang up and think to myself how much Jenny hates driving at night in the winter. But she will just have to do it.

The most difficult call is the one to Bob's sister, Donna. Her shock and fear are palpable. She has suffered so much loss in her life. I feel a sense of responsibility for adding to the list that has included both her parents and an infant son. The fact that I have no clear idea of how Bob died makes me feel worse.

Suddenly my knees are weak. I steady myself against the back of a chair, then slip into it to wait out the waves of dizziness. A nurse produces a warmed blanket that I wrap myself in.

Shelley calls my brother David in Victoria. I weep as I hear her trying to speak the unspeakable. He will go to my mother to tell her. She cannot be told over the phone. I can see this is going to get away from me. It's too big for me to control. I let them do what has to be done.

More police officers begin to arrive, and it is obvious from their conversation that something went terribly wrong at the party Bob had gone to check on. One young officer gently tells me I need to see Bob before the coroner takes his body away. He will stay with me, but warns me that because the police anticipate they are dealing with a crime scene, I cannot touch Bob. I need more support for this and ask him to wait a few minutes.

Shelley calls the minister of the United Church I have just started attending. Claire Bowers is nothing like the menacing Catholic priests of my youth. She is small, vibrant, and the very person I need by my side. Within minutes she is there with me. Her cool, careful words soothe the scorching fear I am trying to swallow away.

Supported on either side by the officer and Claire, I move slowly into the trauma room. Slipping behind the curtain that encloses the cubicle, I look first at Bob's feet, hoping to gather more courage as my eyes move up his body. The familiar musky aroma of his leather jacket lingers under the pungent hospital smells. When my gaze reaches Bob's face, I am stunned. He has been intubated in an effort to find an airway. The tube protrudes crudely from his mouth, held in place with adhesive tape. While there is no glaring sign of injury, little things do not seem right. There is a small cut I do not recall on the back of his hand, and a quarter-sized bruise on his right temple. I am confused by the vomit smeared on the side of his head and dripping from his ear. Someone explains that it is normal for the stomach contents to be expelled as the body shuts down.

And then a sense of peace envelops me. As I take in the image of Bob's dead body, I feel calm. This person who has been the center of my world for so many years is definitely gone. The life is gone from those unforgettable blue eyes. The battered shell that remains knows no pain. Wherever Bob is now must be much safer than where he has just come from.

There is nothing more that can be done at the hospital. The police explain they're launching a thorough investigation with the coroner and will tell me as soon as they know what caused Bob's death.

It's four in the morning. I leave the hospital to wait for Emma and Sam to wake up so I can tell them their daddy is dead.

chapter 2

family gathering

A widow bird sat mourning for her Love
Upon a wintry bough;
The frozen wind crept on above,
The freezing stream below.
—Percy Bysshe Shelley

The drive home from the hospital is surreal. Throughout our neighborhood there are groups of teens gathered in bunches. Three here, seven there; they are everywhere. I think they know something I don't.

My sister Jenny's car is in the driveway. Breathe in, breathe out. I walk up my own front steps. It will never be the same in this house. Our home. My home. My oneness is everywhere. Jenny is there at my door as I walk in. She takes my coat, guides me silently to the couch, and holds me in her arms.

Darkness envelops the sleeping house except for the glow of the gas fireplace and the light from the aquarium Santa brought Emma on Christmas morning. Staring into the bright blue water world, I see that all four fish are floating motionless on top of the water. I am trying to fathom a dead husband. Dead fish are too much right now. I click the tank light off.

The kettle whistles from the kitchen as Jenny makes the first of hundreds of pots of tea we will steep as we try to make sense of life and death. I wrap myself in a nightgown, as if it were an enormous bandage that could contain the hurt, and curl up on the couch under my sister's arm. No one else could do this with me. She doesn't ask anything; she just listens. The tears come. My emotions veer from shock to fear to disbelief. I cannot grasp the reality or the finality of what happened. All I can do is cry.

Shauna and Gordie move quietly around the periphery. I am worried that he is in shock. Their daughter is still asleep upstairs. I try to imagine what is going on in their minds, but it is too much to think about. We are all helpless.

I realize there is so much I do not know—so many pieces of a horrible jagged puzzle that we will have to try to make fit. I slowly tell Jenny what I do know. Bob, Dave, and Gordie went to check on a party at the Cudmores'. Bob didn't come home. A police officer came to the door to tell me something had happened. She took me to the hospital, where I watched the doctor trying in vain to resuscitate him. I can still smell the vomit as I recount the scene.

Standing in the hall, I can see into both Emma's and Sam's bedrooms as they sleep through the end of dawn. When they wake up, their innocence will be gone. They will come down the stairs and ask where Daddy is. Why is Aunty Jenny here? I want to stop the clock while I figure out how I am going to tell them. My legs begin to shake and I return to the safety of the couch.

Emma is the first to appear. Sleepily, she nuzzles into me on the couch, pleased to see the fire. Her damp, curly hair smells of peaceful slumber. Lily, our dachshund, leaps up to snuggle her. When Emma notices Jenny, she straightens up and realizes that things are not as they should be. I search for the simplest words to say. "Emma Bear, I have something hard to tell you. Something bad happened last night to Daddy." Inhale. Pause. "He is dead." Done. All I know. How could there ever be the right words to say this? She is quiet for a time, trembling under my arm. I want to be sick.

"Mummy, you have a big problem. You need to find a new husband, because I will need a new daddy," are the words she finds. And so it is with Emma, the first of many words of wisdom. Unabashed honesty, reality, and innocence all packaged together in one four-year-old girl. She willingly goes to Jenny and is soothed by her cuddles and whispered assurances.

Minutes later, Sam comes down the stairs. He is quicker to detect the tension in the air. Immediately he asks where his daddy is, and I can feel his anticipation and dread. I hold him by the shoulders and stare into the brilliant blue eyes his father gave him. "Sammy Bob, you have to listen carefully while I tell you this. Something bad happened to your daddy last night, and he is dead." It is no easier to find the words a second time. I brace myself for his reaction, knowing it will not be like Emma's.

The shouts and the tears rip through the protective cocoon of tea, firelight, and suspended time Jenny and I have created. He pulls away from me angrily and dives into a ball behind a chair. "I don't want Daddy to be dead," he screams. The questions to which I have no answers tumble out. "Where was Daddy? What was he doing? Who called the ambulance?" Desperately trying to make real the unreal, Sam, the four-year-old man of the house.

All of a sudden it is daylight. I creep upstairs to our bedroom and hesitate before entering. The neatly made bed stands awaiting us. Bob and I should be lying there proposing New Year's resolutions, making love. I tell the bed to stop waiting, that he is gone. The radio has turned on automatically and the local news is playing. "A well-known Squamish man was found dead at a local house party. Police are suspecting foul play. His name has not been released pending notification of next of kin." I barely make it to the bathroom before I throw up.

I can't bear to think that people are going to hear about Bob's death from anyone but me. Sitting on a kitchen stool by the phone, I begin methodically working through our address book. Jolted out of the few hours of sleep they have had since ringing in the New Year, everyone reacts in much the same way —shock, disbelief, asking questions for which I have no answers.

Shauna Markham is my closest friend in Vancouver. We met when I was at university and she hired me to work for a summer government employment program. We hit it off instantly and fell easily into a friendship full of generosity and inspiration. I know that Shauna and her husband, a lawyer who often met Bob for a beer on Fridays after court, will be devastated to hear of Bob's death. But I also know that Shauna will be able to find a place for her grief and still be there for me.

Ever since she was a child, Shauna has dealt with the loss of her mother. Her mother didn't die. She suffered from mental illness and came in and out of her daughter's life repeatedly until just after Shauna's second daughter was born. Since then she has chosen to have no involvement with Shauna. I've been inspired by the way Shauna has carried on, carving out a fulfilling career, building a happy marriage, and being a great mother in the face of such loss. Her example inspires me now.

There is someone I do not know how to begin to find: Bob's ex-wife, Joanne. They were married for barely a year in the early 1980s, and he told me the relationship had ended badly. There were no children, so there had been no contact after the divorce. I hope there will be someone there for her when she hears the news. Even people who are no longer a part of our lives make a mark when they leave this world for good.

Sam asks for Cheerios. At this moment I realize that regardless of the grief and horror swirling over my family, I am still a mother. After breakfast my children will want to play in the snow. They will need lunch, dinner, a bath, and stories read before bed. And tomorrow they will need those things all over again. I look into their eyes and decide that I will not allow their lives to be about Bob's death. Finding their favorite plastic bowls, I pour the cereal. Breathe in, breathe out.

Sitting across the kitchen table from Emma and Sam, I tell them, "Somewhere underneath all this, we will find a gift. I cannot imagine right now what it will be, but I promise we'll find it. And when we do, we will hold it close to our hearts. Maybe one day we will be able to share the gift." Wordlessly, they both nod.

Emma turns her attention to the darkened fish tank. With a tone of exasperation, she asks why all four fish are floating on top of the water. I apologetically explain that they seem to have died. She rolls her eyes at me and wanders away to contemplate one dead father and four dead fish.

It is late in the day. The winter light lies flat on the snow. The thought of darkness makes me uneasy. I am alone in the living room. Its high ceilings give me some breathing space, though my lungs never seem to fill up fully. Curled up in the corner of the couch, I listen to Jenny reading to Emma and Sam by the fire across the hall in the den. My sister is a librarian. She will sit with the children for hours, patiently reading, repeating favorite passages over and over—their rhythm keeping us all afloat. Her marriage is over. My marriage is over. Jenny will keep reading to my children.

I watch my brother David's car pull up in front of our house. He has brought his wife, Heather, their two teenagers, my other brother, Greg, and my mother. After Shelley called him last night, David went to find my mother at her friend's home, where she was staying to celebrate New Year's Eve. He gently told her of Bob's death, watching as pain and grief blanketed her like a thick fog. Then he gathered his family together to come and bear witness. As they slowly climb out of the car and fill their lungs with the snowy January air, I know they are wishing they were anywhere but here. I want to call out to them that they should turn around and go back to Vancouver Island, that I am sorry about the mess. I cannot find the words, and they keep coming.

My mother comes straight to me on the couch. She holds me silently. I bury myself in her embrace, inhaling the warmth, trying to ignore for a moment the intensity of her shaking. She has suffered from a near constant tremor in her hands since a bout with rheumatic fever in her teens. When she is nervous or upset, the movement becomes more intense and harder for her to control. Now it reminds me why she is here.

The rest of the family finds Jenny and the twins, distracted for a split second by the pleasure of being together. I hear Emma say matter-of-factly, "My daddy is dead. We have to find a new one." I can feel her audience cringe.

The phone rings constantly. Some calls I take, others I do not. Periodically I hide in the bathroom and cry. I peer at my face in the mirror, amazed at the lines and half-moons of darkness shock and grief have placed there. I am someone else. I am a widow. I cannot remember eating today, but I still continue to vomit.

David finds me and tells me the police have phoned and they need me to come and give a statement. He will take me to the station. In the car, I remember the drive we made together nine years before. We were going to my wedding. He and Greg were giving me away because my father had died of cancer four years earlier. David brought I Ching sticks in the limousine and told me my fortune. I tried to calm my bride-white excitement to take in his thoughtful, important words. He spoke of passion, pleasure, conflict, reconciliation, and a changing spiritual vision of the universe. I vowed to remember the fate he predicted and tucked the sticks into my bouquet, where they could later be dried for posterity.

This time there are I Ching coins instead of sticks, and David's calm, reassuring words again help me get where I am going. "You are a dragon. A perfect blend of the best of both you and Bob. You can, with confidence and success, move forward with great impact in unexpected directions."

I struggled when I stood looking at Bob's body in the hospital, thinking my strange feelings of peace and empowerment were wrong. But David's reading tells me that the way I'm feeling is okay. I am profoundly hurt by my loss. I will grieve. But I can also find a new and meaningful way in which to see myself in the world.

The staff sergeant reiterates the suspicion expressed the night before by the officer at the hospital. It will take autopsy results to confirm, but the police believe Bob died because he was assaulted. The sketchy details they have been able to put together suggest a huge, out-of-control house party. Bob walked into the middle of it. The staff sergeant gently asks me to recreate our evening, scribbling down the who, what, when, and where of what was supposed to be the start of a fresh new year.

When we leave the station, David tells me that he will be with me for many parts of the journey upon which we are embarking. He will be there at home for me, he will be there for my children, he will support the rest of the family—but he cannot handle being there to witness the reality of the criminal investigation. I am neither upset nor surprised by his admission. My father's gentle and caring nature lives on in my brother.

When we return to the house, Jenny and Heather are getting Sam and Emma ready for bed. Greg and Mum are making tea and toast. They have been writing down messages as they receive them, filling the pages of a notebook beside the phone. Without discussion we are creating a process to manage the business of death.

Suddenly it is too much. I need to be alone, to see if sleep is even possible. My family makes me promise that I will call down to them if I need anything. Lying in bed, I think of the things I need. I need my husband to be beside me where he belongs; I need my children to stop asking where Daddy is. I do not need to be hosting this holiday gathering. I need my family to be in their own homes and beds, not strewn around my home as if it were some kind of horrible work camp. At last I find sleep.

When I wake up, Bob's death sits on my chest like an invisible weight. The magnitude of the loss presses me deep into the mattress. It puzzles me that my body can feel intact when my heart is so broken. The waves of fear begin, and my tears do nothing to wash them away.

Emma's face appears at the door, but she runs away when she sees me struggling to compose myself. I can hear her in the kitchen telling David, "Mum is crying again." He appears beside me and slides onto the bed to hold me as I sob. There is nothing to say. At last it is enough. I want to get up and face the day.

Examining my face in the mirror after I shower off the tears, I think I look sixteen again—childlike and vulnerable. I feel like I am sixty, worn thin by loss and sorrow. I dress in black. It is a protective shield. It will warn people not to ask.

Downstairs, Jenny and Mum are making more tea and mounds of toast. All anyone can stomach is comfort food. Sam is finishing a tantrum that began when Mum poured milk over his Cheerios after he asked to have them plain. It was the last serving in the box, so she is doing her best to dry them out for him. She tries microwaving them, and they shrink into inedible nuggets. He is screaming for more cereal and to have his dad come back.

Greg and I decide to drive to the store for more cereal and to replenish the toilet paper supply, which has reached a critical low. It feels bizarre to be doing a mundane chore when all hell is breaking loose and my life has come tumbling down. I am sure people can tell just by looking at me. This is in fact true, since word of the identity of the body found at the party has spread rapidly around town, even though police have not officially released the name. The young grocery store clerk stares awkwardly at me, trying to hide her reaction, but then dissolves into tears as she reads the name on my bank card. I wonder if she was at the party.

By midday the phone is ringing constantly. My family scribbles notes in the book by the phone. The police call to confirm that the autopsy is being performed that afternoon and they are hoping for results by the next morning. I call my boss to say that I will not be in to work for a while. He is crying so hard that I cannot make out his reply.

The dogs are not managing well. They are looking for Bob and are agitated that he is not here to perform their accustomed rituals. I call the kennel we use when we go away on vacation and ask if they can board Lily and Max until I can get my life in order. They come over immediately to pick them up. Both the dogs and I seem relieved by this arrangement.

Gordie returns from the police station, where he has given his statement. He and Shauna look frail and exhausted, and they decide to take Delaney back to Tsawwassen. I am unable to imagine what this must feel like for them. It is hard to let them go. I hope their own families will build a cradle of support around them.

Shelley and Dave have been trying to reach the Cudmores in Mexico to give them the news. Because of the holiday, it is difficult to get through to the resort. Shelley is now in touch with the Canadian consulate for help. There will be no right words to say. I want to cushion the blow for them, for everyone.

An endless procession of devastated friends and neighbors passes through the house. Clutching lasagnas, casseroles, pots of soup, or baskets of freshly baked muffins, they look at us in stunned shock and disbelief. I try to spend a moment with each of them to reassure them that we are going to be all right.

Rumors that Bob was killed by one or more people at the party he was checking on have begun circulating. By early evening, the story is being reported on the television news. Sketchy details, the suspicion of foul play. The police are investigating.

I think of the number of times I have watched similar news coverage, imagining that I would be totally incapacitated if something so awful were to happen to my family—I would shrivel up and die from grief. But now I am watching the story and it is about us. It does not feel the way I expected. I do not feel incapacitated. There is no shriveling. It is almost the opposite. I feel as though I have expanded in order to take in the immense pain for myself, for my children, and for everyone around us.

A car pulls into the driveway; a man walks through the snow toward the front steps. He carries a flower arrangement. It is the first of over seventy to be delivered. We end up with vases on every available surface. The scent of the flowers becomes overwhelming and their beauty ghastly. In the end I plead with the local florists to divert them to the local hospital or seniors' home.

Shelley has brought her daughters over to play with Emma and Sam. Morgan, who is nine, was at our home on New Year's Eve when her father went to check on the party with Bob. She is coloring with Emma. They are making a small sign, which Emma has dictated to Morgan. They affix a ballpoint pen to it for a handle, like on a placard. Emma strides past me, showing her sign to anyone she meets. It reads, "I need a new daddy." No one knows what to think. I'm not sure that the words need to be taken literally, but I am glad her honesty and innocence enable her to articulate her feelings.

Bob's partner, Doug, appears. His face is ashen, distraught. He goes through the motions as my lawyer. He has likely done this task for hundreds of clients, only this time the name he's reading on the will and insurance documents that I produce from our impeccably organized file cabinet is that of his friend and partner. He is devastated. I search for words to comfort him. There are none.

Sam is afraid to go to bed. I can completely understand. Someone devises an elaborate pirate game that turns Sam's bed into a galleon and has his perfect little cherub face covered in Halloween makeup so that he resembles a buccaneer. I am too exhausted to protest, but in the back of my mind I realize I want to regain control of my family and move them quickly through this hell.

The next morning, I wake up when Shelley calls to warn me that the town is filled with media. I peer out the window and see news trucks parked in our cul-de-sac. Bob's name has been released, and our lives are about to become part of the public domain. I cannot shower it away, and I emerge ready to do battle.

Emma and Sam are tucking into a platter of cinnamon buns that appeared from nowhere. In the living room, two friends are quietly taking down the greenery, lights, and ornaments from the mantel. How will I ever celebrate Christmas again? It has always been my favorite time of year. I insist on having our tree up and the house totally decorated by December first so that we can spend the days leading up to the twenty-fifth listening to Christmas carols and baking endless batches of cookies. I know already that it will never feel the same again.

During the evening news broadcast, it is as if the walls of our home have been lifted away. There is no protection, nothing to lean against. Emma requests cat makeup and joins Sam in his pirate ship to listen to Jenny's bedtime story. The rest of us discuss what has to be done next.

I have managed to contact almost all of our friends. They set up a network of communication amongst themselves, knowing that we cannot keep them all informed of the moment-by-moment developments. Tonight after the late news, I get a frantic phone call from one friend I was not able to reach. He was skiing in Alberta and found himself watching the tragedy unfold on the television beside all those other stories that we think will never happen to us. I feel hopelessly responsible for all the anguish and pain. I do not want to put anyone through this. I retreat to my bed.

I wake up suddenly at 4:30 A.M. Grief and fear wash over me, my nightmares less scary than my reality. I try to rearrange myself in the middle of our bed but cannot stop clinging to my side, afraid to face what is not there beside me. The doctor in emergency gave me a bottle of sleeping pills, but I cannot bring myself to take them. I am afraid that if I do not let the shock and pain of Bob's death come at me with full force now, it will hit me later, distorted and intensified by time.

The rest of the house is quiet. Every bed, couch, and inch of floor is covered with exhausted family. Sleep eludes me, so I pick up a pen and begin to write. The words seem to arrive on the paper before the pen, and an hour later I have written a eulogy for Bob.

Sun shines through the den window. Emma's knees are tucked up into her flannel nightgown as she sits on the window seat. She is immersed in a book about owl babies. My perfect daughter, quietly soothing her soul. This scene fills my heart with hope and tells me we will be all right. We will have a funeral, we will bury Bob, and with him we will bury some of our sorrow. Our family and friends will drift back to their own lives, the snow will melt, and we will be all right.

con te partirò

We know where you are, Bob—You're in all of us, and anytime we're wondering over a choice, or pushing the envelope of our endurance, you'll be called into service.
—David, writing in the guest book at the funeral

A shiny white casket is covered in a blanket of blue-dyed carnations. There is organ music

Suddenly I sit up, my chest tightening as I remember the dream that pushed me from deep, exhausted sleep into the dim stillness of my bedroom. I worry that if I do not stay focused, Bob's funeral will look exactly like that nightmare. Again the tears begin as soon as I turn on the shower. I wash some of the sadness down the drain. I know there will be more. Some of it may not wash away.

The first visit of the day is from the funeral director. He tells me that he cannot confirm a date for the funeral until the autopsy is finished, but he wants me to start thinking about how the service might look. I know from my dream what it is not going to look like. I shiver as I remember.

The funeral director, who is probably accustomed to dealing with people who have no idea how to handle the business of death, appears unprepared for my response. Bob had definite ideas for his memorial tribute and had expressed his feelings to me on several occasions—most recently only a week earlier. One afternoon we were enjoying that delicious space of time between Christmas and New Year's, those days when even if work must resume, it is treated differently. Feelings of expectation and celebration linger in the air. Bob had been testing the small stereo system I gave him for Christmas. He was a lover of music of all kinds and had put in a new CD by the blind Italian tenor Andrea Bocelli; I had tucked the CD under the Christmas tree as a gift from the dogs. Many of the lyrics were in Italian, but there was enough English in one piece to make its haunting sentiments perfectly clear, and when "Time to Say Goodbye" blasted at full volume through the white winter air, Bob determined that this was the piece of music he would want played at his funeral. As he waved his arms like a conductor, he reminded me that people must wear black to funerals and that he wanted to be buried, not cremated. He was so full of life and promise that the consternation in his voice made me laugh. At the time, I promised that I would oblige, sure that I would not have to worry about it for many, many years.

The funeral director takes notes and promises to call me as soon as we can set a date. As he is stepping carefully down our icy front steps, I notice a small crowd gathering in front of the house. The coroner, a police officer, and my minister—Father, Son, and Holy Ghost. Reporters and TV cameras are following them toward the house. It looks like a scene out of a movie, and I wonder what it is doing in my life.

My mother holds me in her arms, flanked on either side by my brothers, as the visitors tell me what we have already feared to be true. The autopsy has confirmed that Bob died of a massive brain hemorrhage. They believe the injury was caused by a blow to the head, likely a punch. The officer explains the police are continuing the painstaking process of interviewing the young people who were at the party. It will be slow going, since investigators believe there were close to two hundred people in the house at the time.

After they leave, I retreat once again to the sanctuary of my shower, where I can say the words aloud. "Why, why, why?" More tears down the drain. I wish for a moment I could follow. Instead, I towel off and wrap myself in layers of warm, black clothes. Things are looking up. I didn't vomit this time.

As I walk down the stairs, the town's coroner, also a family acquaintance, is standing alone in my living room. He is removing the ornaments from my Christmas tree. Slowly he turns each one in his hands before tucking it in the box at his feet. He must think this is one of the last tasks I can cope with. He's right. My mind jumps ahead and I shudder, imagining how I will feel when I bring the ornaments out again next Christmas.

Looking through to the kitchen, I watch as my brother Greg serves a bowl of soup to Harvey Oberfeld, a veteran reporter who has been sent to cover the story. The two men share a hushed conversation over the steaming soup, and I wonder how long my world will be stretched out of shape to accommodate vignettes such as these.

Richard and Lois Cudmore, along with another couple, Peter and Gill, who are mutual friends of ours, have been able to get an earlier flight back from Mexico. Shelley is in contact with them and tells me they will arrive in Squamish after midnight. She and Dave promise to bring them over right away. I need them to know that we will get through this together. I set out a bottle of wine and eight glasses, unable to leave Bob out, following a routine we have observed so many times over the years we have lived in Squamish. On the table sits a candleholder I received weeks earlier at our annual ladies' Christmas party. It is a clay ornament with human figures, hand in hand, dancing around the flame. It is a circle of friends. I count the figures. There are seven. Four times two, minus one.

Richard and Lois, Peter and Gill, Dave and Shelley, and I sit together, trying to comprehend the devastation. Lois announces she will not go back to their house. Peter and Gill will have Richard and Lois stay with them. Dave is quiet and detached. I worry about all that must be going on inside his head. Shelley is sensitive to the fears and concerns of each of us. The same grace and clarity that weaves together their family of six spills over onto our cherished group of friends. We talk about our disbelief, we laugh and cry at memories of Bob, and we plan the practicalities of saying goodbye.

Richard takes me aside before they leave and asks me how Bob's father died. This happened before I met Bob, but I recall hearing that it was a stroke following a series of heart attacks. Richard says he stopped at the hospital on his way to me and read the autopsy report. He wonders aloud if there could be an error in the findings and if, in fact, Bob suffered a fate similar to his father's. I am stunned at this suggestion and think that stress and the long day of travel must be clouding Richard's medical judgment.

When he leaves, I call the police to tell them I am uneasy with his comment and with the fact that he had access to the autopsy report. While I understand that he is our family doctor, surely, since Bob's death occurred in Richard's home, there should be some measures in place to manage sensitive information.

The funeral director and I are seated side by side at the computer as I compose the obituary. A few feet away, the bathroom door is open. Emma is in there doing her thing, and I am apologizing for the odor. He laughs and explains that he has children himself—this would be a common occurrence in his home as well. Just then Emma announces that the toilet is plugged. As the perfect words to memorialize Bob swim around in my head, I watch the funeral director, tie flipped over his shoulder, plunger in hand, resolving the problem. I find solace in the contrast between my sorrow and simple acts of humanity.

One of the TV reporters has asked for some film footage of Bob to accompany coverage of the police investigation. Knowing that the images the station uses will become part of its archives, I do not want to simply hand over our precious home videos. Somehow I figure out how to transfer a selected series of video clips onto one VHS tape and give it to the reporter. Bob would have been impressed by my sudden burst of technological expertise. Up to now it was all I could do to stop the VCR flashing 12:00.

The constant stream of visitors continues throughout the weekend. I spend time with each person, and then they often curl up with family in another part of the house to work through their shock. One man walks up to the door, leaves a box on the step, and leaves. I carry the package into the house and unload its contents on the kitchen counter. Duct tape, light bulbs, batteries, bungee cords, a screwdriver, string—man things from a man who did not know what else to do. Bless him.

Our next-door neighbors deliver an envelope. They are a young couple who, like Bob and me, moved from the city to experience life in a small town. Unfolding the note, I read:

Observations of the Next-Door Neighbor

Bob McIntosh was just our next-door neighbor.

He was the one that we saw enthusiastically hosing down his wet suit on the front driveway after a grueling yet triumphant triathlon.

He was the one that had to drag one of the twins kicking and screaming down the street so that the whole entire family would be participating in the walk-the-dogs routine.

He was the one that spent what seemed like hours meticulously washing, waxing, and buffing his cherished baby on four wheels.

He was the one that was omnipresent while edible morsels sizzled on the backyard barbecue and he would poke his head around the side of the house to chat.

He was the one that headed from the house on training runs with his buddies way too diligently every Sunday morning!

He was the one that, after coming home late from a hard day at the office, theorized that a glass of wine would solve all the problems of the world.

He was the one that coached and encouraged Emma on her form and technique during the summer makeshift front yard nude waterslide event.

He was the one that we met on the trails taking Sam real backwoods mountai.n biking, training wheels and all!

He was the one that joined Kate in hosting many social gatherings filled with music and laughter from numerous friends and family. (...Later some evenings, faint voices came wafting across the backyard from the hot tub.)

He was the one that agonizingly watched us cut the back grass with an old push mower and ended up mowing our front yard for us, while we secretly calculated how much that would have cost if he were to charge us his lawyer's rate.

He was the one that practically leapt across the rock garden that separates our properties just to hug us when we announced our engagement.

He was the one that always had a wave and a smile.

And he wasn't just the next-door neighbor, he was a friend, and we will miss him.

I am told that the local funeral home will not accommodate the number of people anticipated for Bob's funeral. I ask about a church instead and watch the funeral director and his partner exchange sideways glances. They gently suggest that the civic center might be the best venue. I cringe, thinking of saying goodbye to Bob in the gym where Sam, Emma, and I attend Mums and Tots each week.

Weeks earlier we celebrated Richard and Lois Cudmore's wedding at a local hotel. Now it will be the setting for the wake. No one has any idea how many people will attend. Bob loved a good party, and I am determined to make this send-off an event he would never have wanted to miss.

I go to the funeral home to pick Bob's casket. I am confident with this decision, since we have a long-standing family rule to follow. It was my Aunty Jean who came up with the best strategy in this department. Always choose the second-least-expensive casket. No exceptions. I shop quickly and return home.

In June we had celebrated Bob's fortieth birthday. At that time, I went through our photograph albums and put together a slide show that we shared with friends and family. There are images of Bob growing up, on our honeymoon in Europe, taking part in his sporting pursuits, and playing with our kids. The last shot is of Bob at our wedding, flipping up his kilt and mooning the guests. The perfect ending. I put together a compilation of music from Bob's enormous collection and plan to run the slide show at the funeral.

Shauna and Gordie have come back. Their daughter is staying with her grandparents, and they have had some time to process what has happened, but I am sure they are reluctant to be back to the constant reminders. Like everyone else at my house, they must be looking forward to leaving the funeral and returning to their own lives.

When Shauna Markham arrives, her embrace brings me renewed strength and resolve. Sensitive to the shock and grief that has taken up residence with me in the form of family and a constant stream of visitors, she manages to stand back slightly and retain her perspective. She finds a place to hold her sadness over Bob's death and is present for me and for my children in a way no one else has been.

She takes me aside and gently asks me what I am going to wear to the funeral. Taking her into my walk-in closet, I gesture at all the black clothes and assure her I will find something suitable. Suitable, apparently, is not enough. Shauna tells me it has to be fabulous. Bob would want me to look spectacular. She suggests we drive into Vancouver and look for the perfect ensemble. I smile at her ability to suggest a road trip in the middle of a crisis, but I can't do it. Just being in the grocery store or at the police station is more than I can handle. However, she is on a mission, and she recruits the other Shauna, whom she barely knows, to accompany her.

The Shopping Shaunas, as they immediately dub themselves, relieve me of my credit card and make a list of my rapidly shrinking measurements before they depart. Later that afternoon, I find myself seated in a cloud of tissue paper as I unwrap the wardrobe they have brought back to me on spec. There is simple but beautiful lingerie, hosiery, shoes, a great suit, and a light wool dress. There is even a perfect linen hankie.

It does not stop there. They have also outfitted my sister, who walked out her own door with only the clothes on her back. And they brought Emma the most beautiful tiny dress. Long-sleeved, soft black velour with tiny bunches of periwinkle-blue flowers all over it. The flowers are the color of Emma's eyes. The eyes she got from Bob.

I want to deliver the eulogy myself but worry that I may become paralyzed by emotion at the funeral. I call on a friend who runs the local radio station. He and I meet at the studio on Sunday night and tape the words so they can be played back at the service.

On my way home from the studio, I notice neighbors all along our street tying bright blue ribbons, the color of Bob's eyes, to the winter-bare trees in their front yards. I wonder how long the ribbons will hold us together.

I have found the words, assembled the photos, taped the music, and laid out the perfect outfit. Bob would like this party; I wish I was not going to be alone.

The odd calm that has evolved as people sink into their grief is shattered on Monday, January 5. The police make an arrest. Witness statements indicate that a punch was thrown by a young man named Ryan McMillan. I am so thankful that the criminal justice part is going to happen swiftly. I remember Bob saying that if an arrest is not made within the first days following a crime, the chances of identifying the culprit are drastically reduced. Bob deserves this aspect of the tragedy to run smoothly.

The images on the evening news push everything farther into the realm of unreality. We watch in sickened silence as a tall, heavyset young man in handcuffs is taken from a police van. I am frightened by him. I cannot believe this person has anything to do with my life. A charge of manslaughter has been laid and there will be a court appearance in the morning. The people around me sigh with relief. I feel anything but.

We have become accustomed to functioning within the protective cocoon of my home as if it were a base camp on a difficult climb. We feel exposed and vulnerable when we venture out to the courthouse. Ryan McMillan's appearance is over in minutes. Bail is set at $25,000. He is not allowed any contact with his girlfriend or a number of other key witnesses. There is a curfew in effect.

Our layers of black clothes do not shield us from the raw chill as we stand, shivering, outside the courthouse. A crowd is huddled near the doors as both families emerge. Young people yell obscenities at the media from across the road and call out their support for their friend Ryan. Charlie McMillan, Ryan's father, directs an angry tirade at my mother, who had been looking toward his family in empty disbelief and despair. I do not want this for anyone. This is all bad, all painful. We need to go home.

When my father died of cancer in 1985, I was twenty-four years old. Chasing a long-distance lover to Philadelphia, I was not there with my mother and siblings to say goodbye. I made it back for the funeral, stopping at the visitation the night before to see his body and convince myself that he was really gone. And now, the night before Bob's funeral, family and friends are gathering to convince themselves that he is really gone.

Sam cannot wait to go see his dad. Emma is very clear: "I do not want to see Daddy in a box." Actually, I don't want to see him in a box either. I suggest to Emma that she come with us, but she does not have to look. She asks if she can bring the dead goldfish with her so they can be buried together. I love the suggestion, but I know that some others may not see the humor. I explain that we will have to hold a separate memorial for the fish at a later date.

We arrive at the viewing. I feel light-headed and nauseous and try to concentrate on the Pat Metheny music that I sent ahead so there would be some quality of Bob in the room. Deep breath in. I open my eyes and see the shell of what once was. They have done a good job putting Bob's head back together after the autopsy.

Bob's black suit is beautiful. He never had the chance to wear or enjoy it. We bought it on Boxing Day. It was still at the shop being tailored when Bob died. When I called the menswear store three days after his death, the owner weakly said he knew why I was calling. Choking on his condolences, he explained that the suit was already being couriered up to me.

Emma and Sam have written goodbye notes for Bob. I tuck those, along with a family photograph, into his breast pocket. Someone has already slipped a good cigar in there as well. I find out later that the lower half of the casket has been loaded with bottles of Bob's favorite wines. One for the road.

Sam is in my brother David's arms, and he tries to crawl into the casket to hug Bob. My other brother, Greg, carries Emma. Her head is buried in his shoulder as they walk past.

Just as my family did for my father's funeral, we sit across from one another in the limousine. I remind everyone about the Clorets incident. Desperate to rid our mouths of the ghastly taste of nerves, we shared an entire roll of the dark green mints en route to Dad's funeral. When we arrived, just before stepping out in front of the church, we realized that our tongues had turned green. The fits of laughter that erupted, and our urgent efforts to suppress them before leaving the car, have become part of the family mythology.

As the limousine drives through town, I notice that although it is midmorning, many businesses are closed. Their doors are festooned with blue ribbons.

I am not prepared for the scene when we enter the civic center. There are a thousand people packed into the cavernous gym. Standing room only, it is a sea of black. The media have set up in a cordoned-off area, promising to film the service from behind the family.

Bob's casket sits at the front, draped in a length of McIntosh tartan, remnants of the cloth used to make the kilt he wore when we were married. A white banner across the red and green plaid reads "Life Is Large," the title of a song we loved to sing as a family and a phrase that says it all about Bob.

The minister, Claire Bowers, begins her address:

Bob, the athlete—runner, swimmer, cyclist, skier. Bob, the lawyer—passionate, detailed, caring, concerned. Bob, the lover of wines and fine foods—chardonnay, merlot, a tour of Napa Valley. Bob, Katy's husband—words and acts of love filled their lives. Bob, daddy to Sam and Emma—"Daddy-O is home!" Quick and light their feet come running. Bob, the friend—the friend of so many. Mentor, trainer, days and evenings of laughter, wine, and good company. Bob, the music lover—a quiet house was not a home. Music was the language of the soul. A soul that was daring and risking and passionate, savoring all that life had to offer. For Bob, life was large.

*Never taken for granted. Never wasted. Never lost. Not
for a moment. For one such as this, we have come to
honor, to say farewell, to grieve, to remember in the
company of friends. May the divine light be with you all.*

Expressing her condolences to Emma and Sam, Claire asks
them to join her at the front. Sam reaches into his pocket, producing a triathlon medal Bob won recently, and proudly lays it
against the spray of white roses and heather. Emma, with
Claire's help, lights a white candle that rises from the circle-of-
friends holder atop the casket. I am so proud of my brave
children.

The music of Gordon Lightfoot, Diana Krall, Eric Clapton,
and Loreena McKennitt is interspersed between Claire's words,
my eulogy, and the slide show. Sam sits next to me and dabs at
the tears streaming down my face with a hankie. No child should
have to be here doing this, but I am so thankful he is.

Claire finishes the service with a reflection:

*Bob loved justice. He made it his life's work. Justice for
Bob was intrinsically wrapped up in social issues. He
was deeply concerned about the social issues that loom
large in our time. He wanted to do something about
them because this was his way. A commitment for Bob
meant action. His death—tragic, untimely, so, so
unnecessary—is a wake-up call to us all. We must ask
ourselves what kind of society we want and then with
passion and commitment do something to make it
happen. Giving up, abdicating our responsibilities, is an
act of cowardice. Finding ways to creatively, with hope
and love, heal our collective brokenness is an act of great
courage and an act that Bob himself would applaud.*

*Bob was a man with a daring heart. We all need to
be people with daring hearts. Hearts that are loving, that
understand how difficult it is to change and to grow, and
at the same time require change and growth to happen.
A door of opportunity has opened for us. Rare insight*

has been given to us. Seize the moment, and enter through the door. You will never regret it. It may be painfully difficult. Your heart may ache. And if you are not used to living from the heart, this will be frightening. But you will live closer to the depths of life and experience more of life's beauty and mystery, for these are the gifts given to the daring hearts. If Bob's life gives you this, I cannot imagine a greater gift. I know so many of you are devastated by Bob's death. Be a community for each other. Isolation and anger are poisons. Let your pain be pain and love each other.

Katy, your courage is truly amazing; your love for Bob complete and wholehearted. I know that you know how much support and love surrounds you. And I know that you know the path that lies before you. In the days that come, I pray your path be lined with beauty, light, and love.

And still there is today. There is goodbye, farewell, God-be-with-you, Bob. We will miss you terribly. We will miss your face. We will miss your laughter. We will miss your presence. We will miss your passion. We will miss you.

An army of Bob's male friends and family members assemble an honor guard the length of the room, through the foyer, and out into the parking lot. Emma, Sam, and I walk together behind the casket. The Andrea Bocelli piece begins and I hear my Italian friend's gasping sobs as she hears the phrase "Con Te Partirò." Time to say goodbye.

At the hotel the tension dissipates somewhat, since we have chosen not to permit the media inside. The fireplace crackles with a huge wood fire; wineglasses are filled. In a meeting room, we have set up a gallery of photographs of Bob. People walk slowly past, tears and laughter mingling at the memories conjured up.

A favorite sitter whisks Emma and Sam away to explore the hotel. I stand close to the fire and a receiving line forms.

For two hours, I embrace a continuous stream of family, friends, neighbors, and colleagues. People have traveled from all over the world to pay their respects. Despite the sadness we are all wading through, there are beautiful glints of joy and connection throughout the afternoon. I hope people can leave remembering the love and friendship in that room, and not just the tragedy that brought us here.

It has been a long day. Many people leave as darkness begins to fall. A group of Bob's friends moves through to the brewpub for an evening of storytelling and camaraderie. I go home with my family and collapse from sheer exhaustion.

The next day is the interment. I have dreaded this part all along. While there will not be nearly as many people, I expect the ritual to be frightening and empty. Emma is sure that she does not want to see her daddy put in the ground. Jenny is happy to stay at home with her and curl up by the fire with a stack of books. I wish I could stay home too.

After an hour's drive down the Sea to Sky Highway in a limousine, we arrive at the cemetery in North Vancouver. A lone piper stands near the plot. Amazing Grace. Bagpipes have always marked important passages in my life.

The service is brief and the wet cold is bitter. A shovelful of earth is dumped over the casket. Sam is given a bright blue helium balloon to send up to Bob. We stand in a circle and watch it disappear into the gray sky. I turn away from the dark ragged hole in the ground, preferring to look up and imagine Bob being set free into the air we breathe. I feel reverence for all this. But I am also determined that it is not going to define me. I fill my lungs and remind myself that somewhere in all this, there will be a gift.

A small group of family and friends gathers at our home for the evening. It is time for people to get back to their own lives. I am ready to start rebuilding mine. Guy, a doctor friend, asks if there's anything he can do for me before he leaves. I remember some unfinished business in the corner of the den. Net in hand, he bravely extricates the four dead goldfish from their watery morgue and flushes them down the toilet. Emma agrees to a brief bowlside eulogy, and we are done with funerals at last.

chapter 4

libido manor

Bobs wise up in their second marriages. They have moved, in three separate stages of connubial awareness, from total innocence to total antipathy to total acceptance. When they try again, Bobs avoid marrying restless women—even though they understand that there will always be some restlessness. Women who are successful at being wives of Bobs must be strong, self-assured, self-reliant. And able to amuse themselves when their Bobs are out in the garage. They must also be masterful at calling their Bobs in from the garage when they can stand it no longer.
—David Rensin and Bill Zehme, *The Bob Book*

No one who grew up in Vancouver would admit to meeting a future spouse at the nightclub Richards on Richards. Except me, of course. I could say that Bob and I were introduced to one another by mutual friends. But to be completely honest, even without that brief introduction, we would have ended up kissing in the alley behind the club the night we met.

I was sharing an apartment in downtown Vancouver with Jackie, a girlfriend I had met at Simon Fraser University. We had both done business administration degrees, focusing on marketing and organizational development, and had graduated in 1983 with impressive transcripts and good jobs. Jackie went to work as the assistant to a fashion buyer for a large department store. I took a position as a sales representative for a trucking company, but shortly after accepted a job offer from one of my clients, Mr. Jax, a large clothing manufacturer.

The back end of the fashion industry fascinated me. It was not the glamorous job some might expect. There was no travel, no schmoozing with models or huge expense accounts. Instead I was exposed to the nitty-gritty details of the manufacturing process. We could have been producing auto parts as easily as high-fashion women's apparel. My responsibilities were to purchase and schedule the arrival of the raw materials that kept the factory going.

My boss and mentor was a street-smart, charismatic man named Louis Eisman. He had worked in the huge garment factories of his native South Africa and ruled with an explosive temper. I learned more from Louis in my first months at Mr. Jax than I did in five years at university. We became close friends, and Louis gradually delegated tasks to me that he had only trusted himself to handle.

My job quickly consumed me. We ran through three complete business cycles each year as we conceived, sold, produced, and released the collections for spring, fall, and holiday. The company grew from a small designer house to a publicly traded company with several factories and an extensive import/export program. I couldn't have been better positioned to add practical experience to the theory I had learned in business school.

Both Jackie and I drove white 1984 Pontiac Fieros and had fallen victim to some of the more regrettable fashion trends of the 1980s, big blond hair being the most glaring example.

We were often mistaken for sisters and enjoyed the attention we got when we went out together.

In the spring of 1986, The World Exposition was in full swing and Vancouver's nightlife was buzzing. One May evening we found ourselves at the infamous Richards on Richards, where Jackie ran into Jamie, her favorite aerobics instructor. Jamie was out with his roommate, Bob, who was celebrating the end of his law-school exams. The mood was festive, music blared, cocktails flowed, and the four of us danced for hours.

There was an instant chemistry between Bob and me. I could not stop staring at his eyes. They were the most brilliant shade of turquoise blue I had ever seen. His facial features, while angular, were almost pretty. Soft, thick, dark curls framed his face and brushed the top of his collar. I knew without asking that he must be athletic. His body moved with a quick and natural grace. Watching other women in the club looking at him, I sensed that he was accustomed to the attention.

After a walk outside, where we could talk without competition from the raucous dance music, that chemistry boiled over. As good as it felt, I put the brakes on the passion and suggested that we revisit the attraction in the cool light of day. The truth was, I was drawn to Bob both physically and, to the extent that one can be in the space of a few hours, intellectually. If it was meant to be, he would call the number I penned on a scrap of paper and pressed into his hand as Jackie and I got into a cab to go home.

Bob did not call. I moped around for a few weeks and then began dating a lawyer I had met on a ski trip to Whistler. He was kind and extremely smart, but I was bored. The entire time I was with him, I was thinking about Bob. To make matters worse, his apartment was just around the corner from the house Bob shared with Jamie, and I often saw Bob and his current date driving around the neighborhood in his little red convertible. I could not get him off my mind.

Early in the fall, as I was realizing how unfair it was for me to stay in a relationship I was less than enthusiastic about, Bob left a message for me at my office. The secretary who took the message knew of Bob and his reputation as a rogue. She scrawled a note across the bottom of the pink message slip, suggesting I think carefully before returning the call.

Not only did I call Bob back, but I suddenly found the courage to break things off with the other poor man who had been doing his best for the last few months to capture my heart. With the path cleared, I was ready to put my energy into gaining Bob's full attention.

And what a challenge that was. Bob and Jamie's rental house was dubbed Libido Manor by their friends. It was the scene of weekly parties frequented by a crowd of young, single professionals who liked to work and play hard. Both Jamie and Bob were attracted to fair-haired women, and their parties became known as the "all-blond revues." To my delight, I found I was Bob's regular date, much to the chagrin of Jamie, who preferred not to narrow his field of play.

Soon after we got together, Bob began an internship with a midsized law firm in downtown Vancouver that specialized in litigation, and we settled into a routine of seeing one another several nights each week. I suspected there were some straggling relationships Bob still had to end. Trying to be mature and self-assured, I convinced myself that he would soon wind them up and we would see one another exclusively.

As we spent more time together, I got to know the person hiding beneath the flawless packaging. I came to the conclusion that as great as Bob was to look at, the visual impact of his appearance made it hard to get to know the person within. I also saw that it made it difficult for Bob himself to grasp who he really was. He struggled with the way people saw him and, in turn, how he saw himself.

Bob had told me that his father, who died of a stroke just before Bob entered law school, had once had a drinking problem. Bob exhibited one of the common characteristics of adult children of alcoholics: a need to seek the approval of others. His father had been tough on him, never satisfied with Bob's

achievements. While Bob seemed like the last person to be dealing with self-esteem issues, he was still desperately trying to
please his father. He pushed himself relentlessly in both his
studies and his athletic pursuits. To compensate, he required
substantial downtime. He craved quiet space where he could lose
himself in a book or listen to music with no interruptions.
Those became some of my favorite times with Bob.

He described his closeness to his mother but told me that
his older sister had chosen in recent years to have little contact
with the family. Tight bonds with his male school friends and
their families filled a void that existed within his own family. He
was a loyal companion to a number of men he had known since
elementary school.

Bob's aspirations for the future were modest considering the
size of his public persona. He told me he wanted a home and a
family of his own, and he joked that he would know he had made
it when he had a Subaru station wagon and a dog named Stan.

Bob was adamant that his life be as balanced as possible.
He saw the important physical and emotional benefits of spreading his energy smoothly over his commitments to work, sport,
family, and friends. On more than one occasion, that philosophy caused difficulties with his employer. Bob simply refused to
dress up in a suit and spend his Saturday in the office unless
there was real work to be done. Unfortunately, many other
interns competing for jobs were happy to do so. He grappled
early on with the expectations the legal career he had chosen
placed on him.

I spent Christmas 1986 with my brother Greg and a family
friend. Jackie was with her parents, and my mother had gone to
be with my sister, her husband, and their children. I proudly
produced a full turkey dinner for the three of us from the little
kitchen in the apartment I shared with Jackie. As we enjoyed the
mince tarts and brandy sauce, the phone rang. It was Bob. He
asked if I would like to come for a nightcap and meet his
mother. An introduction to his family seemed like a major step
toward solidifying our relationship, and I wasted no time getting

out the door. My poor dinner guests found themselves waiting on the street for a taxi as I left my own party to be with him.

Seeing Bob away from Jamie and their busy party house was an eye-opener. His mother, Amelia, who was called Pam by the family, lived in the heart of suburbia with her gentleman friend, George. Her split-level house was immaculate, and its gold brocade upholstery, swag light fixtures, and thick shag carpeting were comfortable and familiar—the accessories of a typically middle-class family.

Pam was barely five feet tall, with red hair, a mischievous grin, and an unmistakable English accent. As we entered the kitchen, she was moving at lightning speed, filling the punch bowl with ginger ale, cranberry juice, and a generous portion of vodka, then stirring the contents of a pot on the stove. Bob laughingly referred to the concoction as her "famous whisky wieners," and they were indeed tiny cocktail sausages rolling about in a warm bath of ketchup, Worcestershire sauce, and Scotch whisky. Impaled on toothpicks, the minifranks were devoured almost before they hit the table.

Pam's eyes lit up when we entered the room, and, wiping her hands on a tea towel decorated with famous English castles, she came to greet us. There was no doubt she adored Bob and was proud of the fact that he was interning at a law firm. She welcomed me with that wonderful and intimate conspiratorial manner that women develop in the company of men. While Bob greeted some more friends in the living room, I stayed with Pam and helped her clear the counter of glasses and crumpled paper napkins. Their poinsettia motif matched the paper cloth covering the dining table, and I complimented her on her festive holiday decorating. We chatted easily, as if we had known each other for years.

Over the next few months, I saw Pam and George almost every weekend. It was Bob's habit to have Sunday dinner with them, and they graciously included me in the standing invitation. Bob always called his mother on Sunday morning to make sure she had not yet put the roast beef in the oven—she had

that British tendency to overcook meat. But she would also prepare at least five different vegetables, lightly steamed, rather
than boiled. We ate on TV tables in the downstairs recreation
room and watched rented movies. Often Bob picked the movie,
usually something that would confuse poor George. The most
memorable of those was the cult classic *Big Top Pee-wee*. Bob
laughed about George's reaction all the way home.

Though Bob still slipped into his Lothario ways when in
the company of his male friends, I was seeing more and more of
the serious, steady man behind the facade. He was a voracious
reader and loved music of all types, from rock, jazz, and blues to
classical, big band, country, and traditional folk. Becoming a
good lawyer was important to him, and he cultivated relationships with the more senior members of the firm for which he
was interning. He would spend hours poring over case law so
that he could do the best possible job of representing his clients.

Bob was a natural athlete. From a young age, he had dis-
played talent in almost any sport he played. Ice hockey was his
first passion, and he played at a competitive level right into his
teens. Though he was small in comparison to many of his team-
mates, he was quick and handled the stick well. He played tennis
occasionally, for fun, and would dominate the court. During his
teens, Bob spent his summers working on his cousins' golf
course in Radium, British Columbia. After tending to the
greens in the early part of the day, he was free to play the course
and developed a respectable handicap.

Skiing was the first sport in which I saw Bob in action.
Because he grew up in North Vancouver, beneath Grouse, Sey-
mour, and Cypress mountains, he had learned to ski as a young
boy. By his teens he was earning extra money as an instructor
on one of the local mountains. I used to speculate that he might
have been the instructor my classmates and I gawked at when we
went on a school ski trip to that same mountain in the early
1970s.

Bob's craving for adrenaline and constant challenge
brought him together with the first group of local skiers doing

aerial work, and he became one of the early members on the Canadian freestyle circuit in the 1970s. The first time Bob and I skied together at Whistler Mountain, he dazzled me with effortless 360-degree spins and dancelike turns between the moguls on even the most challenging runs. Over the years, I had a few opportunities to watch Bob ski down a run while I rode overhead on the ski lift. On one such occasion, the stranger sitting beside me grabbed my arm and exclaimed, "Look at that. That is absolute perfection on the snow." I had to agree.

Skiing was an expensive hobby and limited to the winter months, so Bob looked for another pursuit for the rest of the year that wouldn't be such a drain on the small salary of an intern. He found just what he was looking for in the emerging sport of triathlon. This was the latest in the new breed of multisports inspired by the Olympic decathlon and biathlon. Its elements are swimming, cycling, and running.

A natural runner who had completed numerous marathons, Bob initially focused on training for the other two elements of the race. During the fall and winter, he swam lengths several times a week at the Vancouver Aquatic Centre. In the warmer months, he went to the enormous outdoor pool at Kitsilano Beach or donned a wet suit and plunged into the ocean for an open-water swim.

Vancouver is a perfect training ground for cyclists. The trails around the University of British Columbia are rugged and challenging, yet not far from the center of the city. Motorists are accustomed to the frequent appearance of pelotons of cyclists and usually share the road cautiously and respectfully.

I did not have the temperament or athletic skill to join Bob in his triathlon experience. I have always enjoyed doing sports to keep fit, but am not interested in pushing myself to prepare for competition. For fifteen years, from the time I was three, I had trained to be a classical ballet dancer, which had involved enough intensity and discipline to last me a lifetime. I was content to sit on the sidelines and cheer Bob on.

Bob's social life began to revolve around his triathlon friends, which annoyed me. I was acquainted with the triathletes and socialized with them, but felt somewhat detached because I was not training and competing alongside them. I feared Bob would find romance with a woman who shared his passion for the sport. This led to some tension between us, but by the end of the summer in 1987, my concerns faded and some of the prickly edges of our relationship smoothed out when we decided to move in together. Our first home was a suite in an old house. Our favorite feature was the wood-burning fireplace in the bedroom, even though the first time we lit a fire in it, thick gray smoke backed up into the room and we ended up sleeping on the floor of the living room. We both loved the routine of being together in our off-work hours and looking after the day-to-day running of our little home.

At Christmas, Bob and I traveled to Victoria to join my family for dinner and dancing at the Union Club, a century-old private club on the city's Inner Harbour. This event had been the highlight of the season since I was four years old. I proudly waltzed with Bob and looked on lovingly as he twirled my mother, my sister, and my nieces around the dance floor.

After the dinner, Bob and I returned to my mother's house, where we were staying. Bob expertly lit the fire laid in the hearth and poured each of us a brandy to sip. I was blissfully happy.

Bob moved from my side and went to sit on the ottoman by my mother. "I wish I had been given the opportunity to meet Katy's father," he began. My pulse quickened as I listened. "I want you to know how much I love Katy, and with your permission, I would like to ask her to marry me."

My vision blurred by sudden tears, I watched my mother rise from her chair and give him a hug. She could barely contain her delight as she replied, "My husband would have been so very pleased to offer his blessing, just as I am to offer mine."

Bob knelt beside me and held both my hands as he proposed. It meant so much to me that he asked me this way.

Burying my head in his shoulder, I responded with a muffled but definite yes.

That Christmas season was a wonderful blur of celebration as we shared our news with friends and extended family. We set an August date for our wedding, and my mother generously offered the garden of Raynham, my grandparents' home on Elk Lake, near Victoria, for the ceremony and reception. The property was named after an estate in Norfolk, England, near where my grandfather had grown up.

The months leading up to the big day were busy with the demands of our careers, Bob's triathlon training, and planning a wedding that no one would forget. My oldest friend, Nicola, who I had met in preschool and who now worked as a costume designer for theater and movies, took on the task of redesigning the wedding dress that my mother, my aunt, and my sister had all worn. Nicola had a perfect eye for style and fit and created a stunning gown that seamlessly wove together tradition and my more contemporary taste.

Not wanting to be upstaged by his bride, Bob jokingly suggested he would wear a kilt. That inspired an idea for a wedding gift for him. Mr. Jax had recently purchased a woolen mill that specialized in weaving traditional Scottish tartans. I ordered a bolt of the red and green McIntosh pattern and had a kilt custom made by one of the expert tailors in our factory. The tailor also made a tiny pair of shorts from the same plaid cloth, to be worn by our ring bearer, my nephew Ben. I used the leftover fabric as a runner on the head table at the reception.

I loved looking after the tiny details that we knew would make the event unique. A papermaker on Granville Island helped me design a custom paper for the invitations, and we integrated the colors of my bridesmaids' silk floral suits (from the Mr. Jax collection) by adding tiny crushed flowers and greenery to the heavy cream-colored stock.

Bob and I often met friends after work at a pub in our Kitsilano neighborhood, where patrons were treated to the rockabilly music of Billy Cowsill every Tuesday night. Billy and his siblings had been rock sensations in the '60s and '70s. They had a huge hit with "Hair," from the rock opera of the same name, and inspired the TV sitcom *The Partridge Family*. Years of hard living, substance abuse, and family alienation had pulled Billy pretty close to the gutter. He managed to cling to the edge and supported himself playing pubs on the local circuit. His voice belied his difficult past and moved all who heard it.

Bob had befriended Billy over the years, and they often exchanged comedic banter between the stage and the floor during his sets. One night Billy joined our table as we were discussing wedding plans. He asked who was going to entertain at the reception. Bob joked that maybe Billy would like to, not thinking for a minute that he would agree. To our astonishment, Billy took it as a serious invitation and said he would love to take a road trip to Victoria. We could barely believe it. Having Billy play would make the night unforgettable.

Bob's mother generously gave us plane tickets as a wedding present. We decided to go to Portugal. I had been there twice in my teens while at ballet school and had fallen in love with the colorful history, beautiful beaches, and friendly people. Bob was looking forward to visiting the Grand Prix auto racing track and exploring the tiny villages that dotted the coastline. A textile supplier I had been dealing with for several years graciously offered the use of his villa for our two-week stay.

As the August weekend drew near, we were caught up in a whirl of parties as we both said farewell to our singlehood. Unlike Bob, I did not have a group of friends who had all known each other for years. Instead, I had friends who represented different times in my life. Like a treasured mosaic, they came together that summer to support me. Nicola, my dress designer, had known me since we were four. I could say anything to her without fear of being judged. I met Diana in my early teens. She and I had done many crazy things together over the years, and she was just plain fun to have around. Shauna and I worked together during the summers when I was at university and had become very special friends. Jackie was my newest friend and was the closest to my relationship with Bob. Together they planned an elegant getaway weekend at Whistler where we wined, dined, danced, giggled, and cried for two days.

Bob's stag took place south of the border in Washington State and was a less formal affair. The pictures I was allowed to see featured his closest friends comparing bare bellies while wearing beer cases on their heads like some odd warrior helmet.

At last the day came. The sun sparkled on the ocean as my brothers and I rode with my bridesmaids in a London cab to Raynham. After winding along the country roads toward Elk Lake, we arrived to the sound of a bagpiper as the 150 guests took their seats in the garden encircling the pond that was to serve as a backdrop to the ceremony.

My brother-in-law, his sister, and his daughter performed a number of instrumental and vocal arrangements including "Ave Maria," a family staple for weddings and funerals, and our favorite Chris Isaak tune, "This Love Will Last." After the ceremony, the chairs were replaced with long tables, and a summer feast of salmon and lamb was served.

Bob and I found a quiet moment down by the shore of the lake to discuss the evening's performance with Billy Cowsill. Bob had warned me in advance that the musician would not take kindly to playing requests. In particular, he suggested we let Billy choose the tune for our first dance. I was so thrilled to have Billy and his band playing live in the garden that I was game for anything they performed.

Bob broached the subject. "Have you given any thought to what you might play for our first dance?"

Billy squinted as the smoke from his cigarette curled up past his face. He paused for a moment, looking out over the lake, then slowly nodded. "Yup. It's gonna be Patsy Cline's 'Walking After Midnight.'" He ground his cigarette butt into the grass and turned purposefully toward the house, where his band members were starting to set up their equipment. Bob and I held one another, laughing, and decided we were just fine making "Walking After Midnight" our song.

chapter 5

affordable housing

Ask for what you want and be prepared to get it.
—Maya Angelou

In September 1988, Bob and I returned from Portugal. We were tanned, rested, and, best of all, married. Climbing over stacks of wedding gifts we hadn't had time to put away before leaving on our honeymoon, we collapsed happily on the couch and began to plan the rest of our lives.

On the career front, things could not be better. While Bob was not kept on at the firm where he completed his internship, he was hired by a smaller litigation practice and quickly found a niche in the area of personal injury law, with exposure to both defense and plaintiff work.

Mr. Jax had moved from its small, grimy storefront in Vancouver's Gastown district to a new, refurbished facility on the Vancouver waterfront with factory, warehouse, administrative offices, and showrooms all under one roof. I would arrive early in the morning to catch the European fabric market before it closed. In the middle of the day, Louis and I would run a ten-kilometer loop that took us to Stanley Park and back. Then I'd stay at the office until dinnertime so I could send faxes to the Asian market as it opened for business.

In the spring, Bob's mother, Pam, returned from a cruise complaining that her eyesight had suddenly deteriorated. An ophthalmological exam detected a small tumor in her eye. The specialist assured her that this could be treated with a simple laser procedure, but he suggested she have a complete physical with her family doctor. His fears that the eye problem might be part of a broader health issue were confirmed just weeks later when she was diagnosed with lung cancer that was fully metastasized in the bone. Pam endured only one dose of chemotherapy and then, when her hip broke spontaneously due to the brittle condition of her bones, a painful hip replacement. The cancer spread rapidly, ravaging her tiny frame, and she died in August. Bob was thirty-two and had now lost both his parents.

Pam's death strengthened Bob's resolve to maintain balance in his own life. He continued to fit his triathlon training in around the demands of his growing law practice and worked hard at maintaining his connection with a large circle of friends.

Moving a step closer to his dreams, Bob sold his little red convertible and bought his dream car—a used white Subaru station wagon. Filled with running, biking, and swimming gear, the car became Bob's mobile training base. When we took up windsurfing that same year, the roof rack was laden with boards, sails, and rigging.

Large student loans, one of the results of our combined twelve years at university, absorbed most of our salaries, but the one luxury we allowed ourselves was skiing in the winter. The windsurfing gear was replaced with ski equipment for the weekends we spent at Whistler, where several of our friends had seasonal rental accommodation. We'd pack up the car Friday morning and get on the road right after work.

The drive to Whistler up the Sea to Sky Highway is spectacular. The road winds its way into the mountains, hugging the side of the sharp black cliffs that climb high above Howe Sound. A stop for gas and a coffee halfway up the highway in the small town of Squamish became part of our routine. With a population of about twelve thousand, this tired-looking mill town was feeling the effects of downsizing in the forest industry. But its picturesque location and proximity to both Vancouver and Whistler gave it development potential that was piquing the interest of many local entrepreneurs.

Each time we stopped in Squamish, Bob began a sales pitch, listing the reasons we should be living there. The dramatic scenery and green space reminded him of the part of North Vancouver he had grown up in. House prices were clearly more affordable than those in Vancouver. It would be years before we could manage a down payment for something of our own in the city. Bob talked about raising a family in a small town while enjoying all the recreational possibilities provided by the mountains in our backyard. He envisioned removing ourselves from the daily pressure of the big city. The commute into Vancouver was only one hour each way—not unusual for most major centers, he argued, painting a picture of what he saw as the perfect life for us.

When Bob first began making this speech on our weekly drive to Whistler, I humored him. Then I began to dread his diatribe. I loved Vancouver and all it had to offer. My career and friends were there. While I did enjoy skiing, I was not a real outdoorsy type, and just the suggestion of leaving made me miss the culture and bustle of the city.

I recall stories of my parents' early years together. My father was in the navy, and it seemed that each time my mother finished unpacking the last of the moving boxes, new transfer orders would appear. But my mother went where my father was sent, and she went with a smile on her face. She embraced the challenge of meeting new people and making new friends, of uprooting children and being away from her own mother and father. My parents were happy and flourished wherever they were because they were together.

I thought of my sister-in-law Heather, an intellectual and worldly American city girl, who had made a similar sacrifice for my brother David. His career in the forest industry took him to a small town in British Columbia's Kootenay region, far from the cosmopolitan life she had left in California, but she made it home and carved out a life for herself and their children.

If my mother and sister-in-law could step out of their comfort zones, so perhaps could I. Their willingness to bloom where they were planted, as the old saying goes, was one of the reasons they both had such happy, solid marriages. I thought about what it would mean to Bob if I stopped protesting and got behind the idea of relocating to Squamish. My support could be a wonderful gift for our future together. And as I made a conscious decision to shift my own thinking, I felt a surge of freedom. I could hardly wait for Bob to raise the issue on our next drive to Whistler.

As I expected, Bob launched into his pitch as we passed through Squamish. When I turned to him and suggested he call a real estate agent so we could look at some houses, I thought he was going to drive off the road. He was shocked at my response. I knew immediately I had just done something very right for our marriage.

Within weeks we made an offer on a lovely little house high up in the Garibaldi Highlands. The property backed onto a greenbelt and looked out over a breathtaking vista of snow-capped mountains. We were able to afford a modest down payment, and the mortgage was less than our monthly rent in Vancouver.

I started to see how this move could enhance our marriage in other ways. Bob would be distanced somewhat from his tight network of friends. And the commute into Vancouver would force me to put some boundaries around the time commitment I made to Mr. Jax. This would give us both the opportunity to focus more on one another and our life together.

The one part of the move I was not excited about was that commute we faced to and from Vancouver each day. The Sea to Sky Highway is a challenging drive in the best of weather conditions, but it can be downright frightening when it is raining or snowing. Bob was an excellent driver and assured me that he would be behind the wheel whenever possible. But that plan fell apart before we even took possession of the house. The day the contingencies were being removed from the real estate offer, Bob drove up to Squamish to look at the house and talk to the lawyer at Race & Company, the local law firm handling the transaction. He came home to announce that the house deal was complete and that he had been offered an associate position with Race & Company.

Daunted by the prospect of handling the commute by myself, I advertised in the Squamish newspaper for a car pool and received an immediate response from a forest industry executive who worked just blocks from the Mr. Jax office. He was happy for the company on the drive and the opportunity to share the cost of gas. I breathed a sigh of relief as I managed to clear the first hurdle this move put before me.

We moved into our first house in December 1989. After unpacking all the boxes, we cut down a small fir tree and strung it with lights and strings of popcorn and cranberries. A few evenings later, we walked to the end of the street to the home of Doug Race, Bob's new boss. He was hosting the firm's Christmas party and had invited us to join them. I knew immediately that this group of people would be a good fit for Bob. They were all avid outdoors people, keenly interested in skiing and triathlon. The balance Bob fought so hard to achieve in the city would be much easier to maintain in this new environment.

A few months later, I seriously injured my knee while skiing and changed the course of my future. My recovery from surgery was slow, and even with physical therapy, it was obvious that the daily commute to and from Vancouver would no longer be possible. I had already begun to suspect that I wouldn't be able to keep up the pace and hours demanded by Mr. Jax for much longer. This situation forced the issue, and I began looking for a new job closer to home.

With fortuitous timing, the Community Futures Development Corporation, a local economic development agency, advertised for a business analyst who would help local entrepreneurs put together their business plans and secure start-up financing. I applied and was hired. It turned out to be a great opportunity to both broaden my business skills and immerse myself in the local commercial environment. I worked with a wide range of ventures throughout the region, from tiny home-based businesses right up to large-scale industrial operations.

The Squamish area's potential for economic growth was substantial, but the transition from the deeply entrenched resource-based economy to a more diverse and softer marketplace was not without problems. For several generations, the town's old guard had made their living in the forest and the mills. They did not take kindly to watching their livelihoods dwindle in favor of high-tech and tourism jobs. There were some interesting political debates as the area attracted more and more couples like Bob and me—the symbols of change and often the driving force behind it—but even the staunchest old-timers could no longer ignore the fact that growth and change were inevitable. It was exciting to be joining in at this stage of the revitalization.

Considering I had to make a conscious effort to embrace our move to a small town, I quickly became one of Squamish's proudest promoters. I cherished the more relaxed pace of our lives and the absence of traffic congestion and long bank lines. I could do all my errands on my lunch hour instead of taking one full day each week for such tasks.

Along with the simplicity came new friendships and the time to cultivate them. Bob and I were quickly drawn into a small group of professional couples who shared our enthusiasm for small-town living. Many of them had moved to Squamish ten or fifteen years earlier and had endured the earliest rumblings of change.

Without the vast choice of social and cultural opportunities that Vancouver offered, we learned to create our own entertainment in the company of our new friends. Dinner parties were a weekly event. We put enormous effort into preparing delicious meals and selecting good wines. After the meal, we would push back the furniture to make room for dancing or a well-rehearsed series of Monty Python skits.

We'd take the occasional day trip to Vancouver, and on one of these expeditions we found ourselves in the vicinity of the pound. Bob suggested we go in for a visit. Within an hour, we emerged with a border collie–corgi cross, who Bob triumphantly christened Stan. He was a big dog who stood close to the ground, and people could not help smiling the instant they met him. My husband's dreams were unfolding just as he had envisioned them, and after our first year in Squamish we decided it was home and that we were ready to have children.

At twenty-nine, a woman knows her body well, and something deep inside told me that pregnancy would not come easily. Sure enough, after a year without contraception, I had not become pregnant. My suspicions were confirmed by a series of painful tests that revealed a serious fertility problem. Bob stood helplessly beside me as a doctor briskly informed us it looked as though my fallopian tubes were filled with crazy glue. He assured me I would never get pregnant in this state. Further testing revealed that the problem could not be fixed surgically. Our only option if we wanted a child of our own was in vitro fertilization (IVF).

Close friends who had been through IVF in Seattle, Washington, had given birth to a healthy baby girl. I called them in tears for advice, and they convinced us to attempt one cycle of treatment. We took a collective deep breath and, armed with our credit card, drove across the border for an orientation session at the University of Washington Medical Center in Seattle. The specialists there told us that tubal blockage is one of the easier fertility problems to circumvent with IVF, and the clinic estimated our odds of achieving a successful pregnancy were about 13 percent. The procedure would cost $10,000. It was a big gamble, but we decided we were willing to take it...once.

The nurse showed Bob how to give me the twice-daily hormone injections, and we went home to begin the process.

We returned to Seattle 102 syringes later to begin the daily ultrasounds that would reveal the precise moment for harvesting the ripe eggs. All the medication had made me nauseous, and I could scarcely keep down the poached eggs and mashed potatoes I ordered from the diner adjacent to our hotel. Bob, on the other hand, viewed this trip as a perfect opportunity to sample the cuisine from some of Seattle's finest restaurants. He happily took off each day in search of a new dining experience and reported back to me as I huddled under the blankets, incubating my eggs. This routine lasted ten days before science and nature were deemed ready to square off.

Mellowed out by a small dose of Valium, I watched on a television monitor as a long syringe punctured the individual sacs and extracted the eggs. By the time the doctor finished, he had removed thirteen eggs from the follicles. I rested and had a disjointed conversation with the nurses about shopping for shoes while Bob went off to do his part.

With the two essential components mixed in a petri dish, the doctor told us to go have some fun; he would report back to us in a couple of days. After forty-eight hours, twelve of the thirteen eggs had successfully been fertilized, and we were ready for the implantation procedure. It was almost anticlimactic, no pun intended. In less than a minute, four fertilized eggs were carefully placed in my uterus. The remaining eight were frozen for future consideration. The in vitro team restated our odds at 30 percent. As I lay at a forty-five-degree angle in the inverted bed, listening to the blood rush to my head, they told me the rest was up to me. The following day, as we crossed back into

Canada, the border official asked if we had anything to declare. Bob told him we would let them know in two weeks.

Just days after coming home, I suffered a serious side effect from the fertility drugs. Stimulated by the massive doses of medication, my ovaries continued releasing eggs. I collapsed with excruciating abdominal pain and a distended belly and was rushed to emergency. An ultrasound revealed that an additional thirty eggs had matured on my ovaries. There was nothing to do except let nature take its course. Each egg sac had to rupture and release its contents. It was five weeks before the pain subsided.

After two weeks of bed rest, I was allowed to get up long enough to drive to the local clinic for a pregnancy test. Our friend and doctor, Richard Cudmore, choked up as he read the results aloud. We were going to have a baby. A notation on the lab report indicated elevated hormone levels and recommended a follow-up blood test the next week. That test revealed an exponential increase in hormones, suggesting the possibility of a multiple birth. I was scheduled for a "head count" ultrasound. Even Bob, with his ability to plan and execute his dreams with such precision, could not have called this one. We were expecting twins.

I spent the first few weeks of my pregnancy in total disbelief. Making it through the IVF process successfully was one thing, but achieving a twin pregnancy was the ultimate reward. I suffered severe morning sickness and actually lost weight during those first weeks, since the sight and smell of most foods sent me retching from the room. When a bleeding scare at twelve weeks landed me in the hospital to have my cervix stitched shut, I concentrated my energies on staying pregnant. I had no illusions that the next six months were going to be easy.

Bob was relieved that the process had been successful and returned to his own routine once the initial medical complications sorted themselves out. I soon learned that he regarded the realm of childbearing to be women's territory and had little interest in the day-to-day minutiae that had begun to absorb me. He would happily continue to hunt and gather while I bore the children.

My family and friends filled the gap by connecting with me and supporting me throughout the pregnancy. I stopped working after five months and slowly began making our home ready for the arrival of two babies. My mother, my friend Shauna, and our neighbor Shelley stayed particularly close to me and made sure that I did not overdo it.

The babies were due in February, so by November I was enormous. One afternoon in early December, I was wallpapering the nursery while Bob skied at Whistler with Richard. I began to experience some cramping and low-back pain and called Bob on his cell phone, but it was Richard who skied right off the hill and came to see me. When Bob had described my symptoms, Richard suspected that I might be having contractions. He was right. I was in labor, and he rushed me to Grace Hospital in Vancouver, where the contractions were stopped. I was put on total bed rest. Before I was discharged, the nurses wheeled me through the special-care nursery so I could see the challenges they faced trying to keep a two-pound baby alive. I got the message loud and clear and planted myself on the couch with my feet up over Christmas.

By mid-January I could hardly move. My stomach barely fit behind the steering wheel of the car. I suffered frequent nose-bleeds, and the blood vessels started popping in my face as my body tried to keep up with the drastic increase in blood flow that comes with a multiple pregnancy. At thirty-five weeks, I phoned the obstetrician and begged him to take out the cervical sutures, assuring him that I knew these babies were ready to come. He agreed that it was time and said Bob and I should meet him at the hospital that evening. He was on call and would be able to follow the labor right through to the delivery.

Bob and I had a wonderful day in Vancouver, anticipating the event we had awaited for so long. I sat in the bleachers at the Aquatic Centre and watched him swim lengths, and then we had lunch at one of our favorite restaurants, a place we had gone to often in our early days together in Vancouver. That life seemed a million miles away as we looked at each other across the expanse of my enormous belly. Bob signed the bill, and I slowly got up from the table. We left the comfortable and familiar surroundings of our past and drove in silence to the hospital.

The high-risk delivery team introduced themselves and we were shown to the room that would be our home until the babies arrived. The first order of business was to remove the sutures and see what happened. As soon as my cervix was released, I began to dilate. I walked laps along the hospital corridor in an attempt to speed things up. After a few hours and little progress, the obstetrician decided to break my water. Things moved along slowly for several more hours. The next step was an epidural. The doctor explained that, with a twin birth, the team needs to be ready to do a caesarean section at a moment's notice. Having the epidural in place ensures they can get one or both babies out fast if they are in distress.

We were now twelve hours into labor, and Bob was exhausted. The nurses, hopelessly swept away by his brilliant blue eyes, wheeled in a gurney for him to nap on. As he drifted off, they covered him with warmed blankets. That image of Bob sleeping in the delivery room will always make me laugh. It so aptly illustrated his view of the division of labor when it came to anything to do with children.

My labor was not proceeding as quickly as the doctors would have liked, so they decided to induce me. I finally began to push twenty-three hours after we had arrived at the hospital. Far from the intimate experience many couples describe, we had fifteen people in the delivery room, including two pediatric teams and our friend Richard.

Tears of happiness and gratitude rolled down my face as a five-and-a-half-pound baby boy arrived. Sam was whisked away by the neonatal specialist—his breathing was mildly labored, which we were assured is not unusual for a premature boy. He had also suffered a small skull fracture during delivery. A CAT scan revealed that there was no neurological damage. Using a vacuum extractor device, the specialist repaired the indentation in Sam's tiny skull. The panic was over almost as quickly as it began.

Our attention was then captured by the arrival of Emma, our four-pound baby girl. Though she was much smaller than her brother, she was strong and clearly determined. Emma squinted right at me with the expression of a wise old woman.

My sister, Jenny, and my mother, assuming the delivery had occurred earlier in the day, arrived at the hospital to visit us. They were escorted directly into the delivery room just after Emma was born. It was magic to share those first moments of motherhood with them both.

The babies were taken to the special-care nursery; Bob, Jenny, and my mother went out for sushi to celebrate; and I was given some time to collect myself physically and emotionally.

Later that evening, Bob held me in his arms as we marveled at the two beautiful, tiny babes sleeping in their side-by-side incubators. There had never been a more complete or perfect moment in my life.

chapter 6

family matters

You've got only one chance to walk this line
And if you should get lost or stuck in time
Just believe this road does not end here.
How do you want to be remembered
A raging fire or a dying ember?
Life is large
It's bigger than both of us
—The Kennedys, "Life Is Large"

My recollection of those first days and weeks after we brought Emma and Sam home from the hospital is hazy, with little distinction between night and day. Life revolved around breastfeeding, burping, changing diapers, and filling the washing machine with endless loads of tiny pink and blue clothes. I would get one baby settled and the other would wake up. Making sure I was nourished and rested enough to keep the four of us fueled and thriving was my biggest task.

What I do remember is the feeling of certainty that mothering was natural to me. The hours spent cuddling and staring at these two beautiful babies made the relentless routine a labor of love. I found the smell of my babies' warm little necks as I nuzzled them intoxicating. Every gurgle and coo they made was the music that put my world into perspective. Motherhood was my best career choice to date. The same organizational skills that had helped me excel in the workplace enabled me to create a well-run home for our family. While my day was certainly less predictable than it had been in an office, I loved the challenge of working out the kinks and keeping everyone happy. If my past employers had any criticism of my management style, it would have involved my reluctance to delegate. This was true at home as well.

Because I was breastfeeding exclusively, Bob felt there was little he could do to help. He poured himself into work and sport, making sure he was maintaining the balance in his own life. Since he had never been able to function well without sleep, he took to wearing industrial earmuffs to bed so the babies' cries would not wake him. For the first five months, I slept in our guest room so I could take care of the nighttime feedings without waking my husband. I knew this was not the way most couples our age divided the labor, but I also knew that Bob simply would not manage if I demanded he share the load more evenly. I feared I would have to cope with his resentment, and I sensed that was not a side of Bob I wanted to get to know.

My friends and family would have been appalled if they had known the full extent of the role I assumed when Emma and Sam joined our family. But just as I had made a conscious decision to support the move to Squamish, I was embracing motherhood with my eyes wide open. I could have insisted that Bob take a more active role in caring for our children, but would it have made us a happier family? I knew Bob perhaps better than he knew himself, and it would not have worked. Instead I chose to see this as an opportunity, similar to what I had faced at school and in my career. My feeling of accomplishment when

Bob arrived home from work and I had managed to look after our children and put a delicious dinner on the table was as rewarding as any A+ paper or corporate promotion I ever received. The difference was that the kudos came from within.

To be honest, there were times when I longingly watched other families go about their days with the father taking a more active role in the care of the children. But that was not our reality. I accepted that and got on with creating the best life I could for all of us. Bob used to say that a happy Bob was a happy Katy. This pattern may have been difficult to sustain as our individual needs changed, but it was working for us at that time.

By willingly taking on responsibility for the practical needs of our family, I allowed Bob to give back in his own way. And he did, uniquely and spontaneously, creating magical times that enriched all of our lives. He was a morning person and made sure he had a half hour each day before he left for the office to curl up on the couch and read stories or play silly games with Emma and Sam. After dinner each night, we would bring the babies into the hot tub for what he affectionately called "the family bath." Their splashing and babbling in the warm water, sheltered from the cool evening air, was a peaceful way to end our day. During those baths, Bob composed many songs with nonsensical lyrics that then became essential parts of the lullaby repertoire.

Bob's triathlon season started again six months after the twins were born. It was a whole new challenge for me to get two babies and all their gear to the race site and keep them happy while their father raced. I suggested maybe the three of us should stay home, but Bob was horrified. He did not understand how difficult the job of mothering was when we were not at home and became exasperated by my lack of enthusiasm. He told me that when we didn't accompany him, he felt it was not worth coming across the finish line, so I tried to make it work.

Perhaps the most exciting race we traveled to as a family was the Escape from Alcatraz in San Francisco. I frantically wheeled the double stroller around the race course so that Emma and Sam could see Bob emerge from San Francisco Bay, ride across the Golden Gate Bridge, and finish up the run through the Marin County headlands. Multisport took on a whole new meaning for me that year, and triathlon regulars got used to the sight of Bob coming up to accept his medal with a baby tucked under each arm.

Things changed the next year once Emma and Sam were walking. It was impossible to contain them safely at races. There was too much danger with water, fast-moving bicycles, and crowds of spectators. Bob could see that it was becoming increasingly difficult for me to cope, so when we went to White Rock for an event in July 1994, he promised that we would leave the moment he came across the finish line rather than waiting for the awards ceremony later in the day, which was our usual practice.

We had to leave the house at 4:30 A.M. to get to the race site in time for Bob to set up his gear in the transition area and warm up properly before the starting gun sounded. I managed to keep Emma and Sam occupied and happy until Bob finished the race, but the effort to hold things together took all my energy. I'm sure the twins sensed this, and they had a huge meltdown as soon as they saw Bob. I was relieved to have his help getting them back in the car for the trip home, but was stunned when he announced that he had decided to stay for the awards ceremony after all. I could take the car with the children now, he said, and he would get a ride back to Squamish with a friend later in the day. I was speechless as we buckled two screaming, tired toddlers into their car seats and he handed me the keys. Instead of falling asleep from sheer exhaustion, both Emma and Sam cried continuously for the three-hour drive home. By the time we pulled into the driveway, I was also in tears.

Clutching the steering wheel tightly, I grappled with the fact that I had allowed this dynamic to develop in our relationship. I loved all that Bob was and how he celebrated life each day by living so richly, but it was impossible to expect two children to be satisfied being his audience. It was my job to speak for them. In order to do that, I had to recover my voice and find a way to convey our needs to Bob without hurting his feelings. It took me several days to get over my anger and muster the courage to confront Bob with my feelings. We rarely attended his races after that.

At a loss without his cheering section, Bob longed for company on the race circuit. One by one he got several friends, neighbors, and coworkers into the pool, onto their bikes, and running alongside him on the local trails. He was a one-man motivating machine. His inspiration was turning people's lives around.

One of the people Bob drew into the sport was Grant Bullington, a local teenager. Grant was a superb runner and cyclist and had been named junior duathlete of the year. Bob encouraged him to add swimming to his workout regimen, and soon Grant was winning triathlons as well. The two became inseparable training partners and began traveling to races together.

Bob found the time to teach Grant many life skills that went far beyond the realm of sport. Ironically, Grant remembered most vividly the lesson he learned when Bob turned off the television following a dramatic scene in a movie where someone had died suddenly. Bob wanted to tell Grant how to make the call to a close friend to let them know someone has died.

Grant became a regular fixture around our house. I teasingly referred to him as my second son, since he had a knack of showing up whenever there was fresh baking. Emma and Sam loved his visits. He was like one of those special cousins you can't wait to see. Watching Bob mentor Grant with such caring enthusiasm made me realize how connected he would become to our own children when they were old enough to do more things with him.

Grant and some other local triathletes joined Bob for a second attempt at escaping Alcatraz. They made the trip without the children and me as cheerleaders, then took a detour to the Napa region before returning home. Hilarious photos showed the exhausted triathletes wrapped in white robes on lounge chairs around the pool at an exclusive spa hotel, drinking good wine and ministering to their tired muscles. Quite simply, if Bob was there, it was going to be fun.

When he returned home, he presented a storybook about the wine district to Emma and Sam. The inscription inside the front cover read "To Sammy Bob and Emma Bear from Daddy-O. You two make my heart melt!!"

I devoted myself to creating a stimulating, fun, and safe environment in which Emma and Sam could flourish. Naturally gravitating toward other mothers with children of similar ages, I found a new social life for myself as well. My own connections within the community of Squamish were deepening, and it truly felt like home.

Bob and I discussed investing in a larger home, but were loath to leave the double-ended cul-de-sac that was filled with our friends and Emma and Sam's playmates. Just after the twins' first birthday, a beautiful home at the other end of our street came on the market. We made an offer that was readily accepted. Same breathtaking mountain views, and more importantly, same great neighbors.

In September 1994, I went back to work for the Community Futures office as a consultant so that I could set my own hours. Emma and Sam loved the day care we found for them. It was run by a warm, intelligent, and creative Argentinean woman and her Canadian husband, who treated the children to a rich cultural feast of play and learning.

With the opportunity to work outside of our home, I finally felt I was creating some balance in my own life. Bob had conflicting feelings about this transition. While he liked the idea that I was again making a financial contribution to the household, he was not happy when my job took me away from him or our children. I worked overtime, physically and emotionally, trying to ensure that I met everyone's needs.

By this time Bob had become an indispensable member of his law firm. Clients and colleagues alike found him professional, compassionate, and a highly capable litigator. He was invited to become a partner and happily accepted the offer.

I was getting a sense of his reputation as he handled more and more work for members of our community and was particularly touched by the skill and empathy he demonstrated in one case. A neighbor out for an early-morning run along the highway was killed when he was hit by a car after the driver, who was speeding on a straight section of road, lost control. Bob represented the dead man's widow in a wrongful death action and became an important support for her as she rebuilt a life for herself and her family. I was equally touched by the kind words she had for Bob and by her willingness to share them with me.

At home, Bob liked to turn everyday chores into special occasions. He would recruit Emma and Sam to help him with almost any project. They would choose appropriate music, put on the right outfit for the job, and away they would go. From the time Sam was barely walking, Bob would carry him in a backpack-style child carrier while he mowed the lawn, taking hours to explain the correct technique for crosscutting the grass. The front garden looked like a sloping golf green, and we had a junior groundskeeper who could proudly explain just how that was accomplished.

Bob was less than enthusiastic about reading typical children's books. Instead he read aloud about things that interested him, like making wine. The twins were enraptured by his animated descriptions of the grape harvest and the bottling process. Instead of teaching them what sounds animals made, Bob taught Emma and Sam what nutrients were found in the foods we ate. Bob would show them a carrot and they would say, in unison, "beta-carotene."

He instigated a special ritual where we would huddle together, our heads touching, and make a noise like a bee. This was the family buzz. Bob would initiate a buzz any time we were doing something special together as a family.

One afternoon when we were all going somewhere in the car, Bob played a new CD he had bought, *Life Is Large,* by a husband-and-wife band called the Kennedys. After one hearing, the title track became our family's signature song. Emma and Sam loved to sing along at the top of their voices. There was no doubt that, with Bob, life was indeed very, very large.

The reality of traveling with two toddlers was daunting, and as a result we stayed close to home for their first few years. Even trips to Victoria to visit my family were an ordeal, so we encouraged people to come and see us instead. As Emma and Sam discovered language and it became easier for them to communicate, we began venturing farther away.

In 1996, when they were three, we took them to Disneyland. Other parents had encouraged us to wait, suggesting the twins would have more fun there when they were older. But we found that they were completely enchanted by the fantasy without being seduced by the well-targeted marketing. It was a relaxing and memorable vacation.

That same year, we had been enjoying a lazy lunch in our garden with our friends Bob and Mary McDonald. Bob was a developer who had found himself in the midst of the leaky-condo crisis in Vancouver. The pressures of his job were immense. Mary was an occupational therapist who had directed her energies to raising their two children. We enjoyed an easy camaraderie with them both. As we sipped wine, the conversation drifted to cars. The two Bobs were in agreement that every man should have the chance to own a Porsche during his lifetime and were taking turns offering preposterous arguments for their position. Mary and I humored them, pointing out that when it came to expensive vehicles, men were able to justify just about anything.

The morning after that lunch in our garden, while working in his office, Bob McDonald suffered a massive stroke. Not knowing what else to do, I left a banana loaf on Mary's doorstep and we nervously waited for word on Bob's condition. It was days before we heard that he would survive but there might be some residual paralysis. Devastated, my husband quietly went out one afternoon and bought himself a Porsche. He said he would be ready and waiting to take his friend for a ride as soon as he got home from the hospital. He kept his word, and months later the two of them went out for a spin together. Though the original conversation about cars had been idle banter, that Porsche became a talisman, reminding us of the fleeting preciousness of life.

Two years later, in a strange twist of fate, Bob McDonald asked me what my plans were for Bob's beloved Porsche. I knew it was not a practical car for me to own, but at the same time I could not imagine giving it up. Bob, who was still incapacitated by the effects of his stroke, informed me that he was going to buy it from me. I laughed and reminded him that he was not able to drive, but he told me that did not matter. The car symbolized Bob—his strength, his good taste, and his pursuit of perfection in all that he did. That Porsche was going to stay in the circle.

Bob traveled with some fellow triathletes to the World Cup in Manchester, England, later in the summer of 1996. The evening before his flight, I was helping him pack up his gear. We had to put his racing bicycle, an engineering masterpiece of titanium and rubber, in a special shipping carton. As I guided the wheel into the box that Bob was holding open, I noticed a small white label on the bike's frame just where Bob would be looking as he rode. Peering down at the label, I read, in his tiny meticulous printing, "Give it 110%."

That phrase summed up Bob. He didn't give just 110 percent to triathlon. He woke up every morning and gave life all he had—and then just a little bit more. He was the most focused, driven, and charismatic man I had ever known.

In the spring of 1997, I surprised Bob with a vacation for his fortieth birthday. We flew to San Diego with the twins and had four days together, playing on the beach. I gave Bob free rein to browse through the triathlon equipment warehouses in and around Carlsbad, the tiny town on the California coast that is regarded as the birthplace of the sport. Then we boarded a cruise ship home to Vancouver. I was pleased with myself for engineering a unique and unforgettable surprise birthday present.

As only Bob could do, when we were disembarking from the ship he thanked me for the special vacation and inquired when the party for our friends would be. Though this had not been part of my original plan, I conceded, and we had a big barbecue to celebrate his birthday one more time. Our home and garden overflowed with friends, and Bob was in his element. I spent days going through our photograph albums and put together a "This Is Your Life" slide show that was a resounding success.

In the fall of 1997, Bob was packing his bags for a trial that was being conducted out of town. Just before he left, we received a call from his cousin Lynne in Vancouver. She told us that her husband, Kerry, had been killed, possibly murdered. Bob was not able to reschedule the trial, so I was left to attend the funeral by myself.

Lynne and I had enjoyed each other's company over the years and had spent some memorable times together. She and Kerry ran a highly successful development business in West Vancouver and circulated with a fast, fun crowd. On the day of the funeral, that same crowd came together in an enormous show of designer black and said goodbye to Kerry. There were rock stars, politicians, professional athletes, and bikers filling the pews at the church.

The experience was uncanny. I stood in the receiving line for over an hour to pay my respects to Lynne. When I finally reached her, she pulled me toward her and asked me to stay by her side. For the remainder of the wake, I felt as though I was experiencing the aftermath of Kerry's death right along with

Lynne. I thought to myself there must be a reason I was chosen to be right there to see the tragedy from this perspective.

When Bob returned home from his trial a week later, I tried without success to describe the impact of Kerry's funeral. He could not grasp what it had felt like to see it from the vantage point I had been drawn into by Lynne. And I thought maybe there was a reason for that, too...

It seemed like the 1997 triathlon season was never going to end. Because I was no longer going to the races, I was more aware of how much the sport was taking Bob away from the family. As the year wore on, I looked forward to the time when Bob would hang up his bike for a few months and give it a rest. Just as I was contemplating that, Bob received a call from the director of Triathlon Canada.

This organization is the governing body for the sport. The director said the group wanted to acknowledge the contribution Bob had made over the ten years he had been racing. Here he was, at forty, competing internationally. He was not a pro but a dedicated amateur. He was raising children, he was a partner in his law firm, and he was mentoring a number of other athletes. The director said Triathlon Canada would be honored if Bob would represent the Canadian team as one of the captains at the world championships in November.

When Bob hung up the phone, he opened his brilliant blue eyes very wide so I couldn't possibly say no to what he was about to ask. Could he do just one more race this year? Of course, how could I refuse? I asked Bob where the race was being held. He took a deep breath before he told me. The world championships were in Perth, Australia.

I knew this was an opportunity of a lifetime. It would be the pinnacle of the sport for Bob. What a perfect way to finish off the year he turned forty. I had spent our holiday budget on the surprise vacation to California earlier that year, so I closed my eyes tightly as I handed him our credit card. We would make it work out somehow. Carefully crating his bicycle yet again, he packed enough gear to last him through the three weeks of training that would precede the race, promised to bring Emma and Sam something made of fuzzy sheepskin, and Down Under he went.

I returned from dropping Bob off at the airport for his flight to Australia on a gray November night and found a note on my pillow.

> *To my dearest Katy and family. You are my everything. When I race, I feel your pleasure and support through my arms, legs, and whole being! This I do for you, as I know I will be a better husband, lover, and father. There is no doubt we are blessed and I can't help but feel there are "others" watching over us. I love you all so very much, Daddy-O xoxo*

Championing his dream was the best gift I could have given Bob. His adventure in Australia was everything he'd hoped for. When he came home, he had finished his racing season emotionally as well as physically. I sensed he was ready to focus on our family and could see in him a renewed sense of joy and contentment. However, once Bob was back, my own adrenaline waned and I ended up in the hospital with pneumonia.

We had the quietest, most peaceful Christmas I can recall, canceling our planned trip to Victoria to see my family. What meager shopping I did was by phone, and the wrapped gifts appeared on our doorstep via FedEx within days. The time we would normally have spent rushing around was devoted instead to reading books with Emma and Sam and watching favorite holiday movies on television. We spent hours cutting out paper snowflakes and hanging them in the windows.

What I remember most from that December was an overwhelming sense of peace. Rather than looking forward to 1998 with a long list of things we wanted to accomplish, Bob and I were celebrating all that we had done in the past and how blessed we were. We had everything we had ever wanted right there in our collective heart. It was the sweetest of places to be.

training wheels

And as the skies turn gloomy, night winds whisper to me,
I'm lonesome as I can be
I go out walking after midnight,
Out in the starlight, just hoping you may be
Somewhere a-walking after midnight searching for me.
—Alan Block and Don Hecht, "Walking After Midnight"

After the funeral, it is hard to say goodbye to my sister Jenny. She has been with us for two weeks, cushioning our free fall, brewing the tea, and reading stories. Now she must go home to sweep up the pieces of her broken marriage. Later I hear about the scene that greeted her on the bleak January day of her home-coming—a dry Christmas tree in the living room. All that was left for Jenny to sweep up were the fallen pine needles. Her husband had left a note explaining he'd decided it was best if he were gone when she returned from Squamish.

Andy, Jenny's twenty-one-year-old son, writes to me:

Right to the chase: When Bob died, I was troubled. Troubled because I loved him very much, but was lazy with our relationship. He offered his friendship many times and somehow I never really took him up on it. I think the way I saw it was that we had a long time to get to know each other. No hurry... I felt really unresolved. Hell, everyone does. What I'm getting to is that you have helped me very much. You have been fantastically open with so much Bob-stuff. You have shared much with me, and everyone. Walking with you the night of the funeral loosened whatever was constricting around my heart... I've seen you give in similar ways to a lot of hurting people, inspiring and real and vital. Now, I think about you and I'll cry. Not from sadness but exultation. I hope this isn't hideous. You make me feel very, very happy. I feel a similar kind of happiness when I think about my mother, freed from stagnant waiting and worrying, and thrust into change.

Jenny's children will give her the strength and resolve to move forward, just as mine inspire me.

The police visit again. The forensic pathologist was not satisfied with the autopsy and decided to investigate the cause of death further. The blow administered to the side of Bob's head was powerful enough to cause his death, but upon closer examination the forensic pathologist found marks resembling the sole of a shoe on the back of Bob's head. When she studied the tissue beneath the marks, she realized the arterial tear that caused the fatal brain hemorrhage was caused by a series of kicks to the head. The police now believe Bob was knocked out by the punch and then kicked while he lay unconscious on the ground. Bob may have been killed by more than one person, and the investigation will continue. This new information leaves me feeling numb. The image of Bob lying on the ground and being kicked to death is seared into my imagination.

Bob's Sunday running group appears for coffee on the bitterly cold weekend following the funeral. They stand around my kitchen, cupping the steaming mugs in their hands as I busy myself clearing away the flower arrangements that have filled the house over the past two weeks. Someone suggests that they take the flowers with them on the run. They can scatter the blooms as a tribute to Bob on this first Sunday run without him. It is a fine idea. Bundling myself up in warm clothes, I walk with the seven of them to the head of the trail to Alice Lake. Like some kind of strange wedding party, they take off through the forest with their bouquets.

In the local bookstore I find a children's book on dealing with death. It is for Monica, the beloved caregiver at our day care. I am hoping she can share it with the other children she looks after. I want Emma and Sam to ease back into a routine while I figure out what to do next, but the other parents must be nervous about the idea of my children returning to Monica's. I want to smooth the way, to help them all understand. Bob's death is not contagious.

Emma and Sam's fifth birthday is one week after the funeral. We planned Sam's party before Christmas, and the invitations have been sent out. A few of Bob's close friends come to help at the pool as ten five-year-old boys swim, play, and gorge on hot dogs. Sam has a good time and seems oblivious to the emotion that hangs in the air. I hate every minute of it and hate myself for my inability to share my son's enjoyment.

I have nothing planned for Emma, and it is too much to imagine putting anything together now. Shauna Markham comes to the rescue with an impromptu dress-up tea party at her home in Vancouver with her daughters, Cody and Tate, and some of their friends. Emma endures the day, but her old-soul character cannot hide the fact that she is in no mood for a celebration. Feeling totally disconnected, I am grateful to be pulled against the tide through these first, and all too soon, milestones by my precious friends.

Each night my friend Doreen appears around 9:00 P.M. She was part of my support network at the hospital on New Year's Eve, and she is the mother of Grant, Bob's triathlon protégé. She lets herself in through the front door and word-lessly begins to brew a pot of tea. We curl up on the couch, where I talk and cry until I am ready for bed. Then she leaves. I look forward to her "tucking in" ritual, as she has come to call it, but as the weeks pass, I worry that she has started to need it more than I do. Sometimes Doreen brings me her journal to read. I pore over page after page of her sadness. Some of it is about Bob, but much of it is about incidents long past. I learn that she is depressed. The farther I feel myself moving away from the hot, painful center of my trauma, the more she seems to be drawn into its core. Soon she is talking and I am listening.

A few people in my life have done everything right. They have been there in the middle of the night when I woke up cry-ing. They have changed the subject when I needed to talk about something other than my widowhood. They have let me laugh.

And there are others, people who have suddenly attached themselves to me. My crisis has become their "cause," some-thing they can focus their energies on in order to leave behind the mundane problems in their own lives. Lives where they have forgotten to be passionate, to seize the moment, and to be grateful.

I had no choice about what happened to Bob. And I have no choice about the way in which some people are handling his death. But I do have a choice about which people I stay close to as I recover.

The biggest casualty in this department is my relationship with Richard Cudmore. I have to believe he is deeply distraught about Bob's death, but his actions and words confuse and upset me. After his query about the autopsy report, which I assumed was a manifestation of his shock and disbelief, I expected that he would come to terms with the situation and support my chil-dren and me as we worked through the aftermath. But when he calls before the funeral to ask me what wine I am serving at the wake, I fear that he is just not getting it. Days after Bob is buried, he calls again to say that he is ordering tickets for an upcoming Irish dance performance in Vancouver. He wonders if I would like to come.

Feeling too vulnerable to convey my despair directly to Richard, I ask a mutual friend to explain to him that I can't continue our friendship at this time. It is my sincerest hope that we will be able to heal better in isolation and maybe reconnect in the future.

The brutality of Bob's death leaves me feeling fearful, exposed, and insecure in our home. I want to create a safe place for Emma and Sam to grow up, and that place is not Squamish. I moved from Vancouver for Bob. The lifestyle he wanted was possible here, but without him I am left only with constant reminders of his dreams—I must find my own. I realize I need to be back near the ocean, where the sand and waves can slowly smooth out the rough edges of our loss. I need to be back in Victoria, where I grew up. My own childhood was so happy, and I yearn to revisit those memories so I can recapture a happy childhood for my children.

When I talk to Jenny about this, she reminds me of my first words to her when I walked in the house after leaving Bob's body at the hospital: "I hate this highway. I'm moving back to Victoria." I know that my family and friends will caution me about making decisions too quickly, but there is nothing left for me in Squamish. Bob's death certificate did not come with an instruction book attached. I am hard-pressed to find another thirty-six-year-old mother of twins, suddenly widowed by the murder of her husband, from whom I can get advice. I trust the daring heart that Claire Bowers spoke of at the funeral and keep moving forward. I arrange a trip back to Vancouver Island.

The ferry rolls over the dark January water and I sit watching the twins tumble about in the play area. Next to me sits another mother. She is very pregnant and proudly holds the hand of her husband. Striking up a conversation, she mentions that they live in Lions Bay, a village just south of Squamish. I remark on what a pretty place it is, and she asks where I live.

When I tell her I am from Squamish, she sighs and says, "Bummer about that lawyer, eh?"

I am frozen. "Yes, yes, it was very tragic," I reply, trying to sound detached.

"Did you know him?" she asks.

I take a deep breath and explain that he was my husband. How could I not tell the truth? My picture has been on the cover of every major newspaper over the last two weeks. She would see it and then make the connection. The woman begins to weep, and I take her hand. "We're going to be okay," I reassure her. Then I remind her to cherish each day with her own family as I gather Emma and Sam up to go for a walk on the deck.

Shauna Markham's brother is a real estate agent in Victoria. She has asked him to show me some houses. The first faces directly onto the ocean. The stormy salt air pushes against me as I walk up the front stairs. I know immediately that I feel too exposed here. The next is a huge old Victorian home. The rooms are chopped up, and there is a tenant living in the basement. He comes out to say hello holding a large iguana. This will not work either.

We pull into the driveway of a third property that is just two blocks from the beach and a small village of shops and cafés. Set back from the cul-de-sac, nestled amongst maples, oaks, and arbutus trees, it looks like a little French cottage, with wrought iron planter boxes off the front windows, and a mansard roof. The minute I step through the front door, I know this is home. I call my lawyer, Doug Race, on my cell phone to tell him I am putting an offer on a house. He urges me to wait but knows I won't. I pacify him by making the deal conditional on his final approval. Standing back from the house, I see what will be a safe and comfortable refuge for my family as we rebuild our lives.

The next stop is a beautiful century-old mansion next to a busy marina. Its spacious rooms are not filled with settees or armchairs, though, but rather with rows of desks. This house and its adjacent outbuildings are home to a small private school. When I was growing up, we would drive past the school on the way to visit my grandmother. I was fascinated by its stately, old-world beauty. Sure that it must be a special place, I fantasized that if I ever had children, they would attend classes there.

The director of the school is visibly moved by our story. I explain that I need to have Emma and Sam in a small, safe, family environment. While I feel very much in control right now, I fear it is perhaps still the adrenaline at work and that I may at some point collapse and suffer an emotional breakdown. The detachment from my children I have felt on occasions such as their birthday parties scares me. I find myself struggling emotionally to focus on Emma and Sam and to be in the moment when I am drowning in a sea of memories and sorrow for Bob. I worry that pattern might get worse. Knowing that they would be lovingly looked after in a school such as this would allay some of my fears. The director promises to get back to me with an answer as soon as possible, and the registrar calls before we leave Victoria. The children have been accepted to begin kindergarten in September.

We study the school's information package on the ferry ride back to Vancouver. I note that children are taught in same-sex classes. I like this idea. It will allow Sam and Emma to establish their own identities, and it will give Sam the opportunity for plenty of male bonding. The list of items that make up the school uniform includes rubber boots for daily recesses on the beach. Now I know for certain that all our jagged edges will be softened by the sand and sea. I am coming home.

It is hard to engage with people in Squamish now that I have made the commitment to leave. I have two months to wrap things up at work and pack up the house. I buy an endless supply of plastic lidded totes in which to neatly sort our messy lives. There are moments when I wish I could crawl into one myself.

My boss at Community Futures has been more than generous about giving me time off. I was away for several weeks before Christmas with my bout of pneumonia, and I want to get back to the office to check on my clients and their businesses. The wheels are already turning in my head about finding a good replacement for the position. It is important for me to leave my job with as little disruption as possible.

Marilynne, a dear friend who was a treasured neighbor until she moved to Kamloops, has been torn about when to visit. I begged her not to come to the funeral, since I knew we would never have a chance to really talk amid the chaos. She comes with her daughters, Lana and Madi, now that things are beginning to settle. Marilynne and I tackle Bob's closet. We set aside his ties. He had a wonderful collection, and I think that his friends would appreciate being able to wrap some of his style around their own necks. There are literally hundreds of T-shirts from triathlons Bob has raced in. I do not want to see them appearing around town, as is bound to happen if we pass them on to a local charity. Marilynne takes them home with her to Kamloops. I chuckle to myself, thinking about where they might emerge and the good karma they will bestow on the wearer.

The garage fills with possessions that will not make the trip to the island. When a neighbor asks if there is anything she can do to help, I hand her my garage door opener and ask her if she could hold a garage sale for us after we have moved. I dread the idea of watching people paw through our life, salvaging memories that we cannot bear to keep.

Lana and Madi are distraught about the dark, empty fish tank. They organize a trip to the local pet shop to replenish the goldfish population. Also included in this thoughtful gesture is a new ornament for the tank. Marilynne rolls her eyes and apologizes in advance for their choice. It is a fluorescent orange skull. We place it amongst the plastic plants, and the new fish explore the skeletal structure. That fish tank becomes my symbol for living with death. I only wish that I could leave the lights on twenty-four hours a day in my world.

I have to deal with the dogs. Lily and Max have been at the kennel for weeks. One part of me wants them to just stay there. I know they will look for Bob if they come home. Lily, in particular, lived for her evenings curled up in the crook of his arm. But Emma and Sam need them back. I cannot keep the dogs away simply because I am afraid of the grief they will trigger. And so, after a few days of waiting by the door for Bob to come home from work, as was their habit, they adapt to the new routine. I welcome their warmth beside me on the bed and the fresh air our daily walks provide.

Each day seems to be a frenzy of manic activity centered on the children, work, and preparing for the move. At night, time slows to a crawl. Doreen's visits have become less frequent as she struggles with the fact that I am leaving. I collapse on the couch or tuck myself into bed and allow the sadness to gnaw at me. I decide that if I do not submit to it, it will never go away. The tears come, and I am relieved that each night they eventually stop. When they do, it is easier to be clear about what I am really feeling. Most of the time, what I seem to be feeling is fear. Fear about not knowing what exactly happened to Bob. Fear that he suffered. Fear that my children will suffer. Fear that something will happen to me. Fear about living in a world where people hurt one another. Fear of being alone and having to raise Emma and Sam outside a loving marriage. Fear about what lies ahead for the families of the young people who killed Bob.

Many of my friends and family are getting counseling to help them deal with their grief. I decide I should probably go to see someone so I can be sure I am handling things in as healthy a way as possible. When I call the local clinical psychologist, he brusquely informs me that his waiting list is long given the recent tragedy that occurred in Squamish. When I explain who I am, he apologizes and agrees to see me immediately.

I learn that there is an important distinction between grief and trauma. As a result, they must each be treated in a different way. The psychologist feels that addressing the trauma will allow me to proceed through the grief in a less intense manner.

The memory of seeing Bob's body in the hospital is the root of my trauma. The doctor recommends a technique called eye movement desensitization routine (EMDR) to address this. EMDR was developed after the Vietnam War to help soldiers suffering from post-traumatic stress disorder. Quite simply, patients concentrate on the traumatic event while focusing their eyes on a bright light that is moving rapidly across their field of vision. The theory is that this eye movement facilitates the separation of overwhelming and debilitating emotion from the disturbing memory.

For me, EMDR works well and quickly. I even agree to have Emma and Sam undergo a few sessions, with the technique modified for their age and their individual perceptions of what was traumatic about Bob's death.

After these sessions, I find that much of the intense fear I was experiencing is displaced by sadness. Unlike the fear, which was sharp and immobilizing, the sadness is a dull ache. There is little I can think about or do in the course of my day that does not somehow remind me of Bob and how I lost him. I do not want to rush the sad feelings. They are all I have of Bob, and I want to think about him even if it hurts. I need to work out where he is going to belong for me in the fullness of time.

Because friends and acquaintances in Squamish know we are leaving, many of them begin to extricate themselves from us emotionally, putting some distance between us even before the moving truck arrives. Just as I am trying to envision what my and my children's lives will be like in Victoria, they must consider their own futures.

Shelley is in the most difficult position. She is determined to remain close to both Richard Cudmore and his family and to me and mine, all the while raising four children, staying involved in her family's businesses, and fulfilling numerous volunteer commitments. Her natural tendency to nurture has her working overtime to help everyone cope with their own pain over Bob's death. I have no sense of how her husband is managing. She studiously avoids discussing his anguish, but I can tell it is taking its toll on her emotionally. What little I see of Dave reveals nothing of the turmoil that I worry is brewing within. I fear he is a time bomb that Shelley is going to be left to detonate on her own.

I have the same concerns for Gordie. He and Shauna at least have the advantage of not living where the crime happened and can more easily remove themselves emotionally. Like Shelley, Shauna is loath to discuss the impact Bob's death is having on her husband. I choose to accept the distance that this is creating and hope they will reach out and get help along the way.

Rumors swirl endlessly around town about New Year's Eve. Some people feel compelled to keep me abreast of what is being said, while I sense that others are trying to shield me from the constant conjecture. The police continue the painstaking process of interviewing each of the young people who attended the party in the hopes that they will get a clearer picture of what happened. While they have charged Ryan McMillan with manslaughter, they believe there is much more to the story. They say little about the details of those interviews, only that they are getting a better idea of who may have been in the room when Bob was killed. With that information they can narrow the focus of the investigation.

Ryan McMillan returns to court in an attempt to amend his bail conditions. It seems that it is difficult for him to be apart from his girlfriend. I would like him to know that it is difficult for me to be apart from Bob.

Though both our careers involved a relatively high profile locally, Bob and I led private personal lives. Now our lives and the crisis that changed them are the subject of widespread attention and opinion. I get the feeling that when people are with me and my children, they are not really seeing me and my children individually, but, rather, the family we were minus Bob. I can understand the complexity of people's reactions, but I worry about the effect it is having on Emma and Sam. Even though they are just five years old, I fear they will start believing they are different if people continually treat them that way. Everything about their behavior at home speaks to their honest and innocent desire to move past the hurt of losing Daddy. The hand-wringing and emotion that people seem unable to curb in their presence become a constant reminder that we are victims. It makes the process of moving forward difficult.

Leaving Squamish will remove some of the daily reminders of Bob's absence in our lives, but there are some that will be present wherever we are. I struggle watching the simplest rituals between other children and their fathers. Shoulder rides, games of catch, even gruff words of admonishment spoken at eye level from bended knee make me miss Bob.

One afternoon Sam and I are grocery shopping together and find ourselves watching a father and son scooping bulk candy into a plastic bag. Their heads lean in close to one another as they laugh conspiratorially about the treat they are selecting. My arms and legs come alive with goose bumps as I feel Sam's grasp on my hand tense up and see the tendons in his neck grow rigid as he tries to control his emotion. There are no words spoken. We stand still and let the wave pass. Together we are learning to navigate this unpredictable storm.

I convince myself that if I focus as much energy as I am able on Emma and Sam and pay close attention to their emotional well-being, we will get through this. That conviction does not, however, make me instantly capable of Lego construction, backflips off the diving board, or two-wheeler instruction. I think I am a good mother. But I do not know if I can be a good father, too.

I have not yet learned to sleep soundly in our bed alone. Finally I move a TV into the room so I can distract myself from the emptiness wrapped in the sheets next to me. But even my choice of television has been altered by all this. I cannot stomach anything that may erupt into violence or delve into emotion. I resort to flicking back and forth between the home-decorating and cooking channels. After all, in a few months we will be living in a new space, and perhaps by then my appetite for something more interesting than tea and toast will return.

February seems to go on forever. I cannot wait patiently until the time comes to move. I decide we need some sunshine and devise a getaway plan that will include my sister Jenny. I suspect that her own crisis is weighing heavily on her in the stillness of winter. After some brief inquiries on the Internet, I book Jenny, the twins, and myself on a seven-day Caribbean cruise. From bed one sleepless night, I shop by phone for warm-weather vacation clothes to fit the gaunt frame that has become the visible symptom of my grief.

Jenny arrives at the airport with a suitcase loaded with children's books. For her, a week immersed in a floating world of storytelling with Emma and Sam will be therapy. I look forward to sitting quietly on the deck without being recognized as "that poor woman."

Sam is delighted to splash about in the ship's pools, but we quickly learn that Emma has an entirely different agenda. As soon as we board the ship, she is looking for unattached men, potential mates for her mother or her aunt. Each time a woman leaves her husband alone for a minute, Emma is speculating about his possible availability. Jenny and I gently explain that a cruise is not really a place where single men congregate, but we let her know her efforts are truly appreciated.

The kids love the children's activity programs on board and make lots of new friends. The four of us snorkel in Grand Cayman, survive a wild taxi ride in Cozumel, and come face-to-face with armed guerrillas in a Guatemalan market. On board the ship, Jenny and I spend hours playing Scrabble. Both of us rediscover our taste buds and regain our appetites as we enjoy the gourmet cuisine. We drink tea in the morning, Southern Comfort in the evening, and lick our wounds. We argue, tongue in cheek, about which is worse: having your husband of almost thirty years walk out the door or having your husband of almost ten years murdered. Thankfully, there are no witnesses to our black humor.

Though we lost our father after a seven-year battle with non-Hodgkin's lymphoma when he was only sixty-four, neither of us has seen divorce or sudden death firsthand. The parallels we are drawing at these early stages of our journeys pull us closer together. Our eleven-year age difference fades quickly as we share this brief escape from reality. Jenny says that we are brave and gallant. Inspired by that perspective, we adopt it as a mantra and get off the ship rested, nourished, and ready to take on whatever lies ahead.

Returning to the middle of winter in Squamish, I wrap up everything I can at work. Community Futures has hired an experienced banker to take my position, and I am confident she will do an excellent job.

A friend returns a triathlon magazine Bob lent her when he went to the world championships. She feels I should have it back. I have never opened any of the similar publications that were piled high on Bob's side of the bed, but for some reason I sit down with this one.

The magazine falls open to a photograph of a man coming across the finish line at a triathlon. He is dressed in typical racing garb but has a bandana tied around his waist. On the facing page is a photograph of a little girl and boy. I read the caption under the picture. They are four-year-old twins. The hair on the back of my neck bristles and a chill shoots from my head to my toes as I begin to read the article.

The man, who is the father of the twins, is competing in the Ironman Triathlon, a full-distance event held each year in Hawaii. The bandana contains the ashes of his wife, who was killed while on a training ride near their home in Washington State. He is scattering her memory along the race course.

Before I know it I am calling directory assistance to locate the phone number for this man, who is identified in the article as Larry Little, a dentist from Port Townsend. I have an overwhelming urge to connect with him, as if somehow he needs to hear my story—or I need to hear his. I leave a message on his voice mail, introducing myself and asking him to return my call because I have a story I need to share with him. Larry calls me back the next day and I tell him everything.

Larry says something to me that I will never forget. He begins by explaining that what he is about to tell me will be hard to hear, but he promises that in the weeks and months to come I will find solace in these words and they will help me move on. He pauses, takes a deep breath, and then says, "Katy, you must remember one thing. Bob is very dead."

Larry's words are the permission I need to find my own way. They are the answer I've been afraid to give all those people who ask if I feel Bob's presence. The same people who want to imagine Bob's spirit sitting on my shoulder, like a guardian angel overseeing my every move. I don't feel that, nor do I want to. That prospect is too frightening. I can, and I will, continue this journey alone.

The house empties quickly as I decide to sell most of our furniture rather than move it. I can no longer bear to sleep in the bed Bob and I shared nor dine at the table we bought just after we were married. At last the day arrives when the movers come to pack everything that is left. There is so much finality attached to this last act. I stand in the house for what seems like hours after it is empty, replaying Bob's voice in every room. The memories of who we were and all we had together as a family seem to float out the door around me as I close it for the last time. We are leaving now.

Emma calls from the backseat as we follow the moving van out of the driveway, "Goodbye, house. Goodbye, street. Goodbye, Squamish."

Sam adds, "Goodbye, Daddy."

The tears have soaked down the front of my sweater by the time we reach the highway.

When we arrive at our new home, the movers quickly fill the house with my carefully labeled boxes while Emma and Sam excitedly explore the garden. The only time they have seen the house before, the yard was blanketed by a light layer of snow—a rarity in Victoria. But now spring is in full bloom and there are plenty of leafy green hiding spaces in which to play.

Looking up from a tangle of garden equipment, I see Sam engaged in a serious discussion with one of the movers. His partner produces a screwdriver and wrench. Within a few moments, the two men are standing in the cul-de-sac watching Sam pedal his bicycle around in circles. They have removed the training wheels. He is riding all by himself. For a moment I wish that Bob were watching, then catch myself, reflecting again on what will never be. *I* am so proud of my son—*that* is what this is about. I wonder if I have a set of invisible training wheels that will help me learn to ride solo.

We stay with my mother at the lake for a week or so until a few small renovations are completed. I drive in early each day to oversee the work as bathrooms are updated, rumpus room floors are laid, and bedrooms are painted. The plumber, electrician, drywaller, and painter fall over one another to look after me. I jokingly suggest a new career for myself as a general contractor, and Jenny laughs when I tell her about the business cards I would have printed: "Crack the Whip Contracting—No one messes with the black widow."

It is a strange and wonderful thing to be able to make all the decisions myself and not have to negotiate around someone else's taste or priorities. I call this my chic house and do exactly what I want. There are cozy places for the three of us to sit in every room. We build a nook in the kitchen so Emma and Sam can be playing games or doing crafts while I am cooking or tidying.

Underneath the excitement of creating our new space is a layer of fear. It reminds me of how scared I was to go into the basement when I was a little girl. Once I finally summoned up the courage, I would go in, get what I needed, and then run for my life up the stairs. That feeling returns in our new house, and I know I have to be brave so Emma and Sam will not sense my fear. It becomes a metaphor for living without Bob. Each of us has to find a way to bravely move about within our house. There will be those moments of fear, but we can always run upstairs again to where there are people and light and it is safe.

chapter 8

the walrus

A gentle zephyr caresses every strand that is the fabric of my soul;
painlessly, it pierces my heart—
reaching to the core of my being,
igniting a flame that envelops me,
not scorching,
not consuming,
bringing passion to every cell that is me.
It is the tenderest death,
Awakening me to life,
Giving me reason to be a man.
It is your smile.
—JMH

Doug Race has done what he can with my personal legal and business matters and has wrapped up the business end of the law partnership to the extent that it affects Bob's estate. We both know there will be more legal issues to deal with in the aftermath of Bob's death, not least of which is a decision about the merits of launching a wrongful death action. We have no control over the criminal proceedings, but a wrongful death action will address the issue of the civil responsibility for Bob's death. A lawyer needs to decide if there is a strong case that Richard Cudmore (the homeowner), Jamie Cudmore (the party's host), or the person or people who assaulted Bob are liable for his death due to negligence, malice, or recklessness. If someone is found civilly responsible, that person may be required to pay a financial settlement awarded by the court. I am not able to equate Bob's death with monetary loss at this point, but Doug warns me that the costs of raising two children in the lifestyle that Bob established for us will be high. He recommends that we at least lay the groundwork for an action.

Losing Bob has been especially hard on Doug. They were friends as well as business partners, and their shared love of triathlon and skiing meant they spent many hours enjoying one another's company outside the office. Bob was gregarious, spontaneous, and bigger than life, while Doug is quiet, independent, and a master of careful planning. Opposites attracted, and a special friendship was formed.

When our move to Vancouver Island is imminent, Doug gently suggests that I look for a lawyer closer to my new home. He gives me the business card of a Victoria lawyer with whom he went to law school in the 1960s. While he is not sure if Michael Hutchison will represent me, he is certain his old friend will at least help me find good counsel. I promise I will call him as soon as the children and I are settled in our new home.

Tucking the card into my wallet, I ask Doug what this lawyer is like. Doug grins as the memories of law-school antics come alive in his mind. He tells me, "Michael is a good man, and he has practiced in Victoria forever. You will like him, Katy. He's a rugby guy—looks a bit like a walrus."

Weeks later, when we have moved in and the renovations to our new home are complete, I pull the business card from my wallet. After booking an appointment for the next afternoon, I head to my bedroom and rummage through boxes to find an appropriate outfit for a meeting with my new lawyer.

My black funeral suit is in the first box I open. I brighten it up with a pale pink blouse from another box and brush the drywall dust from my shoulders. My mother looks after Emma and Sam, and I gather up my file of important papers and head for town.

The law firm is located in a restored heritage building. Exposed brick walls make a distinctive backdrop for the contemporary office furnishings. I nervously flip through an ancient copy of *Time* as the receptionist announces my arrival. Minutes later I am greeted by a stocky gentleman in a well-tailored gray pinstripe suit and a whimsical floral tie. He has white hair and an enormous white moustache curling above a warm and welcoming smile.

The words are out of my mouth before I can stop them. "You *do* look like a walrus!" I exclaim. Michael does a double take, not expecting to hear this from a person he has pictured as a fragile young widow.

His kind green eyes sparkle as he introduces himself and leads me to his office. I seat myself in the armchair he pulls out for me across from his and tell him that I am not used to sitting on this side of a lawyer's desk. I don't think Michael was prepared for that remark either.

He expresses his sympathy for the tragic loss of my husband, and we discuss some of the general legal and financial issues I am dealing with. I tell him I want to be sure that the choices I make affecting Emma and Sam's future will be good ones and explain that I feel a huge burden being their sole parent. He reassures me that what I have done to date is prudent and says he will look over the upcoming matters to ensure that the planning is sound. We make an appointment to start discussing the question of a wrongful death action the following week. As we wrap up our meeting, I notice pictures of his children on his desk: a handsome teenage son and a gorgeous young daughter with almond-shaped dark eyes. I imagine him going home to his family for dinner and feeling sorry for me.

Michael is so easy to be with at our next meeting that I find my emotional guard completely let down. The tears fall more freely with him than they have with anyone else. I suspect this is because he is not grieving Bob's death. I do not have to protect him, and his professional shoulders are wide. He takes notes about the chain of events that led to the murder and plans a trip to Squamish to interview some key people.

Over the course of the next three months, I find myself in Michael's office every week. He calls frequently to request additional information, and I look forward to dressing up like a working woman and getting out of the house for a few hours. Through the pleasantries we exchange during our first meetings, I learn that Michael is a single parent. His seventeen-year-old son Adam lives with him full-time, and Carlie, his eight-year-old daughter, lives with her mother and visits Michael on alternate weekends. His stories of mealtime chaos and bedtime negotiations are familiar, and I welcome the chance to commiserate about the trials of parenthood.

After Michael makes a fact-finding mission to Squamish, he sends me a card. He says he feels compelled to thank me for the grace and support I have shown to all the other people dealing with the pain of Bob's death. Those words, written in the most beautiful handwriting with a Mont Blanc fountain pen, make me feel as though I have found in Michael a trusted friend as well as legal counsel. He makes me feel safe. But more importantly, Michael believes the way I am handling this tragedy is right.

Spring unfolds in Victoria. Pink blossoms rain down from the flowering cherry and plum trees that line the familiar streets. Emma, Sam, and I explore the parks, beaches, and landmarks that were the playgrounds of my youth. This is the perfect place to heal and the perfect place to start over.

It is difficult to spend time away from the sanctuary Victoria has become, but we make an effort to keep in touch with family and friends nearby. In June I take Emma and Sam over to the mainland to visit Bob's sister and her family. We find ourselves in Vancouver on what would have been Bob's forty-first birthday. Packing a basket with slices of cake and a thermos of hot chocolate, we drive to the cemetery where he is buried. The grounds are not well kept, and the rows of flat granite markers make the children uneasy. I remind myself that it was Bob's wish to be buried and it is right that he was laid to rest close to where he grew up. We sit awkwardly on the grass next to the orange traffic cone that marks his grave. I have still not arranged for a proper marker to be made. Nothing about this place brings us closer to Bob. I know there will be people who find peace and solace visiting here, but I do not need to look past the striking blue eyes of my children to remember Bob. We finish our picnic quickly and leave.

At the beginning of July, during one of our weekly meetings, Michael comments that my focus seems to be entirely on creating a safe and happy environment for my children and helping my friends get through their grief. He wonders aloud when I am going to start doing something for myself. I do not know where to begin to answer that. His warm green eyes dance as he says, "I think it's time you let someone do something for *you*. Would you let me take you out for dinner?"

Michael has been the perfect combination of professional competence and gentle, respectful support. I have no hesitation accepting the invitation. Even though I believe he is asking me out because he feels sorry for me, I leave his office with a smile of my own.

I am confident that a quiet dinner alone with Michael will be a much more pleasant experience than the two other social forays I have made since Bob died. The first was to a party at a recording studio in Vancouver. It was crowded with a who's who guest list, and while the dear friends who took me along were easy company, I found making small talk with strangers terrifying. I tried again after the move, joining a group of acquaintances for the opening festivities at the local yacht club. I felt like a stranger in my own life. It was as though I had been picked up off the earth and dropped back down again far, far away. People would lean their heads close together and whisper as I walked by. I could almost hear the words: "There she is, that poor woman whose husband was murdered." Watching single men and women flirt made me uneasy. I couldn't imagine ever being able to engage in casual and easy conversation with strangers again. My attention span was short; I tired easily and quickly lost patience as I watched alcohol warp the atmosphere of the event.

I take out every piece of clothing in my closet before I settle on the simple black shift the Shopping Shaunas bought for me as part of my bereavement wardrobe. I want my outfit to look conservative but feminine enough to show that I recognize Michael's kindness in spending time with me in the evening. My mother is delighted when I call to ask if I can borrow the double strand of pearls my father brought her from Japan almost fifty years before. She is slightly taken aback when I tell her I will be wearing them for a dinner engagement with my lawyer, but recovers nicely by the time I tell her the name of the restaurant (one I am not familiar with) where Michael has made reservations.

It is July 3, 1998. Emma and Sam are curled up on the couch, watching a movie with my Aunty Jean, who has generously offered to look after them for the evening. When the doorbell rings, Emma has her hand on the knob before I can even get down the stairs. Michael is barely over the doorstep when Emma, her hands firmly planted on her hips, asks him pointedly, "Are you going to marry my mother?"

"Well," Michael replies with a laugh, "I thought I would actually take her out for dinner."

Not letting up, Emma counters, "If you decide you are going to marry her, can you please do it before the first day of school. I need a new daddy for kindergarten."

I do not recall how we got out the door, I was so stunned by the greeting Michael received.

There is nothing more spectacular than a drive up the Malahat Highway, north of Victoria, on a summer evening. The sun hangs lazily over the Saanich Inlet, and a rich carpet of green drapes over the mountains and falls seamlessly into the cool blue ocean. We chat easily along the way and soon turn off the highway onto a narrow winding road that takes us higher above the ocean. Suddenly a building appears, clinging to the sloping terrain. Michael parks the car and we stand quietly for a moment, absorbing the magnificent view. It is different without the desk between us.

Once we are seated it is clear why the restaurant is named the Aerie. It feels as though we are perched up in the trees, like eagles in their nest. The inlet glimmers far below us in the setting sun.

Each of the seven tiny courses is perfect. We savor a Californian cabernet sauvignon and discover a mutual love for food and wine. Michael is a wonderful dinner companion. He converses easily and tells wonderfully funny stories. I put the notion that he arranged this dinner because he felt sorry for me out of my mind. I forget to think about how strange it feels to be seated across from a man other than Bob.

Hours later, Michael's hand rests gently in the small of my back as he walks me from the car to my front door. I give him a spontaneous kiss on the cheek and tell him what a lovely evening it has been. Once inside the house, I recount the details of the dinner to my aunty, and she is pleased that I have enjoyed my date. Date. I suppose it was a date.

The following day Emma, Sam, and I have visitors from Vancouver. Shauna and our mutual friend Rosie, along with their husbands and children, are over for lunch in town and an afternoon at the museum. At one point I mention that Michael took me to dinner the previous evening. Shauna's and Rosie's husbands, both lawyers and contemporaries of Bob, are uncomfortable with this, feeling he has crossed a line, but I defend the gesture, speculating that Michael simply felt sorry for me. Though as I reflect on the lovely dinner we enjoyed together, it occurs to me I did not feel pitied.

We return to my house for the evening. Coming up the walk, I can see the sparkle of cellophane encircling an enormous bouquet of flowers leaning against the front door. Shauna and Rosie look at each other with raised eyebrows. I recognize the distinctive handwriting on the heavy cream-colored envelope attached to the arrangement. It is Michael's, and I tuck the note into my pocket before they can see it. My heart is beating so loudly I can barely hear my feeble attempts to dismiss the arrangement as a kind gesture from a casual friend.

After dinner my friends extricate their children from the garden, where they have spent the evening playing, and bundle them into the car. As the headlights recede down the driveway, I retrieve the envelope and unfold the thick paper.

> *Katy, thank you for a truly exquisite evening. I am not used to having trouble talking—but you are quite breathtaking, and I am sure there were times you must have thought I was fumbling for things to say. You are truly an elegant woman, in the very best of ways—from within. How radiant you are—and how lucky I am to have met you! I am most proud to be your friend. In one's life, very occasionally, a genuinely affecting moment can occur, when you know that the deepest and most personal parts of who you are have been touched. The completeness of your beauty and the uniqueness of your substance have done that to me. Thank you. Michael*

Lying awake, I savor the utter surprise of Michael's gesture and the thrill of possibility that emerges from his carefully chosen words. There is neither pressure nor uncertainty. I accept the realization that I may be about to complicate my life as a sign that I am moving forward with the same daring heart Claire spoke of at Bob's funeral.

In the morning, it takes me hours to compose my written reply. I let Michael know the dinner, the flowers, and his letter have moved me, and I accept his friendship. The children and I hand deliver my note to Michael's condominium when we walk the dogs later that day.

That night the phone rings. It is Michael. His rich, deep voice consumes me. He will be away for several days at a trial in Vancouver. The next opportunity we will have to see one another in person is at a press conference scheduled later in the week where we will announce the wrongful death action.

What follows are five days of lengthy telephone conversations and e-mails. Being apart is agonizing, but it gives us the chance to really talk and not let our chemistry sweep us away. As we gently explore one another's hearts, Michael articulates what we both are thinking. I must decide if Michael is to be my lawyer or my lover. While there is no regulation saying he can't be both, neither of us wants that for one another or for our families. If we are going to follow our hearts, we want to do it fully, with all our energies moving in a common direction. I appreciate the care and attention Michael has given to my legal issues, but I know I can find another lawyer. I cannot replace the man he has become to me.

The timing is undeniably bad. But is there ever a convenient time to fall in love? The press conference to announce the civil action has been scheduled, and it is too late to change it. We agree that we will go through with announcing the lawsuit and then officially sever our professional relationship.

I arrive at his office well in advance of our meeting time in an effort to avoid the media, but they are waiting on the street to get footage of me walking from my car. The wait in Michael's reception area seems to take an eternity while he finishes a call with a client. Then he appears, his smiling green eyes repeating in one glance all he has said to me over the past five days. As he closes his office door behind me, I place my purse on the chair and turn to him. He wraps his arms around me. We kiss. It is a perfect kiss. I am suspended for a moment in the depth of that embrace, knowing in my heart that I am where I belong.

I have made the right choice, and those who know me well will assuage their fears by reflecting on my history of good decision making. The rest of the world will not see it that way. I don't care. I have handled what brought me here, so I believe I can handle being here, too.

Stepping apart from each other, we sit at the desk to focus on what needs to be done. Business first. Journalists and camera operators are set up in the boardroom and ready to go. We table the discussion of our personal lives until after the press conference.

Michael explains the nature of the pending civil action to the reporters. The suit names Richard Cudmore and Jamie Cudmore, and because we do not know the name or names of the person or persons responsible for the assault that caused Bob's death, we name three John Does and one Jane Doe. I answer the predictable questions about the anger and vengeance the world wants from me but that I seem incapable of feeling. It is exhausting to have to say, over and over again, that, yes, I loved Bob with all my heart. Yes, I miss him terribly, but that does not mean I have to hate the person or people who committed the crime. Hatred would simply compound the hopeless desperation of the tragedy.

After the news conference, Michael takes me to lunch. The salt air rides a light breeze through the waterfront café while the inner harbor bustles with marine activity. Several of Michael's dark-suited legal colleagues stop by our table to say hello, each of them smiling quizzically at me, eyebrows raised. Over crab cakes and white wine, Michael leans across the table and takes my hands. We stare for a moment as if we have known each other forever. Then I say to him the words we have both decided must be said: "You're fired."

In the garden, Erin, the Australian woman I have hired to help with the twins, is hosting a teddy bear's picnic on a blanket on the lawn. Emma and Sam have assembled an eclectic mix of stuffed animals, action figures, and wildly dressed dolls to partake in the festivities. As I watch the scene, my heart overflows with love for them. I am grateful that the trauma of Bob's death has not stolen their ability to lose themselves in the marvelous fantasies of childhood.

After Erin leaves, we enjoy a cold supper on the deck and walk the dogs along the beach to the playground. Sam asks, "Did Mr. Hutchison help you with some problems today?"

I cannot help laughing as I assure him that "Yes, Mr. Hutchison was very helpful indeed."

I tuck my two blond, sun-kissed babes into their beds and run myself a hot bath. As the bubbles envelop me in a frothy cocoon, I consider how these recent developments might play out. It is too much to comprehend. I recall the sound of Michael's deep, soothing voice during his good-night call and feel instantly at ease. I fall asleep knowing that wherever this next part of the journey takes me, I will not be facing it alone.

A few days later, Michael calls to ask if I would like to have dinner with him and meet his daughter, Carlie. I can't wait to get to know the little girl with the almond eyes who peeks out from the photograph on his desk. Having spent much of her life in the company of adults, Carlie proves to be a delightfully well-behaved dinner companion. She amuses me with her sophisticated palate and polishes off a plate of lobster without difficulty. We spend a considerable amount of time discussing nail polish and the Spice Girls, largely ignoring Michael. He sits backs contentedly, watching the two of us whispering and giggling. I cannot wait for Emma and Sam to meet her.

I have promised my friend Marilynne that the kids and I will drive to Kamloops to visit her family. I can hardly call to say I have just met someone and do not want to leave his side.

Perhaps, I rationalize to myself, a few days away will sharpen my perspective and be a good reality check.

Michael leaves the office in the middle of the day to come over and say goodbye. I load the car with our bags and walk back into the house to find him with both Emma and Sam on his lap. He is quietly reading them a story. I can only wonder who sent this man to us.

I do gain some perspective as I drive the several hundred kilometers to visit our friends. I miss Bob. I am raw from the brutal way in which he was taken from us. My grief and pain have made it hard to engage fully with Emma and Sam. They remind me constantly of what we have lost.

I am in love with Michael. This apparently defies all the rules in that instruction manual I do not recall receiving after Bob's death. It seems, however, that the more I allow love into my life, the better I am able to connect with my children. I am grieving and loving at the same time. One does not negate the other; they coexist.

We are listening to a cassette tape of children's music in the car. It reminds me of family drives with Bob. As a wave of sadness begins to carry me away, I stop and notice that for Emma and Sam it is simply familiar music they love. We adults complicate things with our emotions. I vow to take my children's lead and hear, see, and feel the world around me as they do. Each day will begin with a fresh, new start.

My cell phone rings. Pulling over to answer the call, I am delighted to hear Michael's voice. He is calling to make sure we are safely on the road. Yes, I smile to myself; we are most certainly safely on the road. I tell him I love him.

The following weekend Michael takes me to a cocktail party at his parents' home. They are a delightful couple, and I feel comfortable the moment we meet. Barbara looks like a life-sized version of one of the Royal Doulton figures on their coffee table, with porcelain skin, white hair swept into a chignon, and a strand of pearls skimming the neckline of her soft cashmere sweater. She bustles between their tiny kitchen and the open living and dining area of their waterfront condominium, laying out platters of appetizers and chatting with friends. When I ask if the framed needlepoint portraits on the wall are her handiwork, she proudly shows me a work in progress.

John is a retired anesthesiologist and the former registrar of the British Columbia College of Physicians and Surgeons. Impeccably dressed in a tweed sports jacket, Viyella shirt, and paisley ascot, he deftly tends the bar. Witty quips are served up generously with the cocktails. I can see where Michael gets both the twinkle in his eye and his sense of humor. There is immediate rapport, and John is teasing me just moments after we meet.

They have no doubt heard some of the rumors that are beginning to filter through local social circles about the relationship that is developing between Michael and me, but they maintain a discreet and respectful composure throughout the evening.

Later in the week, we invite my mother to dinner at the Deep Cove Chalet to meet Michael. This has been my family's special restaurant for over thirty years, where we have celebrated milestone events like my grandfather's eightieth birthday and my return from a summer dancing in Britain. It is one of those rare summer nights in Victoria when it is warm enough to dine outside, the umbrella-shaped propane heaters filling in once the sun slips into the ocean. We laugh over the instant bond formed by the shared savoring of a single-malt Scotch before dinner.

I know my mother is struggling with the idea of my becoming involved with Michael. It will take time for her to move past her intense grief for Bob. That grief is layered over her grief for my father, who died in 1985. There has never been another man in her life, and I am sure there never will be. It is hard for her to fathom my ability to open my heart wide enough to grieve and love at the same time.

There are other aspects of my relationship with Michael that will surely concern her. The seventeen years between us means Michael is the same age as some of her younger friends. And his marital history is bound to be a worry. Adam and Carlie have different mothers, and those two marriages followed an earlier brief, childless union.

I want her to see the qualities I treasure in Michael. Some of his most appealing characteristics are a function of his maturity. I value the extent to which he is comfortable in his own skin. Michael is the most "male" man I have ever met, and I have no doubt that his ego is alive and well. But he's not trying to prove anything to anyone, and that makes him even more attractive. This is not a man I see struggling through a midlife crisis. He is settled and content to be the person he is.

My mother cannot help but see how naturally engaging he is. Throughout dinner, Michael moves effortlessly between listening attentively and entertaining us both with wonderful stories. He is a natural orator. That can be said of many lawyers I have met, but none listen as well or with such genuine interest as Michael.

We drop off my mother, and then Michael takes me home. Sam is watching us from his bedroom window as we say good night in the driveway. When I go to his room to tuck him in, he looks at me quizzically and asks, "Mummy, why were you kissing your 'yoyer'?" Hearing his husky little five-year-old voice try to wrap itself around the word "lawyer" is almost as funny as the question itself.

Curling up at the end of his bed, I explain that Michael has become a special friend and that he will not be my lawyer anymore. Sam is immediately satisfied with that answer and nestles down in his bed to sleep.

I meet with Michael in his office later that week so we can decide the best way to handle my ongoing legal affairs. He discusses the situation with his partner, who agrees to take on the work.

With the business matters settled, Michael suggests we take a walk. The streets and cafés are busy with the lunch-hour crowd, and many of Michael's professional acquaintances say hello as we pass. A buzz has developed as it's become common knowledge that a high-profile criminal case has spawned a relationship between the grieving widow and the lawyer handling her civil case. It shall pass. There is always another story waiting in the wings to keep people talking.

Michael leads me into a tiny jewelry store and is greeted warmly by the owner, who slides a small velvet box across the counter toward us.

"If you don't like it, you can pick something else. But I thought it suited your hand," Michael explains as he slips an exquisite ring on my finger. "We had better get things organized if we're going to keep to Emma's schedule of being married before the first day of school. By my calculations, that's less than two months away."

I look down at my hands. On my right ring finger is the gold band Bob gave me ten years before, representing all that we had and the lasting gift of my two children. On my left hand is the ring that represents the future Michael and I will create for ourselves and all our children. In between is my heart—honoring and cherishing what was, what is, and what will be.

Returning to the office, I nervously dial the number for Doug's office in Squamish. He must be the first person we tell. Explaining to Doug that we have him on the speakerphone, we exchange pleasantries and then I inform him that I've had to make other arrangements for legal representation. He is clearly concerned and asks what's happened.

I cannot marshal my words coherently, so I motion to Michael to take over. He explains that a friendship has developed as a result of our professional relationship, and we thought it best to give the file to his partner to avoid a conflict of interest. Taking a deep breath, Michael goes on to tell Doug our news. "As a matter of fact, Doug, Katy and I have fallen in love and we're going to be married." I close my eyes tightly and wait for his response.

Doug asks, "When is the wedding?"

I hastily explain that we are having a simple ceremony at home with our immediate families and the children. Neither of us wants to make a big deal about it. We just want to be together as a family.

Doug repeats the question. "I said, when is the wedding?"

When we tell him that it will be on Labor Day weekend, he says that he'll be there. He introduced us, he explains, and even though this was not what he had in mind, the least he can do is be there to witness our marriage.

I am touched by his immediate acceptance of news that must be hard for him to hear. Bob was his dear friend, and his blessing means the world to me. Suddenly I have a wonderful idea. Since my father died before I met Bob, my brothers gave me away when we were married. It seems fitting to ask Doug to do the honor this time. He graciously accepts.

News of our engagement moves quickly past our friends and families to the pages of the local newspapers. The Vancouver *Province* headline reads "Slain Man's Widow to Wed Her Ex-Lawyer." I am too busy building sand castles on the beach with Emma and Sam to worry about the press. Soon it will be yesterday's headline and we will be able to get on with raising our family.

Many friends do not know what to say. They are shocked by the news of my remarriage. They have no understanding of the strength of my relationship with Michael or my total conviction that this is the right decision for me. The news is particularly hard for my friends from Squamish. Their grief, my absence, and the stress of the polarized opinions regarding the wrongful death action have already created distance in those relationships. Marrying Michael all but severs many of those tenuous ties. I especially miss Shelley. I hope one day the turmoil will settle and we can revive our friendship.

One afternoon Emma and I are doing errands in the mall. She spent the morning digging in the garden and is still dressed in denim overalls and a mud-spattered T-shirt. As we walk briskly past a row of stores toward the pharmacy, she abruptly stops. Turning to see what has caught her eye, I follow her gaze to a child-sized mannequin dressed in an empire-waisted cream cotton dress. The full skirt billows out just above the knee. "That is what I am going to wear to our wedding," Emma announces. She pulls me by the hand into the store, walks straight up to the salesclerk, and asks to try it on. The bemused woman watches as Emma unhooks the buckles of her overalls, letting them drop almost to her knees before she even gets into the fitting room. Emma emerges and the clerk helps her with the zipper and bow. She has transformed from a garden gnome into a tiny fairy. Pleased with the vision in the three-way mirror, she spins in a circle, letting the skirt of the dress ride atop its crinoline. "Do you have the same dress in a larger size for my new sister? She is eight."

Less than fifteen minutes after we made the detour, we emerge with two tissue-wrapped packages. Emma is thrilled with the efficiency of the process and skips the rest of the way down the mall. Clearly my daughter and I are cut from the same cloth.

The night before the wedding, we gather at my mother's home on Elk Lake for a casual barbecue—Michael and I each have three siblings who bring various partners and adult children, and Michael's parents are there. It is the first time our two families have met. Both Michael and I are relieved at the genuinely festive atmosphere of the evening. Any concerns the people closest to us have about this marriage seem to be lost to the pleasures of a good party.

The next afternoon the same small group gathers in a semicircle around our front doorstep as Michael and I are married in a brief civil ceremony. The French doors are open to the lush garden, which is mirrored inside by ivy trailing down the banister of the curved staircase. Amongst the greenery are late summer flowers—zinnias, dahlias, and huge sunflowers.

Sam takes his role as ring bearer seriously and proudly descends the stairs in the new school uniform that he will wear to his first day of kindergarten the next morning. He is followed by Emma and Carlie in their cream-colored dresses carrying small bouquets of sunflowers. Adam stands beside Michael on the step. The amused grin that appears beneath the mop of long dark curls puts everyone at ease.

Doug walks me down the stairs, ushering me from my past into my future. Part of me feels twenty-seven again—another part feels so much older. I have lived a lifetime in eight months. As I look out at our parents, brothers and sisters, and our children, it overwhelms me. There is so much irony and sorrow entwined in the love we are here to celebrate. The grief still deeply etched in my mother's face contrasts with the playful, accepting innocence of the children. I realize there will never be a neat and tidy way to complete this part of the journey. I believe in my heart this is right for me, for Emma, and for Sam. I know this to be true when my eyes meet Michael's.

After the marriage commissioner finishes, Michael manages to say something spontaneous and extremely eloquent about his feelings for me. I am hoping that I will be able to do the same, but the words get caught in the tears, and few make it past my lips.

The most important part of the ceremony involves our children. Michael and I present each of them with a gold ring. These rings bear the Irish claddagh symbol—a heart being held by a pair of hands with a crown above. Michael explains the symbol to them: the hands are friendship, the crown is loyalty, and the heart is love.

Our wedding will forever be captured for me in a photograph taken just as Michael and I are about to kiss. Sam is covering his face with his hands and Emma is rolling her eyes. Carlie and Adam look on stoically.

As the corks pop, what we think is champagne turns out to be sparkling cabernet sauvignon. We toast our rare love with the delicious surprise wine. By 8:00 P.M. everyone is out the door, the dishwasher is running, clothes are laid out for the first day of school, and Emma's wish has come true.

chapter 9

not a story for little ears

*the world is not
respectable; it is mortal,
tormented, confused,
deluded forever; but it is
shot through with beauty,
with love, with glints of
courage and laughter;
and in these, the spirit
blooms timidly, and struggles
to the light among the thorns*
—George Santayana

The burnt orange September morning is spilling through the window by our bed. I wake up curled in the crook of Michael's arm, just as I had fallen asleep the night before. As he slumbers, his chest rises and falls like the ocean in a quiet rhythm next to me.

The transformation of the last eight months envelops me. I lost Bob. I lost my community. I found a new home. I found Michael. Most people would still be stuck on the losing Bob part. Some people would never move past that. Why not me? What is it about me that allows me to suffer and flourish at the same time? It flies in the face of all society's conventions about life and death. I know I want to understand and explain this ability. Not to justify my actions to anyone, but maybe to help other people through times of crisis and loss.

I nuzzle closer to Michael and tuck the thought in the back of my mind for future consideration. We have more pressing things to think about this morning. Today is the first day of school.

After a photo session in the garden, with Emma and Sam proudly modeling their new uniforms, we set off for school. It is a delight to be swept up in the excitement of forty children anxiously settling into their kindergarten classrooms. It feels good to be part of a large group of people engaged in the same wonderfully normal pursuit. Nothing has felt normal for a long time. I think Emma and Sam like that too. I walk away knowing we would *all* do well in kindergarten.

The next morning, I offer to drive Adam to school. I can tell he is apprehensive about being seen with me and dreads the ribbing his friends might give him about his new stepmother. Adam is starting grade twelve and is looking ahead to graduation with that typical mix of excitement and trepidation. I feel for him. He has been with Michael through a number of relationships and was probably hoping he would be away at university before the next one began. We have built a private space for him in our home, hoping that he will benefit from a year or two of a family environment before he sets off on his own. Emma and Sam love having an instant big brother. Adam takes to them both immediately, and I watch a special bond begin to form.

It is indeed a year of firsts. Some, like that first day of school, are wonderful reasons to celebrate. Others are not so easy to navigate. Even though I have Michael, I know I cannot face a traditional family Christmas this first year without Bob. Sensory cues are hard enough for me as I go about my day-to-day life—hearing a piece of music, catching a whiff of a particular scent, sometimes just the body language of a stranger can trigger a wave of grief. I know the holiday season, which I have always loved, will be a constant flow of such reminders.

I remember standing at the bank machine in Squamish in mid-December 1997. At the next ATM stood a woman Bob had represented earlier in the year. A logging accident had killed her husband, leaving her with a young family. I was moved by the profound sadness and exhaustion of her expression. As she finished her banking, she turned slowly to me, her eyes red and tired. Recognizing me as her lawyer's wife, she said hello. We had a brief conversation. Before she walked away, she urged me to go home and hug my family. "Hold on tight," she said. As I left in the other direction, I felt so blessed to think of my family safely going about their day. I could not imagine what it would be like to endure the Christmas she was facing.

One month later, I was that woman. I looked ahead and decided that we needed to be far away for our first Christmas without Bob, someplace where felt nothing like home. I chose a resort in Mexico. I had never experienced a tropical Christmas, and I hoped it would put some distance between me and all the cues that I anticipated would be hard to bear. When I told my family what I had done, they jumped right in and booked their own reservations, making it clear there was no way I was going to be alone with the children for the holidays. Then, of course, Michael appeared on the scene. We decided not to change the plans but to expand them to include him, Adam, and Carlie as well.

When we go through immigration at the airport in December 1998, the officials shake their heads and comment that we are a pretty diverse family. It is a fair comment. There we stand,

Michael with his striking white moustache; Adam with loopy dark curls; Carlie and her beautiful Asian eyes and jet-black hair; blond-haired, blue-eyed twins; and me. There must be some interesting paperwork to back up how we are all connected, the uniformed official surmises. Michael produces the documentation that is required to let us travel out of the country: passports, death certificate, marriage certificate, notarized permission letter from an ex-wife. The new-millennium family.

Within a year, my sister Jenny remarries as well. Her new husband, George, a gentle giant of a man, played professional football during the 1960s and later became a high school teacher. George jokingly refers to Jenny as his princess and treats her like a queen. She is a radiant bride, and I am honored to propose a toast to her at the reception. I get a laugh from the crowd when I point out that she may have broken my record for speedy engagements. We toast the wonderful blessings life bestows when we least expect them.

Living what is essentially a different life refreshes and invigorates me. I realize that I am rediscovering a part of myself that I left behind when I married Bob. We cultivate certain aspects of our character according to the specific dynamics of the relationships we are in, shelving other facets of ourselves. Emerging now are parts of my personality that I had set aside many years before. I feel a renewed sense of clarity and honesty with myself. I do not need to please anyone, and at the same time I am attracting a new circle of friends who genuinely enjoy my company. This is most evident in my relationship with Michael. I feel totally myself with him. There are none of the little games or pretenses that I fell into easily and willingly in my twenties. I know Michael loves me for exactly who I am and not for someone he wishes I would be.

With the twins in kindergarten, I suddenly have time on my hands. I know I am not ready to revisit my career, which ended so abruptly. Until the criminal investigation wraps up, I cannot commit professionally or emotionally to any type of employment. But I can look for some short-term volunteer projects to occupy my time while Emma and Sam are in school.

My childhood home in Victoria was right next door to the local art gallery. It is a wonderfully eclectic establishment in the middle of a residential area—part heritage mansion and part modern institution—and it was my playground as a child. I would wander through the gallery for hours. There I learned to love the West Coast images of Emily Carr and to appreciate the ancient and intricate beauty of the extensive Asian collection. Just the smell of the lobby feels like home. Many of Michael's friends are patrons, and I have no trouble being reintroduced to the institution as a prospective volunteer. I am delighted to accept a position on the board of directors and immerse myself in planning fund-raising events.

My ability to concentrate has been badly affected by the trauma of Bob's death. My mind wanders easily, and I startle at the slightest sudden movement. A therapeutic solution emerges in the most unlikely place. I take up the game of golf. Michael played as a young man and has recently rediscovered the sport. He belongs to the Victoria Golf Club, an astonishingly beautiful course that follows the ragged coastline at the southeast tip of the city. Its clubhouse is a stately building that showcases the club's rich local history.

I become a member and am quickly humbled by the challenge of learning to hit the elusive little white ball. With skiing and windsurfing, I had found that I was not a risk taker. While I wanted to share those experiences with Bob, I had no interest in pushing myself past my comfort level. But the mental challenge of golf appeals to me. Competing against myself rejuvenates my frayed nerves and brings back my self-confidence.

Other members are well aware of my story and our very public marriage, but they show us the utmost respect and discretion. Weekly games with other female members give me the opportunity to make some new friends in a setting where the conversation is light and limited. It is a perfect fit at a time when I do not want to bare my soul outside the safe confines of my new family. As I get to know people better over time, I find a comfortable and supportive social network where I can reveal my new self. Unfortunately, while I thrive socially, my golf game does not improve. On more than one occasion I am presented with the award for the most honest golfer.

At Emma and Sam's school I meet other parents in the playground after classes end, and it is not long before we are making plans to meet socially. Gradually my story comes out and another support system emerges, one that does not include the hidden judgmental component I have sensed with many of my old friends. I realize the difference is that these new friends did not know Bob. While the story shocks and saddens them, they have no emotional attachment to him and are able to consider the life choices I have made without the burden of their own grief.

Getting past the shock is the tricky bit. Before the first day of school, I ask if perhaps we should let the parents of Emma's and Sam's classmates know what has recently happened to our family. The director of the school feels it is best to allow the story to come from the children naturally. It will give them a sense of ownership and control of the information. We can manage the fallout if and when it happens. And it does happen.

At a school orientation evening, I find myself sitting in a group of parents who are discussing their children's first days in kindergarten. One mother repeats a story her little girl had shared about a new classmate. The teacher was using a cat puppet to illustrate what is acceptable behavior and what is not. For example, the cat told the little girls that mouths are for saying nice things to people and not mean things. Hands are for helping and not for hurting. The woman's daughter said that at this point one of her classmates told the cat that he was right—someone had used their hand to hurt her daddy, and now he was dead.

This mother is clearly troubled by the story her child relayed and wonders what exactly the other student was talking about. I can see the doubt, confusion, and fear moving rapidly across her face as she recounts the conversation. Taking a deep breath, I tell the woman that the child she is describing is my daughter and explain what happened to Bob. She is initially taken aback but quickly regains her composure as she more fully understands the details of what occurred. I apologize that the story came out in the way it did. I know that murder is not a topic most parents of five-year-olds are anxious to discuss around their dining room tables.

Sam faces a difficult situation on the playground when an older boy finds out about Bob's death. He begins to ask Sam about the circumstances and then asks him why Bob did not fight back. Sam is stunned by the question and offers no explanation. He comes home from school and raises the question at the dinner table. Michael sensitively works through the scenario with him. It is the first time in months I have felt the need to throw up.

There is a stigma attached to being the family of a murder victim. No one wants to think that type of tragedy will ever happen to them. They distance themselves by assuming that the victim must have been involved somehow in the dark side of society—a place they will never find themselves. Surely the killing was something the victim brought on himself, the result of a drug deal gone bad or a gambling debt left unpaid. It is too frightening to imagine a typical middle-class father being killed randomly. There one moment. Gone the next.

We are not the collective face of a victim that people are prepared for. We are always going to need to reassure them that we are a good family and that the way Bob died had nothing to do with the way he lived. At the same time, they must understand that part of the fresh start we are making includes being free of the burden of pity. Bob's murder is undeniably a part of our story, but it in no way defines who we are. Gradually, each of us learns how to manage the impact our story has when people hear it for the first time.

And gradually my children learn how to control how and when the story is shared. A year later I find Sam retrieving a huge triathlon trophy from a shelf in the basement one morning before school. I ask him what he plans to do with it, and he explains that it is his turn to do show-and-tell. A wave of dread lurches up inside me as I ask him if he is planning an explanation of triathlon or if he intends to talk about Bob and what happened to him.

Sam smiles gently, his blue eyes rolling under the heavy fringe of lashes, as he says, "I know, Mum. I know. It is not a story for little ears."

Later that day I find myself feeling both fragile and blessed. When I approach Sam's teacher to ask how his show-and-tell went, she says he did a wonderful job describing the sport of triathlon. When his classmates asked questions, the discussion moved to queries about Bob. Sam handled them beautifully, deflecting the comments that were uncomfortable and keeping everyone on track.

Michael's family has to deal with the impact of the story too. When his mother is in the hospital for a hip replacement, a woman in the next bed is reading a newspaper article about the criminal investigation into Bob's death. She begins to talk about the story in a way that clearly makes Barbara uncomfortable. She has no problem telling the woman that this is happening to her son's new family and she would rather not talk about it.

This is such a good lesson. It is easy to forget that there are families on the other side of every fleeting headline. Hearing our personal stories bandied about as lightly as the newsprint they are written on is agonizing.

Michael's presence in my life does not erase the huge ragged wound that remains after Bob's death. I need to leave it open to the air so that the parts that can heal will mend themselves. And then I have to find a place to keep the part that will never heal—a place where it will hurt the least, where people cannot always see it. No matter where I try to hide that wound, there are times it will expose itself. I learn that I cannot control when and where that will occur.

I become good at protecting myself from situations I believe will be too much to bear. In August 1999 we are woken in the middle of the night by a phone call from my young friend Grant. His mother, Doreen, is missing. She has left a long letter behind, and her family imagines the worst. The next afternoon their fears are confirmed when her body is found on the banks of the Squamish River. Depression and chronic pain became too much for Doreen. She took her own life. I feel numb as Grant describes the situation. I know how badly he needs me, but I cannot go to him. I promise to be here for him when he can come to us, but I cannot go back to Squamish and attend another funeral for a life cut short for all the wrong reasons.

At other times, the pain catches me unawares. In October 2000 Rob Kiddell, the director from the boys' campus at the children's school, calls to say that Simon Whitfield is coming to surprise the students at an assembly. Simon is just back from the Sydney Olympics, where he won the first gold medal ever presented for the sport of triathlon. Rob is aware that Bob knew Simon and thinks I may want to come to the school in case the event is difficult for Sam. Feeling fortunate to have such caring people looking out for my family, I discreetly tuck myself in the back of the gymnasium where the boys are assembling.

When Simon appears wearing his gold medal, the boys go wild. He quiets their applause and starts running a short motivational video about the sport for which he so proudly represents Canada. The images of competitors rushing into the water in their wet suits, pushing up steep hills on their bikes, and completing the marathon run are set to moving music. While the boys watch in silent awe, I feel the floor dropping away beneath me. My breathing becomes shallow and I think I'm going to faint. I try to get outside for some air, but have to sit down to keep from falling. Sam's teacher, a competitive swimmer who knew Bob, sees that I'm having difficulty and follows me outside. I find myself sobbing in her arms. Poor Sam doesn't even know I'm there until he sees me and the commotion in my wake as I leave the assembly.

As the involuntary physical reaction subsides, the tears keep coming. Sam is in the gym, keeping it together, and I, who have come to watch over him, have lost it. After Simon finishes with the boys, he is invited into Rob's office to meet Sam and me privately. For a moment, as we sit in a circle around Rob's desk, emotion gets the better of all of us. Then Rob composes himself and says to Simon that he understands he knew Sam's father and wonders what he was like.

Simon's reply is perfect. He explains that they traveled and competed together at the world championships in Perth just a month before Bob was killed. Pausing for a second, he turns to face Sam directly and grins as he says, "Well, to be honest, Bob was a real shit disturber!" What seven-year-old boy would not think that was the coolest comment ever? Simon gives Sam the video he showed and autographs the case. We take photographs of Simon with Sam wearing his gold medal. As we are leaving, Simon tells Sam that if he ever wants to do a triathlon, he will help him train for it.

Both Sam and I are exhausted from the emotion of the experience and feeling a bit shaky. I offer to take him out for lunch so that we can collect ourselves. Sam tells me what he really wants to do is go to the office and see his dad. He feels that a bit of one-on-one father-and-son time is in order and hopes that I understand. I don't know if I will ever understand, but I am reminded again how lucky we are to have Michael in our lives.

Michael is always there to pick up the pieces when anyone falls apart. One evening we are having dinner at the golf club with Michael's parents. As we walk into the dining room, Sam freezes. The room has been decorated with a canopy of helium balloons tied with long, curling ribbons. He begins to tremble, and then the tears come. I know immediately that the balloons remind him of the graveside ceremony, when he was given a balloon to send up to heaven with Bob.

We get to our table and Michael gently takes Sam by the hand and pulls him up onto his lap. At the same time he tugs one of the balloons down toward them. "Why don't we write a message to your dad?" Michael quietly suggests as he produces a felt-tipped pen from his pocket. Sam begins to dictate a long note, and Michael carefully pens his words onto the thin, taut rubber. The surface is almost covered with writing when Sam is finished.

Emma has joined them and waits patiently for her turn. Michael pulls down another balloon and asks her what she would like to say to Bob.

"Please write, 'Hope you're having a nice time in heaven.'" So typical of Emma—brief and to the point.

Michael then takes both children by the hand and leads them out into the dark night. They stand on the flat of the putting green and let the balloons go. I watch in tears from the warmth of the dining room as the three of them stand silently, their heads lifted, watching the balloons disappear into the darkness.

I think it is only when you open yourself up to truly feel the crushing sadness of loss that you also begin to see where the real beauty of humanity shines through. It glimmers in the darkest moments. Those who are afraid to lift their heads and confront the pain of their loss miss such moments.

Our journey through grief would have looked very different if Michael were not in our lives to help absorb the shock. It doesn't mean that we get to skip over the painful parts. But it does mean that as we work through that pain, we can find safe shelter in the new family we are building with him. I notice that Emma and Sam, who went from calling him Mr. Hutchison to Michael to Daddy in the space of several months, have now taken to calling him "Dadoo." When I ask them why, Emma rolls her eyes and says, "Mum, didn't you take French in school? 'Deux' means 'two' in French. And Michael is Dad number two. Dad-Deux." It makes perfect sense. The name Dadoo also serves another purpose. It allows Emma and Sam to distinguish between Bob, whom they call Daddy-O, and Michael. It works especially well in public, where they are able to make the distinction in conversation between one and the other without having to draw attention to the fact that they are talking about two different fathers.

Over time, even Michael's connection to Bob evolves. They may never have met, but Michael is raising Bob's children and is getting to know Bob through Emma's and Sam's traits and behaviors. It is impossible not to develop an intimate connection.

During the height of the silence surrounding Bob's murder, an article about the case appears in a Vancouver magazine. Michael is sitting at the kitchen counter reading the piece; I am standing beside him, looking at the article over his shoulder. As I read, Michael's tears are falling on the page. The three of us are connected by an intricate and complicated bond. Michael cannot help being touched by the senselessness of the act, even though it was that act that brought us together. His tears blur the boundary.

There is no road map around the tragedy of Bob's death, but I am blessed that Michael chose to accompany me on the journey. On many occasions we find ourselves staring at one another in disbelief at the chain of events that brought us together. It amazes us how our beliefs about what constitutes a loving and caring home are completely in sync. The similarities in our family histories, our shared moral values, and our strong work ethic enable us to partner and parent in harmony. We have created a new, strong, safe, and happy family from the wreckage. And there is no music more sweet than the laughter that Michael brings home to us every day. He is taking such good care of us. I promise myself I will take good care of him.

Years earlier, Bob and I were recalling the decisions we had made and the coping strategies we'd developed together when we were faced with infertility. I will never forget what he said to me. He told me we were right to focus most of our time and energy on dealing with the problem, but it was important to hold back some energy and emotional capacity. There had to be a small reserve, he suggested, because this would not be the last crisis our family would face. Now I can see how prophetic those words were. I believe life is a series of crises. We all have them. But it is important to remember that in between those crises are wonderful celebrations and opportunities to learn. I believe that the real measure of people is how they move between the crises, celebrations, and learning opportunities that punctuate their lives. It is on this journey that resilience is born and grace flourishes.

the waiting game

A man's dying is more the survivors' affair than his own.
—Thomas Mann

As 1999 closes and we move into 2000, Emma and Sam have slipped happily into the routine of first grade, playdates, art lessons, and soccer practices. Adam has graduated from high school and is taking theory classes at the Conservatory of Music to prepare himself for university. Carlie lives nearby with her mother and stays with us on alternate weekends.

I love being in the center of the busy energy in our home. However, I hold my breath every time the phone rings. I know at any moment the police could call to say there has been some activity on the criminal investigation, and our lives will be thrown into a tailspin.

I agonize over how the waiting must be affecting families on the other side of the tragedy. Surely parents have seen loved teenagers change over the last two years as they have tried to push the events of New Year's Eve 1997 far, far down into the realm of forgotten memory. I imagine those parents watching in isolation, fearing something horrible has happened to pull the light from their children's eyes, but having no idea what it was.

I am removed from what is going on in Squamish. In addition to the physical distance, a significant emotional chasm has formed between me and many of the people I had been close to. My wrongful death suit has caused many people to take sides. Some feel it is unfair of me to go after the Cudmores, while others hope they will finally get the message about the effect their son's aggressive behavior is having on the community. This emotional distance compounds my sense of loss. It was not just Bob who was swept from my life—many more relationships disappeared as well, and I have had to start all over again. I miss the familiar comfort of being surrounded by people who know me. But I also have to look out for the best interests of my family, and if people do not condone the decisions I have made, then that is their problem, not mine.

Hugh Winter, a Squamish detective, has been handling the case from the beginning. I quickly break through his tough cop veneer, built up as armor over years of policing, and we develop a comfortable relationship. Actually, it was Sam who first got to Hugh. Before we left Squamish, Sam told me there was something he wanted to give the two police detectives working on the case. He knew they were working hard to find out who killed Bob, and he thought it would be fitting to give each of them one of Bob's triathlon medals to show his appreciation. There my son stood on our front lawn, clutching the two metal disks, their striped ribbons dangling from his tiny hands. He looked up at the two men and simply said, "Thank you." It was clearly difficult for both detectives to maintain their composure.

With my background in business, I cannot help thinking that this case must be a huge financial drain on Squamish's small police detachment. The staff time needed to interview close to two hundred people who attended the New Year's Eve party would have taxed even a big-city police department.

The sketchy information the police have is inconsistent, but what else would you expect when a large number of drunk and scared kids are questioned in the sober glare of daylight? The town seethes with numerous contradictory rumors about what happened that night, who exactly was in the room as Bob was punched and kicked, and who did the punching and kicking. I cannot understand how anyone could watch a fatal beating and not need to come clean.

I look for ways to help the police with their investigation and, along with Bob's family and his business partner, speak to the Royal Canadian Mounted Police about the idea of offering a reward. They decide that it is worth trying, and in May 1998 the town is plastered with posters offering $10,000 for information that leads to the arrest and conviction of the person or people responsible for Bob's death. I am hoping that someone will be motivated to come forward and connect the dots for the investigators. The reward money will be enough to help some young person move in a positive direction, toward college or better employment. Surely someone will want to break free of the prison of their own conscience. However, while the police receive numerous anonymous tips via the Crime Stoppers phone line, none of the callers is willing to put their name on a statement, even with the incentive of a reward.

I worry that a climate of intimidation permeates teen culture in Squamish and that the town's young people are too fearful to speak up. The teenage daughter of one of my friends made me aware of the bullying that is a way of life for a core group of young men there. She told me that she felt a sense of responsibility for what had happened to Bob. Knowing she was *not* at Jamie Cudmore's New Year's Eve party, I asked her how she could feel any connection to Bob's death. Her reply stunned me. She explained that she watched the same group of young people bully their way through school and on into their young adult lives. In retrospect, she wished that she had done something to expose their increasingly intimidating and violent behavior and make it stop. She always feared that one day one of them would do some real harm. She assumed the victim would be one of their own crowd, not an innocent person like Bob, who was simply trying to do the right thing.

Jamie, the young man who hosted the party, is the most notorious of the bullies. His reputation worried Bob, and his behavior was often a topic of discussion in our home. Ironically, even though he was hosting the party, he is not a suspect because he was not in the house when Bob was killed. He had left his father's home, filled with between 150 and 200 partying youth, and moved on to another gathering. The police corroborate his statement with their own records, which show they gave him a roadside suspension for suspected impaired driving just before Bob was killed. Jamie apparently left his car parked, as instructed by the police, and walked on to another party and eventually to the local Legion.

Shortly after the reward posters go up, Hugh Winter calls to tell me the case has been referred to the RCMP's Serious Crime Unit in Vancouver. Hugh will still be working behind the scenes, but Vancouver will coordinate the investigation from this point forward, and my contact will be with the Serious Crime Unit. Hugh and I have always joked that perhaps I should consider becoming a police detective myself, since I often will guess the very bits of information that he is not telling me. Sensing that I am upset to be losing the easy camaraderie we have developed, Hugh tells me a bit about the detective I will now be dealing with. Don Rinn is the best there is, he says, but his style is different and he will not give me the chance to get close to him the way I have with Hugh. He laughs as he adds that he knows if anyone can get to Don, it will be me.

On one hand, I am happy that the case has been referred up the ranks. The Serious Crime Unit handles most of the high-profile murders in the province. There is a huge backlog of unsolved crimes at any given time, and I know we are lucky they are moving on the case as quickly as they are. It is the first time

I see the politics of policing at work. As in any business, the unit needs to justify itself and naturally will take on those cases that are most likely to produce a good outcome. Clearly there are people lobbying to get our file dealt with. It gives me renewed hope.

On the other hand, Hugh is right. I am going to miss the security of picking up the phone and calling the Squamish detachment, where I can freely ask questions and feel that I know almost everything they know. The officers and staff have all been members of my community and feel a personal connection to Bob's murder and the impact it has had on their town. The case was about the *people* affected by the crime. But now the case is about the contents of box after box of written material. The new detectives on the file do not know Bob or me and cannot possibly feel the loss in the same way. I hope that the separation and impartiality will make it easier for them to get to the heart of the matter.

Over the next two years, Don makes periodic visits to Victoria. We go for lunch or coffee and exchange pleasantries most of the time. Then Don explains that they are actively working on the case but he is not in a position to reveal anything specific about what they are doing. At one of these meetings, I tell him I assume they have gone undercover and that is why he is not at liberty to discuss the details. He is visibly disturbed by my intuition, but relieved at the same time that he can stop the charade. Patience is one of my strongest virtues, I assure him. But I also need to feel I have a small personal connection with anyone who plays such a crucial role in matters that so profoundly affect my life. Don is going to have to get used to my deliberate efforts to get to him. From that point on, he relaxes a bit. I don't ask too many questions about the case, and he lets down his guard and shows me the real person behind the badge.

The rest of the world is not so patient. Because the police are in the midst of an undercover operation, they will not say anything about the status of the case. The public takes that to mean the police are doing nothing, and their frustration plays out repeatedly in the media.

After Bob's death, the Vancouver media quickly jump on any story that puts Squamish in a bad light. Unfortunately, they are given plenty of material to work with. A vicious and unprovoked attack on sixteen young Filipino-Canadian campers at a local campsite in May 1998 is linked to the same group of youths thought to have been involved in the events surrounding Bob's death. Squamish is presented as a small town with a big problem. The media suggest that the town's youth have adopted a code of silence, and the plentiful and meaningful achievements of many young people in the community are continually downplayed as the media focus on the more sensational details of the wanton and destructive behavior of a small group of bullies.

Letters to the editor of the local paper urge anyone who has information to come forward. Some of those letters suggest that some adults may be playing an active role in encouraging the code of silence or at least ignoring its existence. Either scenario is frightening. I understand the sense of helplessness that the community is venting in the letters that are printed week after week.

Before her death, Doreen was tormented by the silence and the opinions that were publicly expressed. She wrote of her feelings to the editor:

This is all bad.

All wrong.

Senseless.

A total waste.

My initial reaction to...Bob McIntosh's death has not changed, nor will it. Because I'm correct in these conclusions.

That someone so good, so kind, so loving, so healthy, so dynamic, so energetic, so cheerful, so athletic, so happy, so passionate and expressive in his joy of living died violently at the hands of another is incongruent. Like others so close to Bob, I am heartbroken. Like others, I have been to hell and partway back; there cannot be an all the way back.

Our world has changed because Bob is no longer in it. It has changed for the worse, because of the loss of this wonderful friend.

A dictionary may define a friend as a supporter of a cause or group, as someone you like, who conforms to a standard. I can see where that can be misconstrued to include groups which are not well-meaning, not positive contributors to a healthy society. The authors of the letters and anyone who shares their mistaken belief that a true friend would ever ask you to break the law or lie for him, would lie for you, could participate in violence or condone it, who teaches by word and action a disregard for a fellow man's needs and rights, even to the extent of his very life, does a disservice to this phrase. There is strength in numbers. I see now that there is weakness in numbers too. Rather, a true friend is a model of integrity, love, peace, happiness, kindness, giving. Loyal for the right reasons. I know because I have many. Because I am one. Because Bob was one.

We are not saying a particular individual is guilty of Bob's wrongful death. But at least one is guilty of violence to his body. At least one is guilty of killing Bob. Perhaps even of over-killing. You know that. Some of you know who. We are each responsible for our choices, our behavior, and the consequences. You are right that some of those choices "bias" onlookers, affect members of society, which has a code of behavior, of ethics. You are wrong that teenagers have been singled out as being out of control. Plenty of adults meet that criteria. In fact,

*the accused is an adult. I cannot agree with you that all
children are fabulous in their own way; some have veered
so far off track that they have lost that part of who they
are. My innocent friend died because of that. The
wake-up call is for you. To turn things around. But it
will be too little, too late. This tragedy cannot be undone
or made up for. It is and remains all bad.*

My friend Shelley is motivated to change the public perception and organizes a Pride in Youth March for June 1998.
Hundreds of young people and adults who care about them take
to the streets. In an ongoing follow-up to the high-profile public
rally, the community of Squamish works hard to raise awareness
of, and provide support for, the positive contributions local
youth make to their town.

Having experienced the carnage of out-of-control youth
firsthand, I develop a heightened awareness of stories of similar
senseless acts. No one else I know has been a victim of violent
crime, so I look to these stories for a sense of commonality and
belonging—belonging to a club that no one wants to join. One
common denominator is the way the justice system protects the
interests of the accused. The victims speak of feeling voiceless
and disillusioned, shut out of the process and kept in the dark.
As much as I want resolution in my own situation, I dread the
process that we will face when that resolution finally comes.

What is usually absent from other stories of violent crime
is any speculation by the victim about what was going on in the
mind of the perpetrator. I want to understand what happened in
the world of the person or people responsible for Bob's death,
how they got to a point where they could kill someone and then
not confess to it. I do not want to experience the disconnect
that is described by other victims, and I believe that understanding the perpetrator's mind-set and motivation is the key to
avoiding that. The label "victim" carries with it a quality of per-
petual vulnerability and an inability to control one's own des-
tiny. I refuse to allow myself or my children to be defined by the
crime that took Bob from us. If anything, I want our lives to be

defined by the legacy of excellence that Bob left behind. Each decision I make to move myself and my family forward is inspired by the way Bob lived to the fullest.

In summer 1998, the detectives arrange for several people to take polygraph tests. When I read about the conditions set out by lawyers representing these individuals, I am disgusted. No matter how much time I spend in close contact with the legal system, it will never change my perception that it is skewed to protect the suspect. The young people being interrogated were assured that they could have family support around the process and that it would take place at a time that was convenient for them. I hear that the police turned a blind eye to one individual who smoked a joint in the parking lot to relax himself before he came in to take the test. I want all of them to know that the last place my family wanted to be was supporting me through this. There was no convenient time for Bob to be killed. And I do not believe for one minute that substance use will relax me and make the pain go away. Someone out there took a life, and now they need to face up to that fact.

In September 1998, the manslaughter charge that was laid against Ryan McMillan days after Bob's death is stayed. There are several inconsistencies in the witness statements, and the Crown counsel fears that the case will unravel. While McMillan may have thrown the punch that put Bob on the ground, it is unclear what happened next. The police tell me that the people who incriminated McMillan are the key suspects in the beating that followed the punch. These people may be telling the truth about McMillan, but the police doubt the accuracy of their accounts of their own actions following the punch.

Several months later, in spring 1999, my lawyer, Michael's partner, receives the police files so he can review them in preparation for the pending civil action. While the client does not normally go through these files, I volunteer to read the material and summarize the key information for him in an attempt to minimize the time he must spend on the case. It takes several weeks to go through four banker's boxes of interview files, and the process is incredibly painful. To read so many accounts of the same drunken evening from slightly different vantage points is excruciating. But there is a part of the ordeal that is enlightening. In the majority of files I read, the witnesses' demeanor, which comes through in their dialogue with the police, is reverent and remorseful. These people had nothing to do with what happened to Bob, and they were sickened to find themselves in the house where the murder occurred.

There are, however, a handful of people who are much less forthcoming and clearly resent the investigation. Reading their statements is frightening. How can these people not imagine what my family is going through? Their refusal to talk pushes the pain deeper inside us. Is it not having the same effect on them? Are they so desensitized to violence that they can blow this off? What will happen when they grow up, move away, and begin real lives of their own? I fear the emotional domino effect this will have over time, on them and on the people who care about them.

Shortly after I summarize the details from the police files, Michael's partner decides to leave the law firm. His departure is swift and acrimonious. I find myself without a lawyer once again.

In an effort to find a new lawyer, I have the file reviewed by a wrongful death legal expert in Vancouver early in 2000. On his advice, I decide to abandon the action. Since the civil suit was launched, the case law has changed slightly. He is not confident that the case that may have existed in 1998 could stand up in court now.

I am relieved. What I know of the early work Michael did on the file has made me dread the process. I have been warned that one of the angles likely to be used by the lawyers for the Cudmores' insurance company would be to suggest that my marriage to Bob would have ended even if he had not been killed. If they could place our marriage on shaky ground in the eyes of a judge, then they could minimize the settlement amount. I knew I did not have the stomach for those tactics. This has never been about money, and I am confident there will be a more meaningful way to raise awareness of the violation of social responsibility that led to Bob's death.

I begin the process of discontinuing the claim, but this is not as simple as I had hoped. Because I initiated the action for the benefit of Emma and Sam, as well as for myself, the Public Trustee has to become involved. I do not have the right to discontinue a claim that my children may choose to pursue years down the road. It means that we will have to negotiate with the trustee to put the whole thing behind us.

A friend points out the irony of the situation. In an effort to pursue the matter of my husband's wrongful death, I found a new husband. Perhaps that is all that was supposed to happen.

For the next year and a half, all is quiet. The undercover investigation continues, I receive sporadic phone calls from Don Rinn, and different media outlets occasionally run stories lamenting the lack of progress and the perceived indifference of the police, but there are no concrete developments.

Then in June 2001, three and a half years after Bob's death, Don phones me again. He says they have secured the information they were looking for and will make an arrest shortly.

I cannot believe that the waiting is over. Part of me is relieved, and the other part fears what lies ahead. Even though I am married to a lawyer, I do not feel equipped to be on the receiving end of the justice process. And I suppose that is the point, really: the victim is not on the receiving end. It is the Crown representing the interests of the public at large versus the accused. The victim comes along for the ride and does what he or she can to feel a part of it all—but mostly does what he or she can to avoid being revictimized by the process.

Weeks later, nothing has happened. I bypass Don Rinn and call Hugh Winter, hoping I can draw on our rapport to get an explanation for the delay in laying charges. I sense his frustration with the situation as soon as I hear his voice. It appears that people in the Crown counsel's office have serious concerns about some of the details of the evidence that the police gathered during the undercover operation. While Hugh cannot discuss what the discrepancy is, he does say that the Crown does not want a repeat of the high-profile Mindy Tran case, in which a suspect was charged with the abduction and murder of an eight-year-old girl in Kelowna, British Columbia, but was acquitted at trial. That case raised questions about the RCMP's conduct and evidence. The Crown has learned from these mistakes and wants to be sure that once charges are laid in Bob's case, they will stand up under the closest scrutiny. The Crown has essentially asked the police to get more evidence.

Hugh has been with this file from the beginning and knows that what they have managed to obtain is likely as good as it will get. He doubts a witness will suddenly grow a conscience or have a clearer recollection of what happened the night Bob was killed, and the passage of time is only going to make it harder to piece events together. Evidence will only be as good as the quality of the witness statements, and the fact that many of these young people were drunk that New Year's Eve, in conjunction with a natural desire to distance themselves from the tragedy, is bound to make their statements less precise and more inconsistent as time passes.

The file has been making the rounds of the Crown counsel's office over the past four years, and no one there has the continuity or attachment to the case that the police who worked on the investigation have. The RCMP's position is that they are presenting the best evidence possible and that charges should be laid without delay. They fight that battle with the Crown for the next twelve months.

In spring 2002 I hear a rumor that Hugh Winter will soon be leaving the Squamish detachment to take a position in the Okanagan. Fearing that I am losing my strongest link to the investigation, I plan a trip to Squamish to see if a personal meeting with him will motivate his superiors within the Serious Crime Unit to move forward with charges, with or without the approval of the Crown counsel's office.

Hugh and I have a candid conversation about the status of the investigation. As I suspect, he wants to get the file wrapped up before his transfer. He has meetings scheduled with the Serious Crime Unit in Vancouver and is doing everything in his power to get them to lay charges.

He reveals one element that instantly puts our discussion into another realm. He tells me the name of the suspect the police have focused on in the undercover investigation: Ryan Aldridge.

There is something about hearing the name. Things move from the unknown to the known. They are less fearful on one hand, perhaps more so on the other. Even though I do not know Ryan, he becomes real.

Looking across the desk at Hugh, I tell him that I want to be there when Ryan is arrested.

He looks at me with a puzzled expression. While he has teased me about being an armchair detective every time I second-guessed him, he is not prepared for me to ask for this. He seeks to clarify my request, as if he can't believe it. "You mean you want to meet him? Why would you want to do that?"

"With all due respect," I reply, "even though it is the justice system that has put food on my table for the last fifteen years, I do not think I am going to get any satisfaction from seeing this person taken out of a courtroom in handcuffs one day. What *will* make me feel better is meeting Ryan face-to-face. I need to say some things to him. I need to explain the impact Bob's death has had on me and my family. I need to ask what was going on in his world at the time to make him capable of killing Bob. And then," I quietly add, "I need to find out what we can do together to ensure it never happens again."

Hugh sits back in his chair, slowly massaging his temples with his index fingers. He explains that my request is not an ordinary part of police procedure, and he wonders aloud if he could ever imagine something like this really happening.

Suddenly his gaze focuses. He looks up at me and says, "We can make a tape. We can videotape you having the conversation you feel you need to have with Ryan. I will do my best to show it to him in the event that we can move forward and make an arrest. But Katy, we cannot predict how this is all going to play out. What is of paramount importance is the integrity of the investigation. We have one shot at this. Crown has been against us moving forward with charges since we concluded the undercover operation a year ago. You have to trust me here; I'll do the best I can."

That is assurance enough for me. Just the fact that the police may let me have this much to do with the process makes me feel better. I am so afraid of being revictimized by the justice system. Securing my chance to have a voice this early in the game helps to lessen that fear.

We agree that I'll return to Squamish the following week to make the tape. In the meantime, Hugh will meet with the Serious Crime Unit and will lobby for action.

I leave his office and drive up the highway to Alice Lake Provincial Park. My head pounds with fear, relief, and sadness all at once. Michael is at home with Emma and Sam. I miss him so much at this moment. The only other person who would have known the right thing to say or do was Bob. I miss him too.

I walk through the park and find Bob's Trail. The huge granite marker, a rough stone engraved and erected by his friends, reminds passersby of his untimely death. Even though I don't need to be reminded, it is good to be there.

I return to Squamish a week later. The timing of that visit is perfect. High-level meetings within the RCMP have produced the decision I was hoping for. Hugh tells me that an arrest is scheduled for the following week. I am skeptical about their ability to pinpoint when it will actually happen. I have been waiting for this moment for four and a half years and have been disappointed before. Taking a deep breath, I close my eyes and tell

myself that this is it. We are truly moving forward. I am starting the part of the journey I had been longing to embark upon.
I wonder perhaps if, deep down, Ryan Aldridge will also find
some relief when he is forced to begin this journey.

How do you prepare for the reality of an arrest almost five
years after the fact? I'm coming at this from a place of comfort
and support. In partnership with Michael, I've built a loving,
caring, and safe home for our family. I have checked in with a
grief counselor numerous times throughout the years to make
sure I am processing the experience in as healthy a way as possible. The counselor has given me top marks for the work I've
done to move through the trauma of Bob's violent death. I've
even spent time dealing with the possibility that the crime might
never be solved and have prepared myself for living without resolution. But resolution is coming anyway.

It is harder to imagine that somewhere out there a family
innocently going about its daily life will soon be yanked from its
present reality into this story. I do not know who the Aldridges
are, but I'm about to find out. I cannot know how they'll deal
with the revelation that their son or their brother is being
charged in connection with Bob's death.

The RCMP arrange to make the videotape at Doug Race's
home, on the same street that Bob and I used to live on. Hugh
Winter and another officer meet me there and set up the video
equipment in the dining room. I sit at the table looking through
the window at the steep wall of forest rising above Mashiter
Creek. The water rushes loudly far below in the steep ravine. My
mind slips back to vivid memories of Bob happily working in
our yard, just a few doors down.

It is from that place in my heart that I find the words to
speak to Ryan on tape. He has never met Bob, and I think that
he should know something about the man whose life he took. I
believe Ryan may learn something from hearing about the type
of man Bob was, the largeness with which he lived.

I also want him to know how hard Emma, Sam, and I have
worked to put our lives back together after losing Bob. I tell

Ryan that it is now his turn to do some work. He has created a prison for himself. He has hidden away in Squamish, hoping this whole thing will go away. But he must know in his heart that it never will, that until the truth comes out there will be no healing. I urge Ryan to dig down deep and find the words to say quietly, to himself, "I did this." Then perhaps, in time, he will be able to say the words a bit louder, so that the people who love him can hear. I tell him that I cannot imagine the pain those close to him must be experiencing, knowing something has pulled him away from them. Something must have happened in his world to make him withdraw so deeply into himself. Speaking the truth will begin the healing for everyone. For him, for me, and for our families and community.

I tell Ryan that if he can find the words to confess, I can find it in my heart to stand behind him and ensure that he receives all the support available as he moves through the justice system. I finish by saying, "All I want for you is what you took from Bob—a happy and productive life."

The video camera is switched off, and I sit silently for a moment, reflecting on what I have done. It is what I hope someone would do for my children if they found themselves in the same dark and frightening place.

chapter 11

face-to-face

Anger makes you smaller, while forgiveness
forces you to grow beyond what you were.
—Chérie Carter-Scott,
If Love Is a Game, These Are the Rules

June 2002 is unspeakably beautiful in Victoria. The swirling clouds of cherry blossom petals have blown away, and the gardens are a jeweled mosaic of rhododendrons, azaleas, roses, and peonies. The scent of lilac drifts lazily in the air.

Bob was killed in the cold, bleak darkness of winter. Four and a half years later, we are at last going to speak about truth, healing, and moving forward. It seems fitting that this should happen in the spring, when there is so much warmth, hope, and new growth.

The arrest is to happen on June 21. On that day I cannot bear to be at home. I can no longer watch the phone and wait for it to ring. I have waited too long and been disappointed too often. Instead I busy myself with wrap-up festivities at the school and try to think about anything other than what might be going on in Squamish.

Late in the afternoon, my curiosity gets the better of me and I check my voice mail. My heart pounds so loudly that I can barely hear the message from a police officer who asks me to call the Squamish RCMP detachment right away. Parked by the side of a busy road, watching people go about their normal business, I return the call. The arrest went off without a hitch. There was no resistance. Ryan Aldridge is in custody.

My body takes over. As I hang up the phone, I am shaking from head to toe. Sobs from the most wounded places leave me gasping for air. Ten minutes pass before I can compose myself enough to drive home.

Michael is away on a fishing trip. He and four old friends make an annual excursion to the north of the island in search of salmon, halibut, and male camaraderie. I can contact him only by radio phone. I decide to wait until I have more information before I try to reach him. The police have promised to keep me abreast of the interrogation as it unfolds. I secretly am relieved that Michael is going to be away through this. I know he has found it hard watching me shift this burden, trying to find a comfortable place to carry it. He will be back after it is over, to help me pick up the pieces and reenter the reality of our life together.

Emma and Sam bounce in the door together from the school bus. They are bursting with news about their end-of-year class parties and the sports day scheduled for the next week. Their innocent reality dangles oddly over the serious events in Squamish that have captured my attention. I sit them down to explain that Ryan has been arrested, and their questions and concerns tumble out.

"They won't hurt him, Mum, will they?" Emma asks.

"What will he be eating in jail?" Sam ponders.

"Do his parents know?" they ask together. Struck by their immediate caring and compassion, I reassure them that Ryan is safe, tell them what little I know, and promise to keep them updated as I learn more from the police.

We try to enjoy a regular dinner and take the dogs for a short walk. My cell phone is embedded in the palm of my hand as I wait for word from Squamish. Exhaustion takes over and as Emma and Sam watch a movie, I fall asleep nestled between them. When the phone rings, I am jarred out of a dream that I instantly forget.

The officer describes the progress they have made over the hours since Ryan was taken into custody. Immediately following the arrest, Ryan was shown the video I made for him. For approximately two hours the police interrogated him, hoping to get the answers they have been looking for since New Year's Eve 1997. Ryan then asked for his mother to be called. Overcome by emotion, he broke down and confessed to her. The police have videotaped the meeting and now have what they need.

After putting Emma and Sam to bed, I sit on the back step watching the evening sun drop behind the giant wall of laurel that encircles our garden. I try to imagine the rawness and fear Ryan's mother must be feeling. My relief is her disbelief. I am embarking upon healing just as she is discovering her own wound. I wish I could tell her that I see the irony and wish her well. I hope that her family will be strong, like mine, and that she too has a daring heart.

The phone rings again. The officer tells me that after his mother left, Ryan returned to his cell and wrote two letters of apology. One is addressed to my children and me, the other to the community of Squamish. He has asked the police if he could hand these letters to me himself. Am I still interested in meeting Ryan? The investigative team has met and decided that it will bring me in for a meeting with him if I am game. There will be no police in the room with us, she explains, but the meeting will be videotaped. If I agree, the RCMP will send a helicopter to Victoria first thing in the morning to fly me to Squamish.

I know what my answer is, but I tell her I want to talk to Michael first.

It is ten in the evening when I get through on the radio phone aboard the *Sayonara*. Michael supports my wish to go, though he says he would prefer it if there were an officer in the room during our meeting. With his blessings and a promise that he will be home in two more days, he says goodbye and I tearfully hang up the phone. I make arrangements for the next day with the Squamish detachment and call my brother and his wife to look after Emma and Sam in the morning.

I examine my face in the bathroom mirror. It looks gray. The toll of the past few years is forever etched in lines around my eyes and mouth. I am so tired of waste and loss. I am afraid that meeting Ryan may mean more of the same. Will he be angry or fearful or, worse, will he be indifferent? Will meeting him face-to-face be more painful than turning my back on him? I want to believe in humanity. I want to think I can make a difference and break the cycle for Ryan. And then I remember.

In the early hours after Bob was killed, I promised Emma and Sam that we would find a gift. We all clung to the belief that beneath the horror of what had happened to our family, there must be something worth salvaging. I lie awake knowing that meeting Ryan will show me if the gift exists.

The ride in the helicopter is surreal. The RCMP pilot knows nothing about why I am going to Squamish. He attempts to make small talk but realizes I am preoccupied with my own thoughts and concentrates on the instrument panel before him.

Ironically, today is the day of a popular mountain-bike race in Squamish. I cheered Bob on when he competed in this race six years earlier. As we fly over the steep and craggy coastline, we can see a line of bikes weaving their way along the hilly terrain.

An unmarked car meets us at the airport and drives the back roads to the police station. As I am buzzed in through the back entrance, I remember Hugh Winter's first words to me in January 1998. "We will make someone accountable for as much of the truth as we can prove," he had promised. And it is Hugh who greets me at the door and hurries me into his office. He apologizes in advance for what he explains will feel like a rushed albeit carefully planned encounter. He understands that this is going to be traumatic for both Ryan and me, but the investigators have to maintain the momentum of the interrogation process and will only be available to debrief for a few minutes following my meeting with Ryan. Hugh goes over the information the police are hoping to glean from the encounter. Hugh indicates he understands I initiated this face-to-face meeting because I want to speak to Ryan about the enormous impact Bob's death has had on me and my family. I agree and explain that I am also hoping to get an understanding of what could have led Ryan to kill Bob. Hugh expresses an appreciation for the depth and complexity of what I am looking for, but explains the RCMP's needs are precise. He requests that I specifically ask Ryan what he did to Bob on New Year's Eve. Even though Ryan has confessed on tape, the police are looking for additional videotaped evidence of Ryan admitting to his actions to reinforce their position. After five years of waiting, the RCMP do not want this case to get away. Looking at his watch, Hugh gestures me toward the hallway and promises that he and other officers will be right outside the door if I need them.

I am escorted to a small, windowless interview room. Two chairs, a table, and a large box of tissues are the sole furniture. A video camera mounted high in the corner is focused on the empty chairs. I feel as though my heart is going to come out of my mouth. My legs are shaking uncontrollably.

The door opens. Ryan walks in. He looks small and much younger than I expected for his twenty-five years. It is impossible to imagine he is capable of kicking someone to death. The police have taken his belt and shoes, so his pants sit low on his hips as he shuffles in his stocking feet to the chair opposite mine. Slowly he lifts his head. Sandy blond hair falls away to reveal the eyes of a frightened child. His body begins to curl around itself as he slides into the seat.

We face one another. There are no words for a moment.

I break the silence by sitting forward in my seat and telling Ryan that everything is going to be all right. The worst is over. We can both begin moving on now that the truth has been told.

He begins to speak, but the sobs break the words apart. I hand him a ball of tissues and fight the urge to rise from my seat. It is all I can do not to reach out and hug him. He looks like he needs that more than anything right now.

Ryan tells me he is sorry for what happened. When I ask him what exactly *did* happen, he has difficulty finding the words to tell me. There is no explanation. He can only give a disoriented account of a beating that was over before it started: drunken bravado acting out pathetic cowardice.

Acknowledging that we both have to accept the justice process and the judgment the system will mete out, I assure him that I will support him through the process. I talk about my family and ask him about his. Explaining my fear of putting the people we care about through the trauma of a trial, I beg him to take his confession one step further and plead guilty to the charge of manslaughter as soon as a court appearance can be scheduled.

Ryan hands me two white envelopes, the letters he wrote the night before. I ask if I can read them now, and he nods. I scan the pages. The words "sorry," "nightmare," "secret," "family," and "heart" tumble from the paper. I will read them over and over, but it is enough for now. I put the letters away. There is so much more to say, but neither of us can climb over the heaviness and find a way to speak. We sit for a moment, feeling one another's despair and fear fill the room. One of the detectives enters and tells us gently that the meeting is over. An officer escorts me out of the room, leaving Ryan alone. As we move toward Hugh Winter's office, where the debriefing is to take place, I pass a closed-circuit monitor that shows the room I just left.

The image of Ryan alone, sobbing, clutching the framed photographs of my children the police have left there, is burned in my memory. It will stay there beside the scene of Bob lying dead in the hospital. One life wasted; another hanging in the balance. I am determined that Ryan will not be another casualty. I also suspect that my perspective will not be shared by many others.

The debriefing is rushed, and I can tell Hugh is keeping his distance emotionally so that he can continue with the investigation. I am back in the helicopter less than an hour after I arrived. The pilot, who had waited at the police station and watched our meeting on the closed-circuit television with the investigative team, turns to me and says, "I had no idea why I was flying you in. That was the most amazing thing I have ever seen. You are one strong woman." We put on our headsets and I am asleep from exhaustion within minutes of our departure. He flies me back from my past to my present life.

The twenty or so minutes I spent privately with Ryan mean more to me than any courtroom process I can imagine. The fear falls away, to be replaced with profound sadness. What could have gone on in his world to make him capable of something so horrible? I think even Ryan doesn't know the answer to that question. But I do think he realizes he would never work through it in the prison of denial he had created for himself. While he may have far less control over the way things unfold for him now, he must understand on some level that what emerges will provide a better environment for the soul-searching and healing to begin.

Emma and Sam had a wonderful morning with their aunt and uncle and have all but forgotten why I hastily arranged for them to be there. It is a relief to hear them describing their antics on the trampoline and the tricks David's cat can do. I cannot begin to explain the intensity of my meeting with Ryan to myself, let alone to two nine-year-olds.

My answering machine's message light is blinking furiously as I collapse on the love seat in our kitchen. News of the arrest has hit the wires, and I am being chased for interviews. I have become accustomed to handling the requests for comment and am proud that the media have always treated me with the utmost respect. From the early hours after Bob's death, I resigned myself to the fact that the public was going to be fascinated by this story. Bob was not a typical murder victim, and many of the circumstances surrounding Bob's death teach valuable lessons; the media are the perfect vehicle to spread those lessons.

I respond to many of the calls and answer the reporters' questions about my feelings on the arrest, but I do not plan to divulge any details about my meeting with Ryan Aldridge. The police will need to use the tape of his confession in court, and any public discussion of our meeting before the court process begins could hinder the investigation.

I hold my emotions in check until Michael returns two days later. As he wraps his arms around me, I feel the floodgates open. Thirty years in the legal profession have given Michael the opportunity to see crime, policing, and justice from many angles, but he admits that he has had no experience with what I have done.

I show Michael the letters that Ryan gave me. We decide that we should release the one addressed to the town of Squamish to the local media. They can do with it what they feel appropriate. The second letter, the one directed personally to our family, we tuck away for the time being. It would be difficult to explain an apology from Ryan to Emma and Sam if he enters a not-guilty plea. If, however, he finds it in himself to plead guilty and save us the heartache of a trial, we will revisit the notion of sharing his letter with the children.

Dear Sam, Emma, Katie,

I am writing this letter from my heart. I have no idea how to apologize to you and your family. I know you don't half to read this letter but please do. For the past few years I've been keeping this lie from you, Sam and Emma. Lately I've been having nightmares about that terrible night. The secrete has been destroying my life as well as yours. The reason why I didn't come forward

right away is because I couldn't remember all what had
happened that night. I guess I wouldn't let myself believe
that I could've done such a horrible thing. I know there
is nothing I can do to change what I did that night nor
what I can say to make things better. Seeing Sam and
Emma without there [sic] dad made me accept what I
did to come forth with the truth. I owe Sam and Emma
my life. Today I needed my mom and dad and they were
there for me. Sam and Emma only have you, and
realizing that really hurts me. I am so sorry for the grief
that I caused you and your family. I just hope in time
you could maybe accept my apology. Because I am truly
sorry.

So sorry,

Ryan Aldridge

There is also the issue of Ryan McMillan to deal with. The
police indicate they will be laying new charges soon and he will
be brought back into the picture. Unlike Ryan Aldridge, who
seemed genuinely remorseful and frightened when I met with
him, Ryan McMillan came across as angry and indifferent when
I saw him in the courtroom. There may have been something
much different going on under the surface, but the man I saw
scared me.

I let the system take over. Court dates will be booked, can-
celed, and rebooked, and the process will gradually unfold. There
is no more silence, no more waiting. We stay close to home to
await developments but are also able to distract ourselves with
typical family summer activities. The feeling of suspended ani-
mation that has not left me since Bob was killed has disappeared. I treasure its absence.

For the first time in many years, I look to the new year
with a sense of guarded optimism. I am confident that the legal

process will be complete within six months and that 2003 will be a fresh start. I have hung in limbo for so long, protecting myself from disappointment and abandoning any long-term dreams. But now I can begin to think about revisiting my career and creating a vision for our future.

As summer winds down and we prepare for the start of another school year, I look for something to do with my time. Golfing has been a therapeutic pastime, but I miss the routine and order of working. I know that until the case is truly wrapped up I can't commit to outside employment, so I jump at the chance to take over the bookkeeping in Michael's office. The law firm needs a new accounting system, so I research software and train myself and his staff for the switch. I love the checks and balances and how everything in an office has its place. Michael is an easygoing boss, and his staff have an enormous amount of respect for him. Because of that, the working culture is pleasant and we function well together. It is also an opportunity to build on my limited exposure to the business of law and good preparation for what lies ahead in my own case.

Ryan's bail hearing is scheduled for the third day following his arrest. I believe the broken young man I met in that interrogation room is in some small way relieved to have been caught. He does not seem to be a flight risk, and I assume the court will release him into the custody of his family. I am sure, though, that if this happens, the media will decry what they perceive as an injustice.

The hearing will be held at the Squamish courthouse on its last day in operation. Recent provincial budget cuts have scheduled the closure of a number of small-town courtrooms, including the one in Squamish. All subsequent proceedings will be conducted in North Vancouver. This is a relief to me, since I find it emotionally draining to return to Squamish. My best friend Shauna, who lives in North Vancouver, promises she will be there for me whenever an appearance is scheduled.

As I expected, bail is granted with several conditions, including a stipulation that Ryan have no contact with his girlfriend or a group of other young people who will likely be called as witnesses. The anger at Ryan emanating from spectators in the courtroom gallery is palpable. Squamish has had enough of the silence, enough of the negative press, enough of being bullied by the group of thugs it believes Ryan represents.

Ryan and his family leave the courthouse in one direction, and I leave with my sister Jenny and her husband, George, who have come to support me, in the other. The media and their cameras follow us down the street, hoping to get a clip of me condemning the court for not keeping Ryan in custody. They want me to be angry.

I reflect on all the emotions I have felt since Bob's death—and I have worked through a variety—but anger was never one of them. I was devastated to lose Bob, and it is still painful not having him in my life. Moments that should be happy are suddenly sad because Bob is missing from the picture: Sam's first swim meet, Emma's dance recital. As proud as I am of our children, I am distressed that Bob is not there to share their milestones with me. It does not matter how solid or loving the new foundation I have built with Michael is. Bob's death still causes me anguish. But that is not the same thing as anger.

There is fear. It was frightening having my life ripped apart by a violent crime. Dealing with the aftermath is frightening. I suspect that parts of this experience will continue to be frightening forever. But again, that is not the same as anger.

Anger is a dead end. Anger tears away at you and stops you from moving forward. It was anger that got Bob killed. When the police asked Ryan what was going on in his head the night he killed Bob, Ryan described it as an "angry moment." That struck me as such a hopeless waste. And now the silence has been broken and anger is emerging all around us. I want the anger to be over. I want to break the cycle.

I've heard the suggestion that my lack of anger means I did not really love Bob. If I did, some argue, then I should have been consumed by anger, bent on vengeance. But for me, the way Bob lived his life, each day 110 percent, inspires me to want the best for myself, for our children, and for the community of Squamish—including Ryan and his family.

chapter 12

doing time

"How old is Dad?" he asked me one night.
"He doesn't have an age now."
"Why?"
"Because when you die, sweetie,
you don't have any more birthdays."
"No birthdays? No birthday parties in heaven?" He frowned.
—Ana Veciana-Suarez, *Birthday Parties in Heaven*

The days are getting shorter as fall gradually pulls the life from the trees that stand between our home and the ocean. After a summer of camps and lazy days on the beach, Emma and Sam happily join their friends back at school. It is hard to believe they are already entering fourth grade.

I am settled into the rhythm of Michael's practice, taking care of the money that comes in and the money that goes out, preparing his month-end financial statements, and making sure there is enough paper in the copier. It is not a particularly challenging job, but the predictability is reassuring and gives me a chance to regenerate some of the concentration skills that were damaged when Bob was killed. The best part of the job is being able to see Michael throughout the day. His calm, thoughtful manner wraps around me like a warm shawl.

The routine of after-school soccer practices, swimming, and art lessons distracts me from thinking about the court process that looms ahead of us. Ryan enters a guilty plea during a brief appearance in the North Vancouver court on October 17. With the plea in place, the judge sets a November date for a sentencing hearing. A blank victim impact statement form stares up from my desk, daring me to find the words. They will come, just as Bob's eulogy came to me in the middle of the night. I thought I would never find those words, but when they did come, it seemed they would never stop.

Besides, this statement is not something I could have composed before now. The impact has evolved over the years since Bob's death. Certain memories of the family that we were, and our emotional responses to those memories, have faded and softened like old jeans. Michael's presence in our lives has naturally eased, without replacing, the day-to-day missing of Bob.

Other parts have grown harder and continue to stick into us like broken glass. The reality that Bob was taken from us violently compounds the fear we have for our own community when we hear that a violent crime has occurred. We cannot dismiss some devastating scene we see on the news, as most other people are able to do, by thinking it could never happen to us. We know it *can* happen. We will always be more sensitive to bad news because we have been bad news.

Media coverage since Ryan's arrest has renewed the public discussion of crime and punishment. In the grocery store and bank, people who know little of me beyond my connection to Bob's death gently prod around the issue, hoping to hear first-hand the bitterness and vengeance they are sure must have a firm grip on someone who has been victimized by violence. It surprises me that casual acquaintances would initiate a conversation about something so difficult when they really know nothing about me. I disappoint them when I explain that the brief face-to-face meeting I had with Ryan following his arrest was all the justice I needed. I confirm that I will, of course, be there in the courtroom out of respect for the legal system that Bob worked for and that Michael is still involved in, but I state that the outcome is not likely to alter where I am in my heart.

I struggle not to take their judgmental attitudes personally. I cringe whenever I hear "If I were in your shoes..." I want to reply, "Well, you're not. And even if I found myself in *your* shoes at another time in my life, I hope that I would not be so presumptuous as to second-guess the response of the person who has been victimized." I can only deal with events based on what I know to be true in my heart at the time. The continual lessons of humility and tolerance are an unexpected gift on this path.

Other people assume that somehow the criminal justice process will bring us closure. Whoever came up with that idea could not have been a victim. There will never be a process or meeting or ritual or anything that will close the wound left by Bob's death or make what we have been through any less traumatic. We all have to learn to live with what has happened and find a place in our hearts to contain the sorrow, for it will last forever. The thought of Ryan facing a long and isolated term in jail does nothing to make me feel safer or any better equipped emotionally to handle living with Bob's death. In contrast, my hope that Ryan may now receive the help he needs to face his demons and create a new and healthy life for himself does give me some sense of safety and healing.

I am deeply troubled imagining what the waiting must be like for Ryan's family. How do you prepare for the prospect of your son going to jail? I imagine the world and all its expressions of hatred and punishment slipping away for a few brief moments so I could sit with his mother and listen to *her* reality and to *her* pain. No one wants to know that I think about this. As if stepping over to "the other side" somehow proves I do not value the life I had with Bob.

Surely by humanizing Ryan and his family I am moving closer to embracing the legacy of love and security that Bob left behind. Bob always rose to the occasion in the most difficult situations, whether it was a conflict in the courtroom or a grueling triathlon course. Inspired by his tenacity, his demand for excellence, and his innate sense of fairness, I am, in my own way, doing the same thing. For me there are no "sides" in all of this, just loss and waste all around. If our society spent less time blaming and dividing when faced with conflict, wouldn't we be in a better position to find solutions that more closely meet our mutual needs? And isn't working with the people who come at the problem from farthest away what builds true community?

It is November 28, 2002, and fog hangs over the water as Michael and I drive to the Victoria seaplane dock. This is the morning of the sentencing hearing, and Shauna will pick us up in Vancouver and take us to the North Vancouver courthouse. My heart sinks as the pilot announces that he can't fly in the present weather conditions. We rush to the heliport to get the last seats available on their service to Vancouver. While the helijet manages to take off, we aren't able to land in downtown Vancouver and are diverted to an airport outside the city. It means a two-hour cab ride to the courthouse.

The hearing is well underway when we slide into the seats Shauna has held for us in the front row. Bob's sister, uncle, and cousin are there, as well as my sister Jenny and her husband George. Ryan's family is on the opposite side of the room, and the media fill the back row. Ryan sits with his lawyer at a table below the bench. The same black-and-white wingtip shoes he wore to the earlier proceedings peek awkwardly from below the cuffs of his dark suit pants.

We have missed seeing two hours of video taken by police in the interrogation room following Ryan's arrest. There are three more hours of tape to watch. It is unbearable. At one point in the video, we can hear music from Bob's funeral, the videotape of which is being played on a television while Ryan is questioned. That is too much for me. I curl into a hard ball under Michael's arm and wait for it to be over.

The interrogation process is relentless and terrifying. Bit by bit the detectives strip away the armor Ryan has spent five years building to shield himself. In the video he appears both tired and scared. The ground is steadily slipping away beneath him.

We watch Ryan viewing the video of me speaking to him. It is almost five years since Bob's death, and at last the silence begins to break as Ryan asks the police to call his family. I see the image of his mother entering the interrogation room. Ryan chokes on his words as she stoically bears the weight of the truth that finally spills out. "I killed him," Ryan sobs.

I think of how desperate I felt for Sam the first time we caught him in a lie. I wanted to sweep it all under the rug for him, but I knew I had to be still and allow him to find and then tell the truth. I ache for Ryan's mother and the years of silence burying the truth that are now being ripped away before her.

Court breaks for lunch. The awkward dance begins as each family tries to leave the building without stepping into the other family's space. The media is hoping for a visual image of just such an encounter. Shauna and Michael whisk me away via a back route to a tiny café for soup. I am chilled to the bone, wrung out, and deeply conscious of missing Emma and Sam. I hunger for a sense of normalcy in my life. There is no bowl of soup that will feed that need.

As we drive back to the courthouse, I think about how open-minded and creative the police were when they allowed me to take part in the process immediately following the arrest. They met my need to connect with Ryan, and that in turn helped them secure a confession. It was brave thinking that paid off, and I hope we will see some of that vision emerge in the courtroom.

As the afternoon session begins, the victim impact statement sits folded neatly in my lap. I struggle to imagine the transition from the words that have been said by the judge, Crown

counsel, and Ryan's lawyer—words that follow the legal require-
ments of the proceedings—to the words that I will say, which
simply speak from the hollow place in my heart. Nothing will
make them any easier or harder to say or hear—they are just
what is true for me.

"Do you feel you can do this?" the judge asks as I rise, suddenly feeling unsteady, from my seat. I know that the prosecutor
could read the statement on my behalf.

"Thank you, but no, I need to do this," I respond as I
enter the witness box.

All the faces in the courtroom fall away except for those of
Ryan, his mother, and Michael. I center myself so I can maintain steady eye contact and begin to speak. A voice I was
unaware I possess slowly and carefully peels the words from the
paper and lets them fill the breathless airspace:

> *It is difficult to find the words to describe the emotional*
> *impact of my husband's murder. I still relive the horrific*
> *scene in the emergency room as the doctor tried in vain*
> *to resuscitate Bob. I could not imagine how I was ever*
> *going to make sense of what was going on—it was so*
> *frightening. I was scared to go and see Bob's body after*
> *they had pronounced him dead. I had no family there*
> *with me—I saw him with an RCMP officer at my side.*
> *It was just after midnight on New Year's Eve 1997 as*
> *I began making phone calls from the hospital to our*
> *families and close friends. I don't know where I found*
> *the words to tell them what was happening.*
>
> *Returning home just before dawn, I faced the*
> *horrendous task of telling my four-year-old twins, Emma*
> *and Sam, that their daddy was dead. I stood in their*
> *doorway while they slept away the last few moments of*
> *their innocence and tried to find the right words to*
> *explain the unexplainable.*
>
> *The next weeks were a blur of police, media, family,*
> *friends, a cold double bed, and a gut-wrenching pain that*

would not go away. I had to explain the words "murder," "massive head injury," "jail," "funeral," and "widow" to two children who should have been learning nursery rhymes. We had to put our private turmoil and pain on hold while we made way for the very public display of shock and grief shown by the 1,000 people who attended the funeral, and scores of others who needed to make a personal connection with us in order to deal with their own grief.

Because the murder took place at the home of our good friends, allegiances were challenged and my closest circle of friends imploded. People found it impossible to be supportive of both families. When I lost Bob, I also lost the relationships we valued the most. The damage has been irreparable.

The enormous loss quickly extended beyond close friends to our community. The code of silence with respect to the crime made it impossible to tolerate living in Squamish. I could not imagine raising my children in a town where the person or persons that killed my husband were living freely. Every time we were in public we would have to endure people staring, making uncomfortable comments, or simply crossing the street to avoid us. I resigned from my position as a business analyst for the Community Futures Development Corporation, uprooted the children, and moved to Victoria.

The decisions I made, and my personal journey through grief, were closely scrutinized and judged by my friends and family. Very few relationships remained unscathed, as there was rarely harmony between my choices and their own experience in dealing with Bob's murder. Many of his friends who initially promised to "be there" for us have not been heard from since the funeral. The loss spread far and wide.

In the four and a half years since the murder my life has been about learning to live without Bob, and to live with the way in which he died. I am not the same person I was before his death. I have lost the ability to concentrate for long periods of time, and doubt that I would ever be capable of full-time employment again. I am fearful in crowds. The sound of sirens makes me shake. My tolerance for stress is greatly reduced—I need to give myself lots of space and time for everything. Sometimes I am simply overwhelmed by the burden of what happened to us and I cry for a day. I have nightmares about not being with Bob when he died. I don't want my life to be about Bob's death.

When Bob was killed it was as though we were suddenly picked up and dropped back on earth to suddenly manage without him. I miss him so much. He gave unconditionally to all of us, and had such a brilliant future to look forward to. There will never be a natural progression of things for any of us. Our lives will always be fragmented and punctuated by Bob's murder. I yearn to just feel normal.

Any activity that evokes memories of the eleven years I spent with Bob is an emotional struggle. Videos and photo albums are painful to look at. Music is often upsetting. My children desperately want to learn to ski, but I cannot bring myself to return to the mountains. Whenever my mind drifts to a memory of my life between 1986 and 1997 it inevitably becomes about what happened to Bob.

When I watch my children accomplish milestones I grieve for the fact that Bob is not here to share in them. It was the moving men who took the training wheels off Emma and Sam's two-wheelers. Every loose tooth, swim meet, report card, Christmas stocking, and birthday party is bittersweet. I feel as though I have a secret wound that will just not heal. I struggle with not slipping into depression in the winter months, and especially the holiday season, when the memories of Bob's murder and the aftermath are so intense. Emma and Sam's fifth birthday was two weeks after his death—it is all I can do just to get through the day each year.

As my children grow, the issues associated with being victimized by this violent crime change. We have to constantly discuss what is appropriate information for them to share with their friends as they begin to seek their own support systems beyond family. They are often confronted by ignorant or insensitive remarks by other children regarding their daddy's murder. I am frightened by how children become desensitized to violence through the media, and have tough rules for Emma and Sam. The constant good example I expect them to set in this regard is sometimes just too much to ask from nine-year-olds. As they push boundaries, and learn to find their own moral code, they cannot help but compare the most innocent of situations to the awful example of denial and unaccountability set by the people involved in Bob's death. I am fearful about my ability to behave as a rational parent when we begin to deal with teen issues.

Emma has internalized her feelings about Bob's death. I often find his photograph or stuffed animals he gave her under her pillow. I try to discourage her stoicism, but she prefers to cry privately. The social stigma of what happened to her daddy troubles her. She is extremely sensitive to aggression and violence. The recent events in the criminal proceedings have been difficult for her to handle. With a sense of moral value beyond her years, Emma has been deeply troubled by the difficulty encountered in solving the murder.

Sam's expression of his loss has been more overt. I have been called to the school on a number of occasions to take him home because he has been overwhelmed by emotion and cannot manage in the classroom. He is fearful of physical confrontation in the playground. Sam asks questions about the mechanics of how someone can

actually be kicked to death. He is envious of close
relationships between his peers and their fathers. He is
very protective of me, and destabilized when I show my
emotion about the ordeal.

   The four and a half years of silence have driven the
grief deeper within us. The constant contact with RCMP,
questions of well-meaning friends, and so many
unanswered questions arrested the natural progression of
healing for all of us. The children and I could not
understand how anyone could be living with himself or
herself if they had any knowledge of the truth surrounding
Bob's death. The murder was devastating, and the silence
from so many compounded that devastation.

   We have, and will continue to receive counseling as
needed to deal with Bob's murder. On behalf of my
children and me, I thank the court for the opportunity to
provide this victim impact statement.

The courtroom is silent for a moment after I finish. I can
hear the sniffing back of tears and the rustle of tissues. As I
return to my seat, Judge Diebolt expresses his appreciation for
my candid statement. He is clearly moved and comments that
the extent to which I have involved myself in the case is something he has not seen before in his time on the bench.

Bob's sister Donna and his cousin Susan also read victim
impact statements. Donna speaks about no longer being able to
see the faces of her deceased parents in Bob's face. She
expresses her hopes that Ryan will grow into the best person he
can be, concluding that he owes it to Bob. Susan, who has advo-
cated tirelessly in the background for this case to be resolved,
speaks from her heart about the horrific loss of her cousin, who
was, in her heart, a brother.

There will never be enough time to hear all that needs to be
said about the impact Bob's death has had on the many people
who were fortunate enough to have him in their lives. But no
more will be said or heard here today. The judge orders that we
will reconvene to hear the sentence on December 11.

Michael and I are swallowed up by the media as we follow Shauna to her car. The reporters are eager to hear what length of sentence I am hoping for, but their questions and speculations leave me feeling empty and profoundly sad.

On the other side of the building, Ryan's lawyer, a young and earnest man who would probably like to be handling any case but this one, is desperately trying to show his client to the scrum of media in a favorable light. He produces from his briefcase a copy of the letter Ryan wrote to Emma, Sam, and me immediately following his confession and proceeds to read it to the reporters huddled around him. Meanwhile, Ryan and his family quietly reach their car and drive away.

Minutes later, as Shauna maneuvers her car through the crush of media, Michael answers his cell phone. It is Sam, calling from home. He and Emma have been watching live coverage of the action outside the courthouse.

"Dad, why didn't you tell us about the letter?" Sam asks Michael. Unsure what he is talking about, Michael asks for clarification. "The letter from Ryan. You never showed that to us. We just heard his lawyer read it on the TV."

It is only then we realize what has been unfolding outside the courthouse's other exit. The letter, which we had chosen not to show our children until the legal process was over, has just become part of the public domain. It is the first time the media coverage has moved so far beyond our comfort zone. We cannot get home fast enough.

Michael declares, "We are bringing the children with us for the sentencing. They can't be following this on the news. I want to be the one to explain to them what is happening as it happens."

I recognize once more how grateful I am to have this man in my life. He takes on these impossible situations and simply does the right thing.

Our next court date is on November 29. Ryan McMillan has now been charged with assault causing bodily harm for the punch he threw that put Bob on the ground. He's being represented by Peter Ritchie, a high-profile and skilled criminal lawyer in Vancouver. Ritchie is also handling the defense for Robert "Willie" Pickton, a Port Coquitlam man charged with murdering fifteen women missing from Vancouver's Downtown Eastside.

Since McMillan's original manslaughter charge was stayed in 1998, he has kept to himself. I am told by friends from Squamish that he spends extended periods of time deep in the bush, working as a helicopter logger for British Columbia's forest industry.

Knowing I do not want to see this matter go to trial, Ritchie has little difficulty negotiating a plea bargain with the Crown. McMillan will plead guilty to the lesser charge of common assault. In a letter he writes to the *Vancouver Sun*, criticizing their suggestion that McMillan was partially responsible for Bob's death, Ritchie says that McMillan's actions, while regrettable, amounted to a small "dustup" that could occur at any party where people are drinking. He claims the punch had nothing to do with Bob's death and should not be treated as if it did. A *Sun* reporter interviews me after the letter appears, and I spar halfheartedly with Ritchie but abandon the exercise because it is so unsatisfactory. Regardless of how the court deals with McMillan, I believe Ritchie has done his client an enormous disservice. Long after the sentencing, McMillan will have to listen to his heart. I cannot help thinking that Ryan Aldridge is already on a course toward healing that McMillan may never find.

With Christmas just weeks away, Shauna and I engage in some serious retail therapy. We are biding our time until the judge sentences Ryan Aldridge and Ryan McMillan. I worry I have developed tunnel vision and am only responding to the legal process as it affects me and my family, losing sight of justice and of society as a whole. Shauna lets me talk through all the things that are worrying me and knows exactly when to offer an alternative, big-picture perspective that helps me see beyond my narrowed scope. I am so grateful that she has a stomach for all that this has become. Many times I do not; a wave of nausea heaves through me as I imagine what Ryan's holiday season may look like. This will be my fifth Christmas without Bob, and it may be Ryan's family's first without him. Loss and waste strung together with tinsel and glitter.

The Wedgwood Hotel is small and known for its highly personal service. It is one of Michael's favorite places to stay when he is appearing before the courts in Vancouver. Emma and Sam approve of the elegant accommodation and busy themselves taking an inventory of the minibar. I am sure many will judge us for bringing our children to this final court appearance, but it feels entirely right to be together. I don't think Emma and Sam will ever know just how much they have influenced the direction we've taken on this journey. Their innate sense of justice is inextricably linked to a caring and compassion for Ryan and the communities in which we live. They've made it easy for us to do what we believed to be the right thing. Their unfailingly positive attitudes, close friendships, and eagerness to learn and express themselves through art and sport are all the proof we need to know we have made good choices in managing the past five years.

We are almost at the top of the courthouse concrete stairs when a reporter turns and recognizes us. "Oh my God, they've brought their kids. Quick, get a shot over here," he shouts to the cameraman who is leaning against the building, enjoying a cigarette in the winter morning sun. They hustle to capture the image. We narrowly escape them and make our way to the courtroom. The cameras are left outside while reporters dash to take in the proceedings. No doubt word is spreading quickly about the children, and the cameras will be waiting for us when we come out, hoping to catch a good clip for the five o'clock news.

The same faithful group fills the hard wooden benches. Silent nods, light hands on shoulders delicately connect us and convey the sadness and fragility of the day.

The same gestures must be taking place on the other side of the room, but I am too afraid to look at Ryan's family. I want them to have breathing space.

Ryan enters with his lawyer and is seated directly in front of me. The black suit seems to be holding him up, and his wingtips keep him attached to the floor. Sam and Emma nestle under Michael's arms, their eyes frozen on the bench, bodies motionless.

Judge Diebolt enters the court and sits behind his elevated desk. The court clerk hands him a stack of documents. The judge speaks about the court needing to send a strong message that acts of violence will not be tolerated. He describes the two sides of Ryan's character: the man seen by family and friends as hardworking and loving, and the young man who failed to come forward because he couldn't remember what he had done. In contrast, he describes what the police knew of Ryan as a bully who abused drugs and alcohol and hung out with a negative peer group.

"It was an unnecessary waste of a human life," Judge Diebolt declares. "I sentence you to a term of imprisonment of five years." His decision is brief and to the point. Five years. An eternity for a mother. A slap in the face for a public that hungers for vengeance.

A member of Ryan's family passes a gym bag over the railing to the bailiff. I imagine what it contains. Clean socks, underwear, a toothbrush. Five years' worth of darkness past packed alongside five years of incarceration to come. How can you possibly prepare for this? I think of what I would want to give my son—to protect him, to help him heal, to nourish him and allow him to grow.

There is no time now for the bag I am packing in my mind. Ryan is helped to his feet. The bailiff is gentle and patient, stepping aside as Ryan turns to face Emma and Sam. "I am so sorry," he whispers. Ryan quickly looks in the direction of his own family before he is led through an exit behind the bench. Someone calls out, "Be strong." The heavy door closes with a loud metal thud.

All the people in the room appear to be steadying themselves. White knuckles grip the backs of the benches; a surge of emotion moves us all off balance. The bailiff asks that we remain in the courtroom to allow Ryan's family to leave. In silence, half the room empties. Even the media move in slow motion, lost in thought.

I take a moment to compose myself, and as we exit the courtroom, Ryan's lawyer cautiously approaches me in the corridor. I do not envy him; this is awful from every angle. This case, so early in his career, will leave an indelible mark of sadness. He discreetly produces a letter from his briefcase and asks my permission to pass it to me, explaining that it is from Ryan's mother. I finger the white envelope in my hands. It is like a bridge across an impossible chasm. Relieved that I accepted the gesture, he walks away in the other direction, and I rejoin my family, tucking the envelope into my pocket for later.

Sam's nails dig nervously into my palm as we make our way down the stairs toward the exit. We can see the throng of media gathered on the sidewalk. Michael and I are like bears protecting our young as we push our way through the double glass doors. Sensing our concern about the impact on our children, the reporters step back and create some space around Emma and Sam. I find some words to express my feelings about the sentencing and stress that it is not how much time Ryan serves but what he does with that time. We need to get our children out of the cold, thank you. Goodbye.

Once inside the protective cocoon of our car, Michael debriefs Emma and Sam, patiently answering their barrage of questions. I take the envelope from my pocket and begin to read Ryan's mother's letter silently to myself.

Dear Katy,

I have wanted to write to you so many times and I have spent many sleepless nights thinking and pondering over the perfect words to share with you and your children. It has taken an enormous amount of courage for me to write this letter because I really don't know what to say; since this is the most difficult thing I've ever had to do.

I know my apologies will never bring back the husband and father that you love and miss dearly; I can't begin to imagine the torment, grief, and pain this has caused you all. However, I want you to know when Ryan confessed to me with such deep emotion that he was responsible for Bob's death, part of me died too. The day of his arrest and learning the terrible truth is an experience I wish on no parent...a memory I can only wish to forget and from which I will never recover. Not to mention the overwhelming impact this has had on our entire family.

Ryan will have to live with his actions for the rest of his life, a self-imposed sentence in itself. He shows complete remorse and is suffering tremendously but I realize this is of no consolation to you and your children. No words can ever bring back what was taken from you, a suspended moment in time that has changed your lives forever.

Through the many tears, I have forgiven Ryan because he is my son and I love him unconditionally, my only prayer is that one day, you, Emma, and Sam may find it in your hearts to forgive him too.

This letter somehow transcends the complexity of emotions I feel as a result of the day's court proceedings. Ryan's mother's words cut right to the heart of my pain, and despite her humble suggestion to the contrary, they *are* an enormous consolation to me.

I suspect I will read this letter over and over in the weeks and months to come. For now, I am reassured to know that, quite simply, this mother loves her son. The power of that love could have everything to do with how things unfold for Ryan from here. Amidst my sadness and exhaustion, I am grateful.

I want to be home with Michael and the children. Now. This is done. For the first time in years, I do not feel the need to look ahead. Our five-year sentence just ended and Ryan's has begun.

With great relief I immerse myself in preparations for Christmas, inhaling the scent of endless batches of cookies while carols blare from the stereo, and dashing happily between school concerts and Michael's office. I think if I create a huge, sparkling holiday celebration I can blot out thoughts of the nightmare this December is for Ryan and his family.

It almost works. It is at night, when Michael snores gently beside me, sure that I must also be sleeping, having run myself ragged baking, writing cards, and wrapping gifts, that I reflect on all we have as a family and all that I wish for Ryan and his.

I had hoped that both Ryan Aldridge and Ryan McMillan would be through the system before the end of the year. I want 2003 to be a fresh start. As December wears on, however, I am reluctant to step out of the festive cocoon I have spun and face Ryan McMillan's sentencing. But I do. Shauna, whom Michael has started calling my "handler," finds the time in her busy December schedule to escort me to the last of the court appearances.

Although I was too exhausted to fight the lessening of charges from assault causing bodily harm to common assault, I draw the line at the court's request to edit my victim impact statement. An objection is raised because it is the same statement read at a manslaughter hearing, while this is an assault proceeding.

We adjourn and I meet with the Crown counsel, who has been asked to discuss the statement with me, to defend my position. I tell him that I will either read the statement in its entirety or not at all. I respect the court and understand it must deal with the charge it is handed, but I hold McMillan just as responsible for Bob's death, and my statement reflects that. To change the wording would somehow diminish what happened to Bob. The mechanics of the punch versus the kick do nothing to change the devastation that resulted. Impact is impact, and the court should hear what I have to say.

Perhaps he anticipates the comments I might make to the media outside the courthouse if I am prevented from having my say, and after he meets with the judge to discuss my position, the judge backs down. I am permitted to read my entire statement. The words come more easily the second time, and I hope they are heard by those who need them most. The judge chooses to reserve judgment, and a final date is set aside for sentencing. Countless appearances down; one to go. Shauna and I finish our Christmas shopping.

December 20, 2002. I step out of the calendar of Christmas recitals and food and gift drives to make one final trip to North Vancouver. Shauna has the routine down pat and is waiting for me as I get off the Seabus that has brought me from the seaplane terminal downtown. The bailiff recognizes us and nods solemnly as we find our usual seats in the front row. I wrap my jacket tightly around me, feeling a chill of sadness. Five years ago Bob had just returned from the World Triathlon Championships in Australia and we were celebrating his fine results. Look at us now.

Judge Gedye makes a brief statement before handing down a three-year conditional discharge to McMillan. She reminds McMillan that he was partly responsible for the actions that led to Bob's death. "You have a small but significant part of the chain of events." She rejects the request of a fine and states that attaching a monetary figure to Bob's life would be inappropriate. I suppress the urge to call out in support of her position.

The judge goes on to say to Ryan McMillan, "You're always going to be the other person involved in the death of Mr. McIntosh." That is for him to live with for the rest of his life.

The conditions of the discharge are typical for the most part. McMillan is to refrain from using drugs and alcohol and is to submit to random testing as required. (A probation officer later tells me that there is no budget for such testing in British Columbia, so it will never happen.) My understanding is that logging camps have a reputation for heavy drinking, and I hope that he manages to stay sober both in and out of that environment.

The second condition is that he not carry a weapon. This is ironic, since he has been carrying a weapon all along—his fist.

And the third condition, which may pose the biggest personal challenge: McMillan is to participate in a victim-offender reconciliation process. Could it be that the judge was inspired by the immediate contact I made with Ryan Aldridge? Does she share my belief that meeting me face-to-face has more chance of making a positive difference in McMillan's life than a jail sentence or community-service order?

This final condition makes me proud of the profession in which Bob loved to work. This is not the legacy Bob imagined he would leave behind, but I think that already people are sitting up and watching what is going on here. We have shown them as a family that we need something different from the system. The punishment that has been ordered may seem lax to some, but I believe sitting down to face me will actually be one of the biggest challenges Ryan McMillan ever experiences.

As we file out of the courtroom, Peter Ritchie suggests to me that we find a quiet space and conduct a face-to-face meeting immediately. Knowing that is not the process the judge has in mind, I politely decline. Somewhere there must be trained facilitators who carry out such orders, and I suspect it may be up to me to find them.

But all that can wait. I've reached a place on the journey where I can rest. I feel like I could spend weeks curled up on the couch with my family, replenishing my soul and not looking backward or forward. And even though winters have been hard to endure every year since Bob's death, I am ready to carve out a warm and light-filled space in my heart that will sustain me through the coming weeks. I bring home from the last court appearance a feeling of peace.

I manage to remain in that suspended state of calm until Christmas dinner. I have stopped qualifying every decision with "once the legal process is out of our way." But as we seat ourselves around our table and I stir the gravy, Sam asks, "What do you think Ryan will get for dinner in jail?" I reassure him that Ryan will probably get a turkey dinner much like ours. What I do not say is that the meal will be served to him in a tension-filled mess hall where you could be stabbed if you looked the wrong way at the wrong person; a place where a five-dollar debt is a life-or-death matter.

That profound feeling of loss is back. Or perhaps it has never left, never will. There is a place for it to fit now, somewhere close to my heart. But it can—and I know now that it will—shift, resurface, and reposition itself, like a bear in hibernation. It is a part of who I am. It will change the way I think about the world around me and the people in it.

live out loud

I just wanted to let you know how amazing I thought your presentation was. You have impacted me immensely,and you provoked thoughts that continue to linger. There is no doubt that when I am faced with a difficult problem, I will remember you. You are a perfect role model of courage, wisdom and optimism. Thank you so much for all you do to make the world a better place. Bob would be proud.
—Grade 8 Student, Burnaby, B.C.

I am what is called a concrete sequential thinker. I like logical conclusions, with everything wrapped up, loose ends tucked in, a neat package. The silence and uncertainty since Bob's death have made our lives anything but neat, and it is not until the weeks following the final court appearances that I am able to intellectualize the experience. There was too much beyond my control, so I simply lived around it, taking care of what I could and gradually rebuilding our family's foundation. As if living parallel lives,

I moved forward and found real happiness creating a family with Michael, all the while knowing that at some point I would revisit the unresolved issues of my past life and more fully process the way in which it ended.

Now that the case is settled before the courts, the path is illuminated for me. Coming from a place of safety and security, I am ready to do the mind work to find peace. I believe it is not possible to reach out and grasp your future with both hands until you let go of your past. I have to begin by forgiving myself for letting go.

Deep inside, the need to understand how Bob's death could have happened is percolating. And it is not something specific to Ryan I am looking for; it is a global question. I am raising children who will be going out into the world. I fear for their safety and the safety of children everywhere. Tragedies similar to what happened to Bob are on the news with alarming frequency. What is going on out there? And more importantly, what can I do to help make it stop?

I am in my car driving past the high school I attended in Victoria when the answer comes to me. "Young people need to hear this story," I say out loud to myself. No textbook can ever take the place of the lessons to be learned from a real-life experience.

I stop at the side of the road, pull out my cell phone, and call the Oak Bay High School career and personal planning department, where I am put through to Reta Clark, the coordinator. Without telling her specifically what my story is, I explain that I have a story about social responsibility that she might want to share with her students. I ask if I can drop by to meet her. (Some years later, Reta tells me she still remembers that call. She admits she had no idea what might be coming through her door, but she had a feeling she needed to listen to what I had to say.)

Reta graciously welcomes me into her office. I sit quietly for a moment, absorbing the memories of being in the same room almost twenty-five years earlier. The clamor in the halls accelerates as classes change. Reta greets every student who passes her door by name, with genuine enthusiasm and respect. This is a good place to start. I can feel it.

We sit silently after my words have tumbled out. Reta is heartsick about what has happened in my life, but she agrees that the story is full of life lessons that fit perfectly into the realm of social responsibility education. We begin to brainstorm about what a presentation to students might look like. She gives me a stack of reading material and videos, along with a list of people she thinks I should contact to help make something come together. The tears come as I walk past my old biology classroom toward the main stairway. I have come full circle and found a new beginning.

A few days later I get a call from Pete Zubersky, an RCMP drug expert. His name is on Reta's list. "I hear you have a presentation for kids," he says by way of introduction.

"Actually, I am just thinking about building a presentation for kids. I would love to talk to you about it," I reply.

"Well, I have some time booked with a class at Parklands Secondary next Thursday, and I have no idea what I am going to do with them. Come and test drive your presentation. If you fall on your face, I'll be there to pick you up and we'll figure out what to do with the kids then."

I figure Pete must not have heard the part about my not having developed the presentation yet. When I try to clarify that, he jumps in and says, "You've got a week. What are you waiting for?"

Right. I do love a challenge, so I tell him I'll see him on Thursday afternoon.

That night I am sitting cross-legged on the den floor, surrounded by old photographs. For five years it has been difficult to look at them. The vibrant images emphasize the contrast between Bob's fully engaged life and the senseless, wasteful way in which that life ended. The notion that these photographs can be put to good use in telling an important story allows me to see them differently tonight.

Using a digital camera, I take pictures of several of them, load the digital shots into my laptop, then dive in and lay out the story using basic PowerPoint software. To my surprise, it begins coming together with ease. The fact that Bob was such a stellar athlete helps. The photo biography is filled with shots of him windsurfing, playing hockey, and flipping upside down off ski jumps. It is also fortunate that Bob loved to play. The shots of him horsing around with his friends and wearing crazy getups will surely create a connection with the audience and make him human. After piecing together what seems like an enormous jigsaw puzzle, I fall into bed at 2:00 A.M., exhausted.

The hard part comes the next day at Michael's office. There is something I need for this presentation, but I cannot begin to imagine how to ask for it. In the course of the civil action I hired Michael to pursue, he received copies of all the police files relating to the investigation. Now four banker's boxes filled with reports sit in the law firm storage room, and I know that in one of those boxes there will be a file containing Bob's autopsy report. In that report there will be photographs. If one of those can show the horrible reality of his death, with dignity and without sensationalism, I know it will be worth more than a thousand words.

I also know I cannot go through the file myself. Even as a child I suffered anxiety over images depicting blood or medical procedures, and it would be impossible to look through such photographs of Bob. I muster up the courage to ask Michael to do it for me. I cannot believe I am making such a request of my husband, nor can I believe his readiness to help. Michael has lived with Bob's ghost for five years, but continues to take on whatever we dish out for him. He is comfortable in his own skin, and confident that even though I have decided to speak publicly about my tragedy, we still have a full and private life that is about today and about us.

Michael approaches the task with the same professionalism and tact I have learned to expect when I watch him with his clients. Within minutes he emerges from his office. Putting his arms around me, he explains that there is one photograph he feels would be appropriate for what I am trying to do. He has placed it facedown on the circular conference table in his office. He suggests I take some time, get some air, and, when I feel ready, go and have a look.

It is not just the graphic image I fear. I am worried that even though I think this is the right thing to do, many people will disagree. But Michael helps make things work for me in the most loving and nonjudgmental way. After several deep breaths, I walk across to the table and pick up the photograph.

If you weren't told that Bob was dead, you probably wouldn't guess it from the photograph. There is little sign of injury, save a small bruise on his right temple. The plastic intubation apparatus is still taped to his mouth. There is a small amount of blood on the crumpled white sheet near his head. An electrode sticker adheres to his chest, an eerie reminder of the flat-lined heart monitor. But to all appearances he could simply be asleep in a hospital bed.

However, I know that Bob is not that vacant, torn body lying before the camera. He is our children's brilliant blue eyes and their gleeful laughter. He is the part of my heart that believes everyone is inherently good and deserves a chance. And he is the realization that I have a job to do to help make the world a safer place. After a moment or two, the picture no longer scares me. The picture of Bob's dead body is what will bring my work to life.

I work on the presentation late at night because I do not want Emma and Sam to see it. Even though they have greater computer skills than I do and could help with the technical issues, they have already lived through this tragedy and do not need to watch the story being reassembled on my computer screen.

It concerns me that I do not have statistics and charts to show kids the emerging trends in substance use and violent assaults. I am not a teacher or an expert. All I have is a story, and I hope it will be enough.

Thirty fifteen- and sixteen-year-olds lumber into the classroom. The back-row seats fill first. Curious eyes peer out from under ball caps and from between earphones at the sight of a stranger in their classroom. When Pete Zubersky enters the room, there is an excited outburst of banter from some of the boys. It is clear that Pete has a rapport with the young people he works with. After a brief introduction, Pete turns the room over to me.

In my mind, I am right back at school. I hated public speaking. My words never seemed to be delivered by a voice that was my own. I remember the sensation of instantly losing the ability to think when facing a room full of people. I let my breath out slowly and remind myself that I am an adult, these are kids, and we have work to do.

With my computer plugged into a projector, an image of Bob as a baby is stretched out across the wall behind me. I introduce Bob and the kids all laugh. Phew! Here we go. Picture after picture of Bob playing hockey, aerial skiing, windsurfing, and competing in triathlon has the room transfixed. More laughter as I describe some of the antics he and his friends were still involved in as adults. The kids are liking Bob more and more as they get to know him. A shot of Emma and Sam as babies elicits big "oohs" from all the girls. What a perfect family. What a life.

Caught up in the biography, the students forget to wonder what the point of all this might be. And then the room falls silent when I advance to the image of Bob in the morgue. Impossible. How could the fairy tale end? How *did* it end? While a video of Bob's funeral plays in the background, I explain our New Year's Eve in detail. You could hear a tear drop in that classroom. Thirty faces are riveted on me in disbelief.

After all the photographs and video, I switch from narrative into a discussion of social responsibility and the risks associated with alcohol and drug use, especially when large numbers of young people are gathered. Introducing the notion of synergy, I compare positive and negative group dynamics, pointing out that a layer of alcohol and other drugs on top of a large gathering of people can be a recipe for disaster.

I ask how many of them have been to a party with over one hundred guests. Many hands go up. Then I ask how many have been at a party where no parent was present. Even more hands are raised. I wonder to myself what is going on with those parents.

Reassuring them that they will likely never see someone killed at a party, I point out the many other things they *will* see. Their friends may drink too much and get alcohol poisoning. They may overdose. Others may engage in unprotected sex and get a sexually transmitted infection. Girls will be raped. There will be unwanted pregnancies. Friends will make the unwise decision to get in the passenger seat of a car driven by someone who is drunk or stoned. Fights will break out. And there will be enormous property damage at unchaperoned house parties.

I watch heads nod in agreement when I tell them the most common risk of all: simply having regrets about their own behavior. They will wake up after a night of drinking and not remember if they said something they may regret or made an advance to someone they don't really have feelings for.

We segue into a discussion of silence and the peer pressure that so often produces it. I provide the kids with commonsense strategies for staying safe. I am careful not to lecture my audience. The story of what happened is enough. I expect them to draw their own conclusions and, I hope, apply those conclusions to their own behavior.

After forty-five minutes I wrap up my presentation by throwing out a challenge: Use the group dynamic I have described to look after each other, and call for help immediately if something gets out of control. Parties happen. Never forget the story of Bob.

There are many questions. Someone asks, "How can you stand up and tell this story without crying?" I do not have an answer for that. Nor am I confident I could tell the story again without tears. Watching the faces of those kids processing Bob's life and the enormity of his death has affected me deeply.

Pete is leaning against the blackboard with a huge grin. He nods his head and gives me the thumbs-up. I can't believe that I have done it.

The adrenaline is still pumping as I wind the cord of my computer into a figure eight and tuck my laptop back in its case. The kids move slowly out of the classroom and make their way to their next class. I wonder if they will have difficulty relaying to their friends what they have just experienced. I know I will.

In the school parking lot, I call Jenny on my cell phone. She is anxious to hear how my first attempt at storytelling has gone. It is hard to describe the impact, but I tell her I see it as completely positive.

When Reta Clark hears from Pete that the presentation was a resounding success, she immediately arranges for me to give a series of talks to groups of tenth-, eleventh-, and twelfth-grade students at my old high school, Oak Bay.

It feels weird to stand in front of a class in the same school where I was a student twenty-five years earlier. I know firsthand where these particular kids come from, and this knowledge motivates me. Of all the local schools, this one really needs to hear my message.

Oak Bay is filled with kids from Victoria's most affluent families. These kids' parents can afford to travel and may choose to leave their teenagers home on their own over the weekend. These are the parents who have well-stocked liquor cabinets, who dole out generous allowances that may get spent on alcohol and other drugs, who provide their kids with cell phones that enable them to communicate and gather at the speed of sound. And these are the parents (and teenagers) who believe that if Jason or Jessica does something wrong, Daddy or Mummy will bail them out.

Not much has changed in the social order since I was there. The feeling of entitlement is alive and well. I predict that these kids will think this story is something they will only read about in the newspaper—something that happens to other people from other places. Surely they are never going to see something so violent happen at one of *their* parties. Surely one of their parents will never suffer a similar fate in an effort to bring a party under control. It could never happen to them. But I am from Oak Bay High, and it did happen to me.

After my first presentation, a beautiful young girl comes up to me in tears and asks if she can speak to me in private. We move away from the group and she explains that just the weekend before, when her parents were away in Asia, she had invited a few friends over. Before she knew it, a few turned into eighty. Within minutes the situation was beyond her control. Precious family treasures were broken, furniture was soaked with spilled beer, and the carpeting was burned by cigarette butts. It was well after three in the morning before she managed to get everyone out the door.

She asks me how to tell her parents about the situation when they return. I put my hand on her shaking shoulders and tell her that she was very brave to come and share her story with me. I suggest she begin by telling her parents about my presentation and what she has learned from it. Perhaps that will be the opening she needs to admit to the situation she created and to let them know she now understands how, for so many reasons, it could have resulted in tragedy. It didn't. By a miracle, no one was hurt. The property can all be repaired or replaced. Her parents may be upset, but surely they will see she has learned from the experience.

As she walks away I realize that the presentation has given me the opportunity to connect. Connection is what it is all about. If I can tell a story that gets kids talking—whether to me, to each other, or to their teachers and parents—it might make a difference in the choices they make about high-risk behavior.

I offer to speak to the senior students at the school that Emma and Sam attend. Some of these students know my children, and the presentation is even more real and personal to them. It is also more emotional for me to share the story with an audience that represents my children's community, but if there is anything I can do to create safety within that community, I am game.

On my forty-second birthday, my best friend Shauna presents me with a tiny, perfectly wrapped gift. Over the years I have been delighted by her thoughtful cards and surprise gifts. They arrive promptly for every special occasion, but often show up in between big days for no particular reason except to reach out and make me feel cherished. Nestled in the small box is a silver necklace. Hanging from a fine chain is a slim silver bar engraved with the words "Live Out Loud." Nothing could mean more than Shauna's blessing for the work I have taken on. The necklace will always remind me that I have nothing to fear by living my truth.

Shauna's sentiments are echoed by another friend who remarks that what has happened in my life should not be seen as my tragedy, but as my purpose. I love that perspective. Just as I love my friends who have found it in their hearts to support me.

By the time school lets out for the summer, I have spoken to over eight hundred kids.

Telling the story is cathartic for me. It is a privilege to share Bob with young people. The way he lived does so much to inspire them. To combine the inspirational message with the cruel reality of how he died leaves a strong impression and stimulates discussion long after my visit ends.

I am proud of the small dent I have made in the impervious shell teens erect automatically as they begin to pull away to form their own identities. As Sam and Emma excitedly look ahead to summer and all that the long, warm, lazy days promise, I wonder if the young people who have heard our story will remember Bob when they are faced with a difficult choice of their own. I feel a bit sad as I put my laptop away after the final presentation. Perhaps I have made an impression, but I know there is more work to be done.

In the fall of 2003, when I return to the regular routine of handling the finances at Michael's office, another local school contacts me. A counselor there has heard about "The Story of Bob" and is wondering if I am available to speak to three hundred ninth-grade students at an assembly to kick off drug and alcohol awareness week.

Three hundred students. I was comfortable perching on the edge of a desk and speaking to a classroom-sized group, but an assembly is a totally different matter. I have a flashback to freezing up during an oral report in a lecture hall filled with my peers in a fourth-year marketing class. I shiver the recollection back into the memory vault and rationalize that I *must* be better able to handle myself now.

When I mention the request to Michael over dinner that evening, he responds, "I think you should go for it. But I hope you are going to charge them a fee. It is one thing sharing the story with our alma mater and the kids' school, but if you are going to take it beyond that, you may need to consider it as a business proposition."

I am stunned. It had never occurred to me that this could turn into something more than an occasional volunteer effort.

Summoning my courage, I confirm my availability and indicate that the presentation fee will be $100. When the confirmation comes back immediately, I really start to wonder where this is all going to go. But first I have to deal with my trepidation at speaking to large groups—and my fear of microphones. Ever since I first heard my voice replayed through the portable cassette player that I so coveted for my ninth birthday, I have disliked the sound of my amplified voice. I can only hope that the power of the storytelling will distract me from my long-standing anxieties.

As the auditorium begins to fill with excited teenagers, happy to be out of their classrooms, a harried teacher approaches me and warns, "This is a lively bunch. It will be a challenge to get them to sit still for an hour. Good luck."

Less than reassured, I focus on finishing an equipment check and taking deep, calming breaths.

As soon as the photographs of Bob are projected, the room is silent. There is laughter at the pictures that illustrate his sense of humor, and there are expressions of awe at his numerous athletic accomplishments. The total silence that falls over the auditorium when I show the photograph of Bob in the morgue is remarkable. I am aware of muffled sobs as I describe how Bob ended up in the morgue. And three hundred fourteen- and fifteen-year-olds continue to listen with rapt attention as I discuss what can cause such a tragedy.

I wonder if there will be questions from this large audience after I speak. It is one thing to speak out in a small group, quite another to put your thoughts out there in front of all your peers. But as I will learn in the months and years to come, there is something unique about this particular age group. They have little difficulty asking questions and often pose the most challenging and interesting ones.

Someone asks what became of the other Ryan. Explaining that he received a three-year conditional discharge, I focus on the ban on alcohol and drug use and the court-ordered victim-offender reconciliation imposed by the judge.

They wonder what became of Jamie, the host of the party. They are aghast to hear that he left his own home filled with people and moved on to another party, sustaining a twenty-four-hour driving suspension for suspected impairment along the way.

I am asked about Emma and Sam. How have they managed since losing their father? The students seem relieved to hear that they are typical ten-year-olds who care more about playing soccer games and enjoying birthday parties than focusing on the tragedy that altered the course of their lives six years earlier.

Emma's and Sam's coping methods give me an opening to introduce the notion of resiliency. I remind them that Sam's reaction to hearing about Bob's death was to ask for a bowl of cereal—not because he felt any less about Bob or the seriousness of what had happened, but because it is natural for children to honestly express their immediate needs. They are not suppressed by social convention to say what they think people want to hear.

Emma's reaction was to become preoccupied with finding a new daddy. It was not out of some deep-seated difficulty coping with how Bob had lived or died, but simply because she wanted to be part of a two-parent family again. Young people laugh, while adults struggle with the thought of Emma on her one-girl matchmaking mission.

In the end, the students agree that it was fortunate all the upheaval and change—Bob's death, our move to Victoria, Michael's joining our family, the first day of school—happened within that first year. It is merely history now. 1998 was followed by years of stable, happy, and normal living. I truly believe that I have Emma and Sam, with their honesty and resiliency, to thank for that.

While few of the young people I speak to will lose a family member the way I did, they will all see families change over time due to the more common upheavals of divorce and illness. My story illustrates how families regroup and heal, and it is often the simple, straightforward honesty of children that moves the process along.

I answer most questions easily, because the same ones come up each time I speak to a group of students. But nothing prepares me for one question. A boy stands and asks if my children and I have considered what our lives would have been like if the kicks Ryan delivered to Bob's head had not been quite so hard.

In other words, what if Bob had suffered a debilitating brain injury rather than a fatal one?

The nauseous wave I have become accustomed to riding lurches under me as the stage floor seems to tilt away. I struggle to find the words to answer and finally tell another story, recounting an experience that took place only a few weeks earlier.

Emma, Sam, and I were walking Lily the dog to the market near our home. As they concentrated on keeping their half-eaten popsicles from falling off their sticks, I gently moved them aside on the sidewalk as a young woman came past pushing a wheelchair. It was actually more of a modified stretcher. A young man lay strapped to the inclined bed, his head lolling to the side as he moaned quietly. His limbs were curled into impossible, rigid positions that suggested a complete lack of mobility.

I checked to be sure the children were not staring inappropriately and noticed that Emma was forming a question to ask after they had passed us.

"That could have been Daddy-O, couldn't it?" she said.

The awfulness of that suggestion stopped me for a second. I led them on a detour to the beach so we could sit and discuss Emma's question together, face-to-face.

Yes. Bob could have suffered a brain injury rather than being killed. That would have happened if Ryan's kicks had landed in a slightly different place on or around Bob's head, or if the kicks had been less forceful. I explained that brain injuries can range from mild concussions—like what you'd get if you fell off a bicycle—to severe and irreversible damage that can affect both physical and mental function.

Emma went one step further. "Okay, so if that man we just saw had been Daddy-O, what would our lives be like now?"

Much, much different, I told her. We would probably not be living in Victoria. If Bob was in a vegetative state and was hospitalized, we would likely be living in Vancouver, close to the hospital, so we could be near him. Our days would revolve around his care. I reminded them of images we had seen on the news of Nicholas Chow Johnson, a young man who was viciously beaten in Victoria when gang members erroneously thought his red jacket meant he was a member of a rival gang. The images of his mother lovingly spoon-feeding his contorted and withering body had burned themselves into our memories.

Sam leaned into me, stroking the dog curled at his feet. "We would not have Dadoo, would we?" he asked, lowering his eyes.

"No," I replied quietly. "I suppose not." There is such complexity in the emotion around all that we have been through. We feel the sadness over losing Bob and the fear that radiates from the way Bob died. But we also feel the newfound happiness and security that came into our lives along with Michael. There is no neat package.

We sat on the beach for a long time, exhausting the what-ifs and agreeing how lucky we were to simply be there together, whole and healthy, inspired to look at the world from a slightly different angle—a perspective I would not wish on anyone, but one we felt belonged to us just the same. We vowed to be there for one another and to talk about all the hard stuff that most people could not face. Always.

Many of the three hundred young people in the auditorium are stunned by all my story brings to mind. However, the boy who posed the question is satisfied with my answer. I wonder what has gone on in his short life to make him ask about such an outcome. I hope he is okay.

The anxiety of speaking in front of a large group never materializes. I realize that the microphone I feared feels strangely comfortable in my hands. The dramatic impact of the story is amplified when the group is larger; the questions are bolder when asked in the darkened and spacious venue.

I have found the perfect legacy for Bob. If he had had the chance to live his life, he would have had a tremendous influence in our family and on our community. He would never have envisioned touching people's lives this way, but he doesn't get to choose. I have to do that for him, and I pick this. Bob and I are working together in a way we may never have managed during his lifetime. Wherever I find a place to set up my computer and a group of kids to listen, I can bring Bob to life and leave behind a powerful and lasting lesson. And after today I realize that the lessons are not just for the audience, but for me as well.

finding the gift

And so
I have made myself a promise;
to look
at my challenges
from a different perspective;
and to find
the gift,
which is enclosed
within.
—Pamela Rosemary Adams, *Searching for the Silver Linings*

In May 2003 I am reading an article written by Liz Elliott, an assistant professor in the School of Criminology and a codirector of the Centre for Restorative Justice at Simon Fraser University. The piece is part of "Crime and Consequence," a series in the *Vancouver Sun*. Elliott describes a concept called victim-offender reconciliation, a formal, facilitated process of bringing together the people most harmed by a crime. The strategy of reconciliation is a key component of the restorative justice movement, which in British Columbia was pioneered by Dave Gustafson and Sandi Bergen from Fraser Region Community Justice Initiatives Association in Langley.

A vague bell rings when I read the term "restorative justice." It was a phrase used by Nancy Reeves, a grief counselor I visited when we first moved to Victoria. She was explaining to me that she thought there was no need for her to work with me any further. I was moving forward in the right direction, and she did not feel she should take my money when we were spending our time discussing the broader issues of how violence and loss affect others in our communities, and the impact violence has on the perpetrators and their families.

Nancy thought I might be interested in the work of her friend, a nun who was working in the corrections system and teaching the nonviolent communication model of Marshall B. Rosenberg. Nancy told me that her friend's work came under the heading of restorative justice, and she suggested I might feel an affinity for this school of thought.

At the time, I was not willing to step out of the protective cocoon of my family. I tucked this idea away with several others, just in case, down the road, I was able to reach out beyond the bruised shell that was holding me together.

But now in 2003, almost six years after Bob's death, I am safely immersed in my new life and making an accidental career out of sharing The Story of Bob. I hunger for any resources that will deepen my understanding of how crime affects our society and what constitute best practices for healing and the prevention of recidivism. I am empowered by the notion that I could participate in a restorative justice process with Ryan and waste no time contacting Community Justice Initiatives.

Dave Gustafson, the organization's codirector, takes my call. As I begin to tell my story, I sense that he is hearing it differently than anyone I have shared it with before. Perhaps it is because he has spent many years listening to victims. There is an absence of pity and an abundance of compassion and understanding in his response, especially when I get to the part about Ryan.

Dave is not surprised when I ask him about the possibility of initiating a formal, victim-offender mediation. He explains that the process happens only after a trained facilitator spends time preparing the people on both sides. It is not something that can be rushed, and both parties have to be willing participants. The first step would be for David to make some inquiries at Matsqui, the medium-security prison where Ryan is serving his sentence. If the institution is supportive and Ryan is keen, we can move forward toward a meeting.

Within days of my contacting CJI, another article in the "Crime and Consequence" series catches my attention. This time I am surprised to find myself referred to in Ian Mulgrew's in-depth commentary. He is discussing reconciliation within the context of the justice system. The bulk of the article highlights what Mulgrew refers to as an age-old cry for vengeance and retribution and examines the sentences that have been handed down for a number of high-profile criminal cases. He then goes on to say:

> I don't want a system weighted only toward retribution
> and punishment, because I believe such sentences sow the
> seeds of future criminality by forging bitter, twisted
> inmates who return to their communities more damaged
> than when they left. And that issue is front and foremost
> for me. Except in the most extreme cases—multiple
> child-killer Clifford Olson for example—almost everyone
> who commits a crime, even terrorists, gets out of prison
> one day. If for no other reason than self-interest, I think
> the system should leaven any victim's need for vengeance
> with enough mercy to lay the foundation for an offender's
> reintegration to society. Consider the case of Ryan
> Aldridge, the twenty-five-year-old convicted and sentenced
> to five years in prison for kicking lawyer Bob McIntosh to

death at a New Year's Eve party. He could have gone to jail for life for such a cowardly crime, but there were mitigating circumstances taken into account at his sentencing for manslaughter. The forty-one-year-old widow, Katy Hutchison, had a veritable epiphany after the young man wrote a letter to her and her two children saying he was sorry: "I know there is nothing I can do to change what I did that night nor what I can say to make things better. Seeing Sam and Emma without there [sic] dad made me accept what I did to come forth with the truth. I owe Sam and Emma my life."... When she saw him sobbing on a police videotape of his confession, Hutchison said: "I wanted to make it okay for him... He seemed genuinely remorseful." She later said she felt "at peace with everything as soon as I met him." That in my mind is a powerful statement from someone whose life has been irretrievably rent by a horrendous crime. I think triggering reconciliation between an offender and the victim should be an aim of any decent system of criminal law. There can be no better outcome. A system that is focused solely on punishment and making an example to deter others will not engender a better society. Perhaps, though, if we emulate Hutchison even a little, and show convicts the key value at the heart of our civilization—compassion —they'll get the message. Speaking to the media about her experience, Hutchison said: "I accept he made a fatal error. But what does forgiveness mean? I expect him to make a difference in someone else's life."

Seeing myself put forward as an example reinforces my belief that I am on the right path. I write a letter to Ryan explaining my desire to meet with him and send it to Dave to deliver the next time he visits Matsqui.

With his codirector Sandi Bergen, Dave speaks to Ryan and learns that he is indeed interested in meeting with me again. Ryan sends a reply to my letter via Dave:

Your letter brought tears to my eyes. To read that you want to encourage and help me to take the right path in life means so much to me. I thank you for that Katy. At times I find myself crying myself to sleep. I picture all the people I've hurt and try to understand why. "Why" is the biggest question I have to answer. And not knowing is eating me up inside. I have to live with the fact of what I did. I can't turn back time, wish I could, but I can't. Somehow I have to make some good out of this. I want to let you know that my prayers and thoughts go out to you and your family. My remorse is truly real and I'm extremely sorry for what I have done. I understand that you would like to come here and talk with me. I would like to have the chance to talk as well.

Over the next few weeks, I have several long telephone conversations with Dave and Sandi about the reconciliation, and we meet briefly at a coffee shop on a day I am working in Vancouver. Dave and Sandi visit Ryan a number of times at Matsqui to prepare him for the process. We are both anxious to schedule a date for the meeting, so when I make plans for a trip to Vancouver during October to speak at several schools, I set aside some time to travel to the offices of CJI. Our plan is to spend a full day at Matsqui with Ryan.

When I meet Dave and Sandi on October 27, I am immediately confident that nothing I have to say will shock them. They have surely heard the most horrific tales, and I imagine them listening to stories of harm with open minds and hearts. They are able to hear what needs to be said by all sides, and they offer nonjudgmental permission to venture into one's conscience. I am secure in the knowledge that they have a firm grip that would prevent me from falling too far.

We stop on the way to Matsqui for a cup of tea. Seated under the harsh fluorescent lights of a fast-food restaurant, I am hit with the reality of where we are going and why. Six years of fear and anxiety come to the surface and spill over the paper cup

I am clutching. Dave and Sandi let me cry. There is no rushing the readiness to reconcile.

I explain that there have been parts of this journey that have been overcrowded. Family and friends clambered over one another to get close to me and to my children, to be a part of the experience. But other parts have been so lonely. Few people could understand or accept the fact that I felt no anger and desired no vengeance, and their incomprehension left me in a solitary place. When it came to actually meeting with Ryan after his arrest, and expressing concern for him and for his family, I was even more on my own. Perhaps people rationalized it as some twisted extension of my grief and expected me to get over it and get on with my life. But now, my determination to foster some type of ongoing connection with Ryan is beyond the comfort level of some of my closest friends, and they clearly express their disquiet to me. I am conflicted. I do not want to disturb people by reaching out in this unexpected direction, but I feel a deep personal need to do so.

Through my tears, I see that Dave and Sandi get it. 110 percent. We sit close for a moment, facing one another around the small, molded plastic table. Our shoulders form a protected space. It will not be the last time the significance of the circle reveals itself. My tears soak through a wad of skimpy restaurant napkins. Stuffing them to the bottom of my paper cup, I push the whole lot through the flap of the garbage bin. Breathe in, breathe out. We continue on with our excursion to Matsqui.

As we turn up the driveway to the institution, my chest gets heavy and I can hear the blood rushing near my temples. Even the people in the parking lots seem to move with a heightened sense of deliberation and caution, alert to their surroundings. Beyond the large patch of asphalt there is a high chain-link fence topped with circular snarls of razor wire as far as the eye can see.

Dave and Sandi walk on either side of me toward the low gray reception building. A guard buzzes us through the first of a series of tall, heavy metal gates that lead us into the prison. The pungent smell of industrial cleanser permeates the air as soon as the electronic door closes behind us.

Both Dave and Sandi wear photo tags that identify them as regular visitors to the prison. I sign in and am given a hard plastic badge to clip to my jacket. It has a large V emblazoned on it. V for visitor, not victim, I reassure myself. A guard escorts us past the reception area to a conference room, where I am introduced to Allie, Ryan's institutional parole officer. Allie has a genuinely caring manner and expresses her support for the reconciliation process. I ask if she is going to be present through the conference. I want to be sure that Ryan has all the support possible. She tells me she is willing to stay if Ryan agrees.

While we wait for Ryan to be escorted from his cell, I try to quell the fear that is rising up within me. It is not the prison that scares me. The wire, the concrete, the smell—they are only temporary assaults on the senses. It is what the prison may be doing to Ryan that I dread. I am concerned that the broken young man I last saw leaving the courtroom ten months earlier will be devoid of emotion. What if he has simply turned off and disconnected in order to survive his jail term, or what if he has slipped into the dangerous subculture of prison life? I don't want any more waste or loss to plague our families.

Ryan enters the room. He looks so young. Time appears to have stood still since I last saw him. I have felt so old since Bob's death. The contrast is odd.

As he seats himself on the other side of the broad expanse of conference table, I am relieved to see, despite his obvious trepidation, a genuine focus and unmistakable sparkle in his eyes. We both look away—fearful, I suspect, of overstaying our welcome within one another's gaze.

Dave rescues us from our momentary discomfort and lays out the framework and guidelines for the victim-offender reconciliation process. He explains that the meeting will be filmed, in compliance with CJI's protocol, but he assures us the film will not be viewed by anyone outside the organization nor without our consent. Ryan is comfortable with Allie in the room, so we begin.

It is through simple conversation about our daily lives and our families that we cautiously explore the ravaged wasteland left behind on New Year's Eve in 1997. We work backward to build an understanding of, and a familiarity for, one another's lives. The chasm between those divided by society's justice system is gradually filled in with stories of worlds that are more similar than they are different.

I can relate to many of the stories Ryan shares from his own youth, scenarios where peer pressure played a key role in bad choices about high-risk behavior. I saw my share of excessive drug and alcohol use in my own peer group. But I never saw the violence that Ryan describes as being so central to his life.

Dave and Sandi sit back and let us fumble through the visit, creating a safe space from which we can speak of the dark corners as we encounter them. Periodically they help us over a hurdle, reframing those questions that stymie us, or setting aside things too painful to tackle so we can try again later.

It is hardest for Ryan when I speak of Emma and Sam. I want him to know how we have worked to rebuild our lives, to recreate a place where they can have their childhood. I want him to know they were, and will continue to be, profoundly affected by their father's death. But Emma and Sam also personify resiliency, and they have kept me moving forward against all odds. Their spirit fills me with awe each day. I want Ryan to know that too, because I want to share that which inspires me. He deserves to know it. He needs to begin releasing himself from his emotional shackles so he can move toward healing.

I explain the new champion I have in Michael. His presence overlies the memories of men who have deeply touched my life and then left too soon: my grandfathers, my father, and Bob. He is unconditional in his support for the path I have chosen. I tell Ryan that Michael understands my need to be here today, while many, many other people in my life do not.

I make excuses for those who choose not to support my decision to seek reconciliation. This is a personal choice. Part of understanding the true impact of the harm is the realization that some people will never come around. The landscape is forever changed. If that is my experience, then it must be the case for Ryan too. His family may be concerned about our choosing to meet, and I am sure his fellow inmates have strong opinions as well. We have come to this day from two very different places, but I point out that there is common ground in some of what we may be experiencing.

I find it difficult to hear about Ryan's family. I can't image how their lives have been altered by this tragedy. As I build a new life, it is only the memories of Bob that weave in and out of the new structure, but the Aldridges must deal with the reality of Ryan's actions and his incarceration as they try to move forward.

The momentum of our conversation is interrupted when a guard comes to the door to escort Ryan back to his unit for a head count. This procedure takes precedence over all other activities in the institution. Dave suggests it might be a good time to take a break. Ryan will eat with his fellow inmates. We will leave Matsqui for a meal and return to finish our session in the afternoon. Allie reassures me that she will check up on Ryan to see how he is faring.

We find a quiet corner in a pub where we can debrief after our morning session. Both Dave and Sandi are pleased by the extent to which Ryan and I have revealed our feelings and explain that it often takes several meetings to reach this level of disclosure. Many people never reach it. Dave reflects on what he feels we have accomplished: "tears and important dialogue; the taking of responsibility; confession; acknowledgment of the pain, past and present; hope of healing and of lives yet to be lived."

I am so glad that Sandi is here to share the experience with me, and I fight back the tears as I tell her so. In addition to her calm and empathetic presence at the reconciliation, she brings a mother's perspective. I am committed to describing to Ryan the impact Bob's death has had, and will continue to have, on my children. But as I do so I cannot help putting myself in the place of Ryan's own mother. My heart aches with the hope that if my son ever found himself in such a place in his life, someone would do what I am doing for him. And Sandi understands this. Without needing to say a word, our eyes lock and we know that there but for the grace of some higher power goes every child, go our own children. As we bear witness, we continue to nurture even the most lost of children. While many men throw up their arms in rage, in disgust, women keep putting one foot in front of the other, cleaning up as they go.

This is the heart of the matter. I believe that when something happens to us in this life—whether it is something that is put upon us or something we bring on ourselves—we all have a responsibility to roll up our sleeves and clean up the mess. Sometimes this means we find ourselves working alongside the very person or people who caused the harm. But what of it? Why do we back away and say, "I do not have to do anything with or near this person," when the potential for such profound change and healing exists? What more powerful alliance could there be than between those responsible for and those most affected by harm?

Before we leave the subdued atmosphere of the pub, Dave suggests I make a list of questions that I have not yet asked and note anything else I feel I need to know as we prepare for our final session at Matsqui. There are a few loose ends for me, but I can already feel that it will be hard to walk away at the end of the day.

In the morning, Ryan had spoken of his love of art. He mentioned that he kept a sketchbook. I apprehensively asked if I could see it, wondering immediately if I had overstepped a line. When we reconvene after lunch, Ryan holds a small, black book in his hands. He sits down beside me and begins to leaf through the pages. His drawings are meticulous. Realistic images in soft pencil, perfectly centered, symmetrical, and filled with intricate detail.

As we move through the sketchbook, photographs of his family slip out from between the pages onto the table. A Christmas dinner, a newborn nephew, a beloved family dog. All held safely in Ryan's book. Frozen in time. Waiting. I weep.

He speaks of his family with great respect and concern. What happened in his world that, in a split second, he could show such wanton disregard for *my* family? I can see that gap in understanding will not narrow if I do not ask the questions. For now there are no answers, but he *does* seem to be willing to look for them.

I want to know that incarceration is going to be more than time standing still. What is there here in this prison to help Ryan answer my questions and those he may pose to himself over time? He tells me that in the ten months since his sentence began, he has received no formal rehabilitation. His sentencing plan, the treatment strategy recommended by an assessment team at the start of his incarceration, includes cognitive behavioral therapy, drug and alcohol counseling, and an anger-management program. Ryan explains that he visits the program coordinator each day to ask when he will actually get into these programs. The answer is that enrollment is based on release date. Ryan is going to be here for a while, so he must wait. What can he say to that? And what happens to you in an institution when you are waiting? Of his own accord, Ryan has completed an English upgrading seminar to improve his writing skills. He is taking an auto body painting course in hopes that he will be employable after his release. He works out regularly and walks six miles around Matsqui's yard each day. I am relieved he keeps moving. What would happen to him if there was no momentum for him to go forward?

I tell Allie how concerned I am that no formal rehabilitation is taking place, and she assures me she will speak to the programming staff to see where things stand. I am aware of the irony that it is me, the victim, who is advocating for Ryan.

And now another emotional hurdle to clear. I need Ryan to know about the work I am doing in schools. The Story of Bob

is also, in many ways, the story of Ryan. It is important to me
that I am not doing this work behind his back. I turn on my
laptop. My hand shakes as I advance through the photographs of
Bob that begin the story. Ryan's head falls into his hands; his
shoulders sag. But he does not take his eyes off the screen.

Dave and Sandi are standing by, ready to catch either of us
if we fall off our precarious emotional perches. Part of me wants
to protect Ryan from the image of Bob lying dead in the
morgue. But for so many years he buried the reality of Bob's
death deeper and deeper in his mind, in a dark place he hoped
he would never have to return to. At some point we all have to
return to those hidden places in our own psyches. We need to
gently extricate the emotional corpses of our past and look at
them head-on. Mindful of what they teach us, we then can give
them a respectful and decent burial outside our subconscious.
We can free ourselves.

Ryan endures the presentation. And I endure the telling of
the story he knows all too well. I share with Ryan some of the
things that kids say after I speak and how they believe the com-
pelling story may make them think twice when peers pressure
them to use alcohol and other drugs or put themselves in the
dangerous situation of an unchaperoned gathering. If this story
elicits that type of response, then this is indeed important work.

Ryan asks what made me want to tell the story. I tell him
about the flash I had while driving past my old high school and
how things quickly snowballed from there. Then, searching for
other ways to describe my work, I suddenly recall a movie I saw
recently. *Pay It Forward* is the story of a young boy whose
teacher challenges him to make a difference in the world, an
assignment his classmates shrug off as impossible. The boy con-
fronts the task and constructs a pyramid-type scheme of giving
gestures that literally changes the world around him.

It is only as I am relaying the movie's plot to Ryan that I
make the connection for myself—Michael and my children gave
me the strength and resolve to live through, and beyond, Bob's
death. They have allowed me to find a fulfilling and meaningful

life. And most of all, they do not condemn me for living it to the fullest. When I began doing the presentations, I'm not sure I fully understood why I felt such a deep need to do so. Now it is clear that it is because I want to pay it forward.

Ryan needs to know that the narrative I share is only half the story. I speculate about the impact it would have if *he* was part of the telling. I explain that I do not want him to feel beholden to me, but I suggest that he may see this as an opportunity to pay it forward alongside me.

I plant a seed. "I do not know what your plans are after you are released from prison, but if you would like to come and work with me in the schools, I would be honored to work with you. Don't feel like you need to even respond, but just think about the difference we could make..."

It's been a long day. We've spent five hours together. So many tears. Our wounds have been exposed, spoken of from the heart, cleaned, and tenderly rebandaged. There was laughter too. We found places where we could connect: family, friends, a sketch, a soccer ball. Bridging a gap of humanity. We have been brave.

Before we say goodbye, I bring out a small book for Ryan. *Searching for the Silver Linings* was written by a woman named Pamela Adams from Salt Spring Island. Emma chose it for him at the little bookstore near our home. She pulled it off the shelf, efficiently flipped through it, and announced, "This is perfect. It is simple, inspiring, and does not talk about God. I think we should buy it for Ryan." Emma is only ten, yet her old soul constantly reveals itself.

Ryan accepts the book and we linger over the wide table, postponing our goodbye. I let Dave and Sandi move past me toward the door. They are speaking to Allie, wrapping up practicalities. Ryan and I are standing next to one another. I take a deep breath of thin prison air. My heart aches. I ask him if I can give him a hug. He nods. I am folded briefly into his arms. This is reconciliation. This is healing.

Ryan goes back to his cell. I go back to the embrace of my family. I hope this has helped Ryan as much as it has helped me. And more than anything, I hope that Ryan will be safe, that he will survive, and that one day he will thrive.

chapter 15

it's all about
the shoes

Dear Katy,

I am seventeen turning eighteen. I was one of the teens present today at your presentation at the custody center. Well, I don't really know how to say this or what words to use but I've been thinking about it ever since the Story of Bob. I'm in here for violent charges, and what led to the violence was alcohol and drugs. I've been to so many groups about violence and listened to so many people talk about it and its affect and what alcohol and drugs do. Never once have I thought so hard about what anyone said or even really cared cause I just thought they were doing a job, they don't know what it is really like. But today the words you spoke touched me. I guess things happen for a reason. Yesterday I was talking to friends about getting out and partying, but after this morning I've decided to make a change and that is to cut violence out of my life and get help for my drug and alcohol abuse and give it 110 percent to make my way back to the person I was six years ago. Then in my future to show kids that if I can change so can they. It just takes some courage. Thank you for your help, you and your family will be in my heart and when it gets tough for me I'll think about your words and look to my family for strength to keep going. You've helped me take the first step to change, thank you and keep up the good work.

—A youth in custody awaiting trial and sentencing for violent offenses

My work in schools evolves dramatically after the reconciliation with Ryan. Layered over the discussion of social responsibility, which uses Bob's death as the teachable moment, is an explanation of the gift I had promised Emma and Sam. The day I spent with Ryan in jail humanized what had been a horribly inhuman trauma. I urge my audiences to consider the possibilities in their own lives. Can they let go of the small, day-to-day annoyances that so often build up into unnecessary conflict? If I can sit across from the person who killed my husband and make peace, what can they do?

This adds a unique dimension to my work, and I begin to get speaking requests from a number of different groups: a recreation center that provides a safe haven on Friday nights for teens who would otherwise be hanging around on the street, a criminal justice conference, a neighborhood parents' group, a school that is recovering from the horror of a student stabbing a fellow classmate, a remote First Nations community battling the ravages of poverty and alcoholism, another school with a progressive administration that has instituted a peacemaking program involving peer-to-peer conflict resolution.

As part of a best-practices component for a justice workshop, I volunteer to give my presentation at the Burnaby Youth Custody Centre in November 2003. I tell the story in a classroom to twenty-four violent juvenile offenders. Their dark green institution-issue tracksuits do little to cover the rough edges of these kids. Many of them seem to be visibly struggling with a short lifetime of demons, some perhaps handed down by past generations. Even within this small group, a class system is palpable, with obvious tension between groups and individuals. The wounds sustained on the streets may have healed, but their eyes betray the hidden bruising of their souls.

I am introduced by Julie Czerwinski, their life-skills instructor, a wonderful woman who will become a special friend. As soon as Julie speaks, a calm settles over the room. Her words and actions convey true compassion and respect for her students. She may be the closest thing to a caring parent that many of these young people have ever had.

The young offenders' reaction to The Story of Bob is much different from any I have seen in a regular school setting. This is not a cautionary tale for this audience. Many of these kids have witnessed this kind of tragedy firsthand. Some have been victims of violence themselves, and many may have been the perpetrators in similar situations. I sense that forgiveness is not a concept they have often considered, either extending it or receiving it. These kids might see themselves, or some part of their own stories, in Ryan's past. But the strongest commonality between these kids and my school audiences is the instant concern for the welfare of my children. My audiences always ask how Emma and Sam have fared. This is what Canadian educator Mary Gordon refers to as the "roots of empathy" phenomenon. No matter how abused or neglected young people may be, no matter the extent of their personal moral agony, their sense of empathy for younger children resonates. Tapping into this empathy has enormous potential for reaching into these kids' consciences.

Workers at the youth custody center tell me later that three of the kids in the audience came to them afterward to ask about initiating victim-offender reconciliations for their own offenses. Even if those meetings never take place, the fact that the kids entertained the notion that someone could meet them face-to-face, speak from the heart about the harm, and possibly offer forgiveness is a move forward. It may be their first step toward learning to forgive themselves. And I have learned that forgiving oneself is where it all starts.

I realize this is a population that will find both healing and hope in my work, so I offer the presentation to the custody center in Victoria. After I speak, I am given a tour of the site, a state-of-the-art facility with well-equipped classrooms, an art studio, kitchens where inmates can learn basic life skills, and lots of outdoor space for recreation. While the individual cells are small and spartan, they may be the most secure personal space some of these kids have ever had.

As I finish the tour, a staff member approaches me with a letter written by a female resident.

I don't know exactly where to begin this letter. So I'll start by thanking you for helping me find the hope that I had lost on one of my darker days here in youth custody. I've spent a year and two months here, with every day to think about the nightmare I so desperately want to waken from. I've asked God and myself for forgiveness so often that I've lost all hope of getting it. I know what it is like to carry the guilt of not helping that person in the most critical of conditions. When picking up the phone to call 9-1-1 was at the very tips of your fingers and the thought of it hanging at the edge of your mind, held by just a thread of hope that everything will be alright. That it's not as bad as it looks, and that maybe, just maybe the person will get up and be living their life, breathing the air I breathe. If only it were that easy. Now I'm sitting in my room built to contain the most nerve wracking thoughts. A room where so many tears have been shed. A room of regret. My room, my cell. The moment that you began your story and said you weren't angry I felt anger burst through every vein in my body because I could not understand. The instant I walked out and finally caught my breath I realized that I needed to write to you. I've given a lot of thought to

*forgiveness but I cannot find forgiveness for myself until
I find it somewhere else. I have been charged with
manslaughter and the sentence is but a few years; but is
to me a life sentence.*

I cannot leave the center without seeking this girl out and meeting with her if she is willing. The staff provide us with a private lounge. We sit curled up on either end of a couch, separated by a box of tissue. She speaks. I listen. Her story is no more remarkable than Ryan's. The same waste. Anguish. Emptiness. There is small chance for a reconciliation, since her victim was an indigent man about whom the authorities knew little.

Out of respect, I look toward my lap as I speak to her, knowing that eye contact has different connotations for First Nations people. Holding her hands in mine, I say, "I forgive you. And what that means, my friend, is that you are not your crime. You are the power and grace of now and the healing you make for yourself for tomorrow. A violent death may be a part of your story, as it is part of mine. But use that to create something good and safe and healthy for yourself and those you care about."

We sit beside one another for a long time. Silence. Tears. For her victim, for Bob, for her, for Ryan, for someone out there who once cared about her victim, and for me. It is hard to leave her.

Some weeks later, a package arrives from the custody center. Nestled in a box filled with tissue sits a cylindrical container made from four different kinds of wood. Its pewter top is decorated with a cutout design of a mother and baby hummingbird. Thick curls of cedar fill the container. Their rich scent fills the room and reminds me of the forest Bob and I used to walk in with Emma and Sam. An enclosed card, written by the girl I met, and signed by several of the youth, thanks me for coming and speaking, and I am thankful once again to have found my voice.

It is harder to speak in some places than others. When I am asked to come to Bob's old high school, I arrive early and find his class picture hanging in one of the hallways. Gazing at his image, captured twenty-eight years earlier, I wonder what Bob, the class valedictorian, predicted his legacy would be. Surely not this. But it is a powerful and honorable gift just the same.

After four hundred students settle themselves into the bleachers, I watch a group of men enter the rear door of the gym from the parking lot. My stomach tightens as I realize it is a group of Bob's old friends. They all graduated from this school around the same time, and some of them, even though they had promised to be there for me after his death, had quickly disappeared from my life.

This is where grief is tricky. It is not a team sport. There is no playbook. No timed intervals. No prize for the best score. Grief is a personal process that can be completely different for different people. I believe that none of these people anticipated how hard it would be to stay close as we each navigated the storm of Bob's loss. But I also believe that none of them understood my grieving process continued even when I remarried. Nervous and curious, I wonder how hearing the story in this context, as audience rather than participants, may illuminate that dark expanse of friendships suspended.

I find out before the final applause dies away. Jamie, Bob's former roommate, wraps his arms around me and his speechlessness says it all. The following day, a one-line e-mail from Mark, the best man at our wedding, reads simply: *You are my hero.*

As school winds down for the 2003 winter vacation, I realize that I have been going flat out. The eight hundred people who had heard The Story of Bob by the end of June have now become eleven thousand. I continue to be inundated with requests for the presentation. At first the sight of days booked on a calendar makes me nervous. Part of my recovery has been the realization that I should not overcommit myself and make long-term plans. I learn important lessons about not overdoing it, but only after losing my voice following a speaking tour that involved fourteen presentations in four days. As I start to get a sense of balance, I can feel some of the old me is back; the busy, connected, looking-forward-to-the-next-thing me is returning to life. I welcome myself with open arms.

I am thinking out loud to Michael one evening about how good it would be to have a Web site where people could go to find out about the presentation. He laughs as he tucks himself into bed and says, "I know what's coming." And he does. When I crawl into bed at 4:30 in the morning, Michael nestles against me and murmurs, "Let me guess. You built a Web site!" He's right. After some quick research and reviews of do-it-yourself sites, I found an Internet tool kit that met my needs perfectly. The loss of a night's sleep seemed a small sacrifice for the ability to provide simple and consistent information to anyone who wants to know about my work.

Dave Gustafson calls me just days before Christmas. He suspects that this is not an easy time of year and wants to check in. We talk for a while about how certain seasons and celebrations trigger traumatic memories. I confess that I feel cheated because I am no longer able to immerse myself in the Christmas season the way I did before Bob's death. I explain that Michael and I are working hard to create new traditions with our children that do not pull at the past.

I thank Dave for thinking about me and reaching out, and he tells me there is something in the mail for me. "I think this is going to be a pretty wonderful Christmas present," he adds as we say goodbye. I am curious about what I will find in the mailbox.

Ryan has sent me two letters. The first is a handwritten cover note that begins, "I hope this short story of my life will help you with your presentation. I am hoping it will reach some young teens and show them that violence is not the answer."

Folded neatly in the same envelope is a typewritten letter.

My name is Ryan and I am currently serving a five-year sentence in federal prison for manslaughter. I hope that by helping Katy with her program I can influence today's youth to make better choices than I did. I would like to talk to you about my life...and hope that you will learn about the price of violence, and how a close relationship with family is so important.

I grew up in the small town of Squamish. After completing elementary school without many problems I moved on to the local high school. Like most teenagers I was concerned about meeting new friends and fitting in. During my early years I was picked on, bullied, and pushed around. Unfortunately I didn't tell my parents and thought I could deal with the problem myself. Eventually I made some friends and the drinking and partying began. After school one day, we were invited to a local house party. We collected money for beer and found someone to bootleg for us. Later that evening while walking home, we were threatened by a crowd of teens. They started pushing us around. I became angry; I punched one of them and a fight broke out. Subsequently three of them swarmed me and they proceeded to beat me up. After they finished I looked around for my buddies, they hadn't come to my aid and were nowhere to be seen. So during my long walk home I decided that it was time to move on and find some new friends.

I began hanging around with a new group of friends; I was impressed with their lifestyle and felt accepted. I guess it was all about status and ego. I went to more parties, began drinking more alcohol, and then started experimenting with drugs. My parents gave me good advice but of course I knew better! Life seemed great, I had new friends, wasn't getting bullied anymore, and felt like I fitted in just fine! Unfortunately along with my newfound lifestyle and the partying came fighting and trouble with the local police—they got to know me on a first-name basis. My school grades were suffering and I barely graduated. I was in three alcohol-related car accidents, and also lost a friend grad night in a tragic car accident. This devastated me and instead of grieving, I became angry and started looking for answers in all the wrong places. I was now nineteen and my life was spiraling out of control.

New Year's Eve 1997 a friend was having a party; the house was unsupervised since his father was out of town. Around one hundred and fifty guests of all ages attended but most of them were teens. Drugs and alcohol were everywhere, the house was crowded, and small fights were breaking out throughout the evening. Several of us were upstairs; I was heavily intoxicated and listening to music. An unidentified guest came up the stairs suggesting that we leave the house. My buddy was arguing with him, then punched him. As the stranger fell to the ground, I kicked him (I was later told four times); we then left the area. Shortly after, chaos erupted—an ambulance, followed by the police. To avoid confrontation with the authorities I left with my buddies and moved on to another party, not knowing that I had just made the most fatal mistake of my life.

The following morning I learned that the man died from his injuries. His name was Bob McIntosh, Katy's husband, Emma and Sam's father. I didn't know what to do, my head was foggy, it seemed like a bad dream. I couldn't believe that I was responsible, what would my family think of me? I was scared—so the silence began. Throughout the investigation I knew I was a person of interest, but unaware that I was the main suspect. I tried moving on with my life; however it was more like the end of my life! Depression set in, I became antisocial and was haunted by nightmares. After four years I began falling apart and finally broke my silence to an undercover police officer. They now had enough evidence to charge me. The media attention was relentless, and my family was devastated.

Now I look back on my life and realize how many bad choices I have made. Because of my poor actions a precious life has been lost. A father was taken from his children, a husband from his wife, and a man from his family and friends. Not to mention how this tragedy has impacted my family and friends.

I have learned how important a close family relationship is. Throughout my darkest days they have loved and supported me. I wish that I had been more open and honest with them; they would have guided me in a more positive direction and maybe my life would have been different. So please...talk to your family, share your feelings, problems, and concerns. Regrettably I cannot turn back the clock and undo what has been done, but hopefully I can influence at least one misguided teen to make better choices than I did. I guarantee there's a price to be paid for violent behavior. If any of you are going through a similar scenario, please consider your options. Stop and think of the consequences. This could happen to you. Don't go looking for advice in all the wrong places because you won't find the right answers.

The biggest question I ask myself is <u>why did I do this?</u> That question may never be answered. However I do know that doing jail time is easy compared to the guilt that I will have to live with for the rest of my life! I consider that a life sentence.

I would like to share with you a poem written by Pamela Rosemary Adams that was given to me by Katy and her children. I read it every night and it inspires me. These words have made me realize that there was help for me and I chose to ignore it. With Katy, Emma, and Sam's forgiveness—maybe I can move on and forgive myself.

In desperation
I cry out

"O.K.
I admit it,
I can't do this alone;
and yes,
I have not suffered alone.
There has always been help,
And there always will be."
Oh what peace admitting this
has given me.
Now I move forward,
with joy in my heart

I read the letter over and over. Ryan's clear and simple description of the factors that led him down a path of alcohol abuse, drug use, and violence floors me. Nothing I say to the audiences I address could have nearly the impact that this message will. I can hardly wait for January, when I can incorporate Ryan's contribution into The Story of Bob.

I have become accustomed to receiving packages of letters from schools where I have given my presentation. The first school that hears Ryan's letter sends not one, but two packages. The second is addressed to Ryan in the hope that I can forward it to him in prison. A note from the teacher asks me to look over the enclosures and make sure I am comfortable with Ryan receiving them. The kids' notes are filled with blunt, logical, and honest sentiments. "Each choice is a drop of water, each sends ripples through the pool of life." "Please consider this fatal mistake a *major* lesson and use this lesson to educate those who may end up committing the same unfortunate deed." "I respect you."

Another student shares a folktale with both Ryan and me. It is the story of two hedgehogs seeking shelter from the rain in a cave. It is cold, and when the hedgehogs try to draw closer to each other to generate some body heat, their spikes poke into each other. Every time it happens they draw away, until finally they find the perfect distance, where they're not close enough to hurt one another, but close enough to tolerate the abiding cold. The young man who sent the story even passes along his mailing address should Ryan feel inclined to contact him. I relish the possibilities that are emerging from this extraordinary exchange of mail.

A television interview with Vicki Gabereau results in my e-mail in-box being jammed with requests for The Story of Bob. Instead of one presentation every couple of weeks I am doing weeklong speaking tours across the country. From big city to small town, public school to private school, the response to the message is unanimously positive.

I find some humor in what has become a predictable reaction to my work. A gaggle of girls, often holding hands, will shyly approach me as the crowd is dispersing. Often one or two of them will be in tears, while another will giggle nervously. A confident girl will step out of the group to tell me how powerful the story was. Then they will all begin to speak at once. They will say I am brave. They will tell me they don't know how I do it. We debrief about my story, and sometimes their own stories begin to emerge. The interactions in a small group are intense and emotional. I try to give them all the time they need to say what needs to be said and ask what needs to be asked. It is hard to wind things down. Invariably, when they feel complete, one of the girls will break the heaviness by looking down at my feet and saying, "Those are really great shoes."

And so I make a point of wearing wonderful shoes whenever I am speaking. The work I do is about so much, but sometimes, it's just all about the shoes...

I take the time to remind these groups of girls that they are often the ones who can make things right when a party is getting out of control. Boys can be easily deafened by peer pressure in group settings, and they have the added complication of ego and bravado to deal with. The girls need to listen to their natural nurturing voices, set aside their anxiety about speaking out, and do the right thing.

I also want them to see me as a positive role model. I am passionate about my work, and I want these girls to realize that you can create a space to flourish, even in the most barren of places. If I can do this, I want them to imagine what they will be capable of.

In April 2004 I am asked to present the Story of Bob at the secondary school on Salt Spring Island. This request stirs up some painful unfinished business from the past.

Shelley and Dave, our former neighbors in Squamish, are now living on the Gulf Islands. Their two youngest children are students at the school where I have been asked to speak. I explain the situation to the school counselor. He agrees to contact Shelley to ask how she feels about my speaking to an audience that will include her children and their peers. The reply comes back quickly. Her kids are anxious to hear the presentation, and she would like to be in the audience as well.

Shelley arrives to meet me before the school gym fills with two hundred students. We have not seen each other since 1998. I immediately want to melt into her arms and restore the broken pieces of our friendship. There is a flood of emotion and so much to say, but it must wait until after I present. We agree to meet privately later in the day.

But it's not simple. We can't merely pick up where we left off, because so much has happened in both our lives. A reconciliation will mean churning up dark waters from the past and navigating through them. Over a cup of coffee in a café by the ferry dock, we decide we are both prepared to make the journey. We promise to take our time and be gentle with one another. I am grateful Shelley is willing to do the work along with me. I have missed having her, Dave, and their children in my life and the lives of Emma and Sam. I look forward to getting to know them over again.

I am curious to see how my court-ordered victim-offender reconciliation with Ryan McMillan is going to play out. For a time, I resist the temptation to push the process. I want to find out what infrastructure exists at the provincial level to deliver the service. But when no one is in touch with me during the year following McMillan's court appearance, I decide to take matters into my own hands.

When I talk to McMillan's probation officer in Squamish, he is not even sure how to initiate the process. As I feared, if there is an established program for restorative processes, not all probation officers in the field are aware of it. I explain I have worked with Dave Gustafson from Community Justice Initiatives and suggest that perhaps he and his partner Sandi Bergen could facilitate the reconciliation. My query is moved up the ranks, and eventually I deal directly with the office of the attorney general. Staff there decide that although CJI usually handles federal cases, the province will contract them for our reconciliation because they have already worked with me. I can see our communities need an advocate for restorative justice.

My victim-offender reconciliation with Ryan McMillan is scheduled for June 2004. Dave and Sandi speak to me frequently on the phone and meet with Ryan a few times in advance to prepare him for the meeting. I am apprehensive about facing Ryan. I cannot imagine connecting with him the way I have with Ryan Aldridge.

As we sit across from each other at the table in a conference room rented from a social service agency in North Vancouver, the conversation is stilted. We are two strangers, making small talk as we move awkwardly toward speaking of the tragic event that connects us.

Steadying myself with a deep breath, I ask the questions that have been burning a hole in my heart for the past six and a half years as I have imagined Bob's last moments alive. "What words were exchanged between you and Bob? Was he rendered unconscious immediately following your punch? Did you see Ryan Aldridge kick Bob? Was there anyone else in the room?"

As Ryan begins to answer my barrage of queries, he struggles to recall the events of the evening. His answers seem uncertain and he appears to be emotionally detached. I realize it is less important for him to answer my questions than it is for me to ask them.

Ryan describes a brief argument that occurred after Bob suggested the young people wrap up the party, but he can't remember anything either of them said that would push the situation from a verbal altercation to a violent assault. Ryan says he turned and left the room before Bob even hit the ground. He had no idea if Bob was conscious or what happened next. That's it.

I think Ryan senses my disappointment, but he seems incapable of offering anything that might shed light on that dark night so long ago. I feel I am choking in the dark. Could anything Ryan says about that New Year's Eve make a difference to me now?

I accept that I may not be able to get through to the drunk young man from 1997 and choose to move to the present, where there is air and light—and maybe sharing and healing. We struggle clumsily to find common ground. Dave rescues us by drawing Ryan out in a discussion about fishing, and the staccato dialogue softens.

As we begin to speak about our families and the day-to-day lives we now live, it becomes easier to let the pain of the past weave itself gently into the conversation. I talk about grief, fear, and the process of rebuilding a life for me and for my children. Ryan explains the effect the incident has had on his family. Despite his ill health, Ryan's father desperately tried to find information to break the code of silence. Ryan believes the stress of it ultimately led to his father's death. I tell Ryan about losing my own father to cancer when I was in my early twenties. In this we find a bond, and, quietly honoring one another's loss of a parent, I feel marginally better.

After two hours, we find little more to say. Dave and Sandi assure Ryan he can come to them for support in the future. I doubt he will. He just wants to go fishing.

In July 2004 there is one more reconciliation. It is one I am not prepared for and is all the more precious because of that. Emma is spending the month with a youth group in Cairo,

Egypt, and Sam and I decide that this, at last, is the year to go to Squamish to watch the triathlon that is run each year in Bob's memory. Since 1998, Bob's friends, led by Peter, Gill, Ray, and Doug, have put on a race that raises money for a scholarship in Bob's name to be awarded to a local high school student. Until now I have never felt able to cope with going to the event, sure that the emotional overload will be too much—Squamish, triathlon, old friends.

But this year I feel strong and ready. Doug invites Sam and me to stay at his home on our old street. It is a perfect, still, warm summer evening. We sit with old friends and neighbors on the front porch, taking in the spectacular mountain view, while Sam reintroduces himself to the kids up and down the street who would have been his schoolmates. It is a brief, strange glimpse of what our life would have been like if Bob were still in it.

We wake up at 5:00 A.M. to help the volunteers prepare the race course at Alice Lake. While Sam sweeps the gravel from the path leading from the shore into the parking lot, which will be the competitors' transition area, I help set up bike frames. The racers begin to appear.

I watch the familiar ritual of a triathlete setting out his gear. With his back to me, he slides his bike into the rack, cleats mounted on the pedals for quick access. Running shoes ready. Water bottle close at hand. He turns to retrieve something from his bag. I recognize the face, deep in concentration and anticipation. It is Richard Cudmore. My heart skips a beat. There, in the stillness of the morning, the air heavy with the scent of lake and forest, it is time to close another gap.

His smile is reassuring and familiar. Images highlighting the years of friendship whip around in my head as I walk toward him. I can tell from his eyes that he is pleased to see me, but I am grateful for his British stiff upper lip and reserved demeanor that will keep the emotional tide from overflowing in both directions.

I keep it simple for now, knowing Richard will be relieved. A hug. I wish him a good race.

Something big that has been out of place for so long has just found its way back.

Sam fires the starting pistol while Peter and I choke back the tears. The athletes enter the lake for the 1,500-meter swim. We watch all the competitors come out of the water and take off on their bikes before we move on to the finish line of the run portion of the race to await the winner.

There are six hundred people gathered by the track of Don Ross Secondary School. Emerging from the forested trails that have been painstakingly cleared for this event, the runners make one lap of the track before passing beneath the timing clock.

The winners are long over the finish line and well into the postrace festivities. Peter is about to start the awards ceremonies, and Sam is ready to present the trophies, when the last runner enters the school grounds. The proceedings are halted and everyone crowds around the track to cheer in the last person over the line. Blinded by tears, I remember Bob returning to the finish line at Elk Lake some two hours after he had crossed it to cheer our friend Shauna Griffiths, my sister Jenny, and my brother David. They had all been inspired by Bob to take on the immense personal challenge of completing a triathlon. He was so proud of their efforts. It is as though Bob has orchestrated this scene in Squamish.

Peter struggles to maintain his composure as Sam stands with him on the stage. Before they hand out the trophies and ribbons, Peter asks the audience to observe a moment of silence in memory of Bob. As I stand amidst the crowd, head bowed, tears flowing, an arm wraps around my shoulder. It is Richard. As we stand together in the silence, I realize nothing more needs to be said.

"You will not believe the story we need to tell you," says an e-mail I receive from an organization called LOVE, an acronym for Leave Out ViolencE. I call the phone number in the message and find myself speaking to Erin Barton, director of the

Vancouver chapter of this not-for-profit organization that works to reduce violence in the lives of youth through the work of a team of young people who teach a message of nonviolence. Erin explains that this group was founded in 1993 by a woman named Twinkle Rudberg. After her husband was murdered by a young runaway on the street in Montreal, Twinkle was looking for ways to break the cycle of senseless violence. LOVE was her answer.

On what has essentially been a solo journey, I am rocked by hearing any story that is similar to mine. Twinkle's story is more than similar. I have to meet her.

But first I meet Erin and her colleague Michael Maxwell and bring The Story of Bob with me to share in their cramped East Vancouver office space, where they provide an evening photojournalism program for youth who are either victims or perpetrators of violence. We quickly establish a rapport as we confirm our work is moving in a common direction.

Over the next few months, Michael and I pass along each other's information to schools and community groups. We even find ourselves working together at a First Nations conference entitled Leaders and Healers.

One of LOVE's most successful programs is its weeklong summer leadership camp, held each August at Camp White Pine in Haliburton, Ontario. Michael asks if I would be interested in coming to the camp to facilitate a workshop based on The Story of Bob. I do not hesitate. My bags are packed. I'm going to summer camp.

Part of the deal is that I, along with two other adult leaders, will accompany and chaperone the group of young people from the Vancouver chapter on the trip to camp. They are not hard to spot when I arrive at the airport. Amidst the generally sedate crowd in the boarding lounge blossoms a pulsing mass of color and energy. Hair in every shade of green, fuchsia, and jet-black sticks up and hangs over the excited faces of the LOVE gang.

When I sit down beside them, they look at me as if I must be lost. Who is this straight-looking mother type, and what could she possibly be doing with us? I explain that I am coming along for the ride and suggest that we'll be getting to know one another pretty well over the course of the next week.

On the plane I sit beside a young LOVE member who is twenty and suffers from ADHD. This is his first plane ride, and he is a throbbing ball of fear and excitement. It is all we can do to keep him in his seat. The takeoff both terrifies and thrills him, and nearly an hour passes before he has settled down for the red-eye flight.

We land in Toronto at five-thirty in the morning and take the bus to the Yorkdale mall, where camp buses will pick us up later in the day. The stores are not open at this hour, so we set up a temporary camp in the food court. Many of the kids are so exhausted that they unpack their sleeping bags and curl up on the floor underneath the tables. A hasty explanation to a mall security guard is met with a sigh and nod of understanding. Apparently the LOVE delegation from Halifax is also at the mall and has set up a similar camp at the other end.

By late afternoon we arrive at Camp White Pine. It is the quintessential summer camp, the site where the movie *Meatballs* was filmed back in 1979. But the eighty-plus campers are hardly typical, with do-rags, dreadlocks, piercings in every conceivable body part, and enthusiasm beyond measure. Many of these kids have never been outside the city. They have come from Vancouver, Toronto, Montreal, Halifax, and New York. And they are all here because of Twinkle.

After a hearty spaghetti dinner in the massive log-cabin dining hall, we gather at the lakefront for a campfire. Someone produces a guitar, and we all join in singing a repertoire of songs, some predictable and many not. After completing a bed check to make sure the girls and the boys are where they belong, we adults crash into our assigned bunks.

I wake up early, still on Pacific time, and make my way to the beach. Alone on the dock that juts out over the still lake, I treat my body and soul to some yoga as the birds call across the water to one another. From the work I have done with high-risk youth in alternative schools and detention facilities, I know The Story of Bob will be hard on these kids. Breathing deeply, I ask for strength in creating safety and healing as I do my work.

Michael shows me to the cabin where I will be facilitating my workshop. Hidden amongst the pines, it is a cool, shady, and quiet space; bare except for a series of rustic wooden benches arranged randomly on the wood plank floor. I imagine the cabin filled with the colorful, crazy-brave kids who were swept out of their cities to these woods. There is nowhere in this large, open room to hide, no long rows of auditorium seating to sink into if the emotional toll is too much when I speak. The kids will need to be there for one another when I tell my story.

Before I lead the first workshop, I join a group of kids who are gathered on the beach to meet Twinkle and hear her story. My tears begin as I see her walk toward us. I know already that something bigger than both of us has brought us together on the shore of this lake. I can hardly listen to her account of the night her husband Daniel was murdered. It is too close, too real. After the kids move on to their next workshop, I am left alone with Twinkle. We can barely speak to one another. We start, and then it is too much. We promise to pull ourselves together and try again later in the day.

Twinkle comes to hear me speak. We sit together afterward and absorb the parallels of our journeys. She says we were meant to be brought together, and we talk about how we might work together in the future to break the cycle of violence for the youth we both care so passionately about. We mull over the suggestion that The Story of Bob might be a good opening act for LOVE's violence-prevention workshops in schools, and as the camp continues, she introduces me to members of her team from across the country.

For the remainder of the week, I share my story once a day and fill the remaining hours with long runs, swimming, volleyball, and camp crafts in the company of the most courageous of young leaders: kids who have found the strength to rise above impossible beginnings of family abuse, gang violence, addiction, and loss.

In the evenings we are treated to improv workshops and a talent show. The creative ability that exists here amazes me. The kids sing, dance, play instruments, read poetry, and perform skits. What shines through each performance is a total lack of competitiveness—they genuinely want one another to succeed and do everything they can to support each other. Kids who on the first day clung to the edges of the group are now center stage, decked out in wild costumes from the bottomless dress-up trunk, basking in the attention of their audience.

Each evening ends with us gathered by the campfire. Seated in a wide circle around the flames, we sing old Canadian folk songs, Led Zeppelin, and everything in between. The strength of the community we've built so quickly radiates as brightly as our fire.

For the first four nights, I am assigned to a bunkhouse with one other adult leader and ten girls. There is little opportunity to sleep, since it is our responsibility to make sure the girls check in after campfire and do not go off in search of the boys, who are housed on the other side of the property. When I do sleep, I dream of simple pleasures—a bedside lamp, a radio, and an indoor bathroom. I spend the final three nights in relative luxury. Swapping accommodations with the other leaders, we move into cabins with private bedrooms and an adjoining communal bathroom.

On the last day the whole camp is in tears from the moment the breakfast dishes are cleared. It is heartrending to see these kids, who've bonded so intensely during the week, say goodbye. Some of them are going back to volatile families, ill-fitting foster homes, or the street. As we board the buses to take us back, we know we have been somewhere sacred and we've experienced true community. LOVE is everything.

chapter 16

sharing the stage

How could anyone ever tell you
You were anything less than beautiful?
How could anyone ever tell you
You were less than whole?
How could anyone fail to notice
That your loving is a miracle?
How deeply you're connected to my soul.
—Libby Roderick, "How Could Anyone"

The experience of taking The Story of Bob to LOVE camp has fueled my interest in sharing the presentation with varied audiences, so when Father Mako, a chaplain from the minimum-security Ferndale Institution, calls to ask if I would be interested in addressing a volunteer appreciation event the prison will hosting late in September 2004, I am keen to accept. The institution wishes to honor the volunteers who escort inmates when they leave Ferndale for family visits or appointments, and who assist with their cultural and spiritual programs. The theme of the gathering is "Growing Safe Communities—A Harvest of Healing," and the program will explore the significance of restorative justice while honoring people from the community who give their time to the men at the prison.

I do have one concern, though. In February 2004, Ryan was moved to Ferndale. When Corrections Canada notified me of the move, I was pleased. Inmates at Ferndale, or fellows, as they are called, live in group housing scattered around the property, and I hoped that these living conditions, which more closely resemble the outside world, would provide a healthier environment for Ryan as he continued his healing journey. I ask Father Mako if he is aware that Ryan Aldridge is now serving his sentence at Ferndale.

Not only is he aware of the fact, but when I ask how he thinks Ryan will feel about my coming to Ferndale to speak, he replies, "I believe that Ryan wants to do the presentation with you." I am speechless.

But before the volunteer event, I need to prepare for another type of encounter with Ryan—his first parole hearing, scheduled for September 8, 2004. I am given the opportunity to read a prepared statement that has been reviewed in advance by the National Parole Board.

Ryan's mother, Marina, and I arrive at the Ferndale duty desk at the same time. Just as we step forward to speak to one another, two parole board officials move in and lead us away in opposite directions. I am immediately assigned to an escort and briefed on the rigid protocol that will be observed throughout the proceedings. This protocol assumes that victims, offenders, and their families wish to be kept as far away from each other as possible. I understand that this is the most appropriate course of action in many situations due to fear and safety issues. But what if things are different? It is uncomfortable being kept apart from Ryan when we have come so far working together. I am also saddened that, although his family is there to support him, we are unable to meet.

My escort leads me into the hearing room after Ryan is seated so I cannot make eye contact with him. When I stand to read my submission, I am behind him. Ryan has been instructed to face forward and not look at me while I am speaking. I begin:

> *My motivation to make an in-person statement at Ryan Aldridge's parole hearing is for reasons that are likely very different than those of most victims of serious violent crime. Having said that, my expectations for Ryan's readiness to be released back into society are high.*
>
> *At the time of this hearing, Ryan will have spent approximately nineteen months in custody. I need to know that this time has been well spent. I need to be assured that all parties concerned feel that Ryan has utilized every resource available to him during his incarceration. I want to feel confident that Ryan is ready for reintegration into society. The following are the areas I would like to be assured he has fully addressed:*
>
> Substance abuse: *Ryan admits that he readily used alcohol and other drugs, and that he was under the influence when he killed my husband. He also indicates that he has a history of alcohol and drug use. Has Ryan been given the necessary counseling with respect to substance abuse? Are the professionals who facilitated that counseling confident that Ryan will be able to function without abusing alcohol and other drugs? Does Ryan feel that he can move forward clean and sober?*
>
> Anger management: *Ryan said he was angry the night he killed Bob. In reflecting on his teen years, he describes a continual need to fit in to an increasingly angry and violent group of peers. Has Ryan dealt with the issues surrounding both the appropriate expression of feelings and his sphere of influence? Has he*

demonstrated the ability to make good decisions and to understand the implications of those decisions?

Ryan's family: *Ryan is lucky to have a family that has stood by him through the most horrific of circumstances. I have no doubt that his family will continue to support him following his release. He has expressed to me a profound regret that he had shunned his family's attempts to influence him during the misdirected years of his youth. Does Ryan fully understand that his family plays a critical role in his future and will he allow them to guide him?*

My family: *Emma and Sam have had to live through a scenario and learn lessons no children should have to. I believe Ryan, through his own relationships with his nieces and nephews, is starting to understand the depth of the trauma he caused and how much he took away from Emma and Sam. I have worked extremely hard to give my children some semblance of normalcy in what remained of their childhood. Emma and Sam fully supported my choice to forgive Ryan and to champion him as he moves through the justice system, incarceration, and his eventual move back into society. The gift, if there is one to find amidst this tragedy, is that Emma and Sam are two of the most aware, empathetic, and socially responsible young people you will ever meet. I have no doubt that they will continue my work in educating people about choices, resiliency, and forgiveness long after I stop telling our story. Ryan must understand that how he conducts himself in the future will weigh heavily on us all. I could not imagine anything more devastating for my children than to hear that Ryan has found himself back in trouble with the law after his release. There will be no second chances for Ryan from my family or me. The hand that I firmly extended to him the day of his arrest will only reach out once.*

The future: *I understand that Ryan has worked on developing a trade while incarcerated. What plans have been made by Ryan to ensure the best chance for employment and a healthy living situation? What are Ryan's feelings about encountering people and negative influences from his past? Has he demonstrated a facility for the life skills needed to move on with his life? What infrastructure and support exists from the Parole Board after Ryan is released and what are the mechanisms for accountability?*

For Ryan, I am sure that nineteen months behind bars has seemed like an eternity. I hope so. That would be the point. I cannot think of a better outcome than for all involved to feel sure that nineteen months is enough. I would like nothing more than to offer Ryan my blessings for a fresh and productive start. On behalf of my family I sincerely hope Ryan finds true happiness in a life with genuine purpose, shares it with a family of his own, and can teach the world something from his heart from what he has learned on this journey.

Ryan, please be inspired by the way that Bob lived his life—each day 110 percent.

The two-member panel begins to ask Ryan questions. They ask how he feels about his involvement in Bob's death. They commend him on recent rehabilitative work that he has done to more fully accept his responsibility for what happened.

Then they ask him questions about some other violent incidents in Squamish. He was never formally charged for these incidents, but police suspect he was involved in them. Ryan is less able to explain what went on in those incidents and, according to the panel, has exhibited less than full acceptance of his responsibility. I begin to suspect that the panel members are not convinced Ryan is ready for parole.

After a brief recess, my suspicions are confirmed. The panel announces that his application has been denied. I am unable to speak to Ryan and am immediately escorted to my car. I can only imagine the devastation for Ryan and his family.

I watch the dark water churning up against the hull of the ferry as it rides the waves back to Vancouver Island. While this was not the answer Ryan was hoping for, deep down he is probably not surprised. Perhaps he is even slightly relieved to know that there is more help available to ensure that when he is released, he will be well and truly ready to lead a productive and fulfilling life on the outside.

As I consider the day's events, I decide the parole hearing was far more valuable than what we went through in the courtroom. Even though the protocol was strict, pertinent information that was not admissible as part of the sentencing process is readily introduced, and the panel was able to discuss all its concerns without any impediment. My needs were met more fully, and I felt my contribution was readily accepted. I wonder if the hearing would have been a better experience for all of us if it had been conducted in a circle rather than in the hierarchical layout of a courtroom. It is not solely about outcome. It is also about healing—something we are all moving toward.

Two weeks later, I return to Ferndale for the volunteer appreciation evening. There are about eighty people in the room: corrections staff, volunteers, my friends Dave and Sandi from Community Justice Initiatives, and the fellows. Ryan is seated with a facilitator from the alternatives to violence program he is participating in. Sarah McLachlan's "Angel" is playing in the background. Just before I start to share The Story of Bob, I catch Dave's and Sandi's eyes for reassurance. I am filled with gratitude for the support they have given me with my work.

It is not easy to bring Bob to life with Ryan and his community facing me. And it is almost impossible to advance to the slide of Bob lying dead in the morgue. I cannot help thinking of the men in the audience who have caused similar tragedies and have witnessed others along the way. Images of wounds and death may be imprinted indelibly on their own consciences. I do not want to retraumatize anyone, but I do need them to see the reality of the death that is our common ground before I can move the discussion to forgiveness and healing.

When I come to the part in the presentation where I would normally read Ryan's letter, I simply welcome him to the podium and take my seat. There is a pause while Ryan composes himself. I can hear individuals choking back tears throughout the otherwise silent room.

We hang on every word Ryan says. The volunteers have their heads bowed as they wipe their eyes; the fellows are looking up and nodding as they recognize scenes from their own pasts in Ryan's story. He is calm, articulate, and, quite simply, real.

I join Ryan on the stage and humbly thank him for being there with me. I acknowledge his courage, his bravery, and his honesty in telling his story. Then I give the audience a challenge: "Bringing together people on either side of such devastating loss is nothing short of remarkable. Ryan and I have been on parallel journeys. The opportunity to stand together and regard that common road and then to share the moment with such a receptive audience is yet another gift. What we are doing is filled with promise. I urge you to imagine the possibilities."

The audience is on its feet. The support and appreciation overwhelm us both. And once again it is hard to leave, though I sense this time, in contrast to the end of our meeting the previous year at Matsqui, there will be more support for Ryan. As I walk through the gate toward my car, I can see Ryan standing on his doorstep, chatting to his housemates. The silhouette of their back slapping and high fives is a hope-filled image to take away with me.

Later in the fall I am contacted by William Head Institution, the federal minimum-security prison located near Victoria on Vancouver Island. The prison staff are preparing for Restorative Justice Week in November and have heard about the session Ryan and I did together at Ferndale. They want us to give the same presentation at William Head. This event will be significantly larger, with two hundred participants expected. Ryan is keen to present with me again, and we negotiate the complicated logistics for his visit to the island with a staff escort from Corrections Canada.

What happened a few months earlier at Ferndale was groundbreaking. Part of me wishes there had been some way to record it, though I rationalize that cameras and a film crew might have stifled the spontaneous quality and the honesty of our first work together. However, now there is a chance to film the William Head event. I have been talking with Sue Ridout, an independent documentary producer and director who is interested in telling our story, and when the institution approves our request to film the event, she quickly puts a crew together.

I am mingling with the crowd when Ryan arrives with his escort. I feel safe in this place, and his hello hug feels good. I am happy he is here to share in the telling again. The larger crowd, the cameras, and the knowledge that this is bigger than both of us pull fresh emotion to the podium with us.

Several people join us onstage when we finish. One fellow presents me with a beautiful beaded necklace depicting an orca. He tells us how, in First Nations culture, the whale is honored for its strength and bravery. It represents goodness and is a guardian. I am proud as I bow my head to accept the piece of art he places around my neck.

The next fellow stands between Ryan and me and speaks about the effect of our shared story. He has carved us each a large, slim, oval cedar box. The top of each box is adorned with a simple raised feather motif, and inside lies the most precious treasure—an eagle's feather. For British Columbia's First Nations, this is a highly sacred object. The feather, we are told, represents honoring, respect, and strength.

As we leave the stage, the Gettin' Higher Choir, a local group of nonprofessional singers directed by Shivon Robinsong, performs two songs, "How Could Anyone" and "Before I Ever

Spoke," chosen specifically for Ryan and me. As we stand together, our tears wash more of the hurt away.

It is hard to see Ryan leave, knowing he is going back to prison. But this time I am comforted by picturing his slow trip by ferry through the Gulf Islands, a route traveled by the orcas and eagles who inspire bravery and strength.

The Internet links me to many teachers and practitioners of restorative justice. I'm reading articles and studies from all over the world and am awed by the devotion of this global community of experts who are working so hard to promote reconciliation and healing. Restorative practice is being used in schools for dispute resolution, in policing, in the justice system, in land ownership and use grievances, and in religious conflicts. The same principles that brought me to peace after my own tragedy are being applied to resolve large-scale conflict, and they appear to be working.

As if I were browsing through a glossy travel brochure, I peruse the agenda for a conference called "New Frontiers in Restorative Justice." It is to be held at Massey University in Auckland in late 2004. Before I know it I am e-mailing the conference organizer to tell him about my work. Within minutes he replies and invites me to speak at a plenary session. The look on Michael's face when I tell him what I have done is unforgettable. He shakes his head and laughs as he tells me, "Of course you should go!"

I get in touch with the New Zealand Police and arrange some school presentations on the South Island through the DARE (Drug Abuse Resistance Education) program to make the trip viable. I also receive an invitation to speak at a Maori community center on the North Island after the conference concludes.

So during the first week of December 2004, while my friends are all busy with the end-of-year chaos at school and Christmas shopping, I am alone on a plane to New Zealand.

The woman coordinating the DARE speaking tour has jokingly insisted that I arrive well-rested because she will be meeting me at the airport and taking me on a hike. She is not kidding. I barely have time to put on comfortable shoes before she has me out of the car, traipsing across the *Lord of the Rings* landscape near Christchurch.

Jet lag is not going to fit into a busy schedule that takes me to schools all along the west coast. I learn that kids are kids the world over. Whether they are packed into a cavernous high school gym in downtown Vancouver or bused from tiny farming communities to a dilapidated 1950s theater here in Hokitika, they all deal with the same issues. Their lives are punctuated by choice and consequences. Just like the boys at home, the boys in New Zealand express their anger at my story and have a hard time accepting my lack of vengeance. The girls, in their floor-length uniform kilts, come forward in tears and then ask me about my shoes.

The conference is officially opened by the governor general of New Zealand, Dame Silvia Cartwright, with a traditional Maori Powhiri ceremony. Delegates from Africa, Asia, Europe, the Middle East, and North and South America stand in a semicircle to witness the solemn and rich performance.

Because my work is neither research nor professional best practices, and thus does not fit into the typical structure of an academic conference, the organizers have scheduled my presentation for the first evening session following the keynote speaker Howard Zehr. Zehr, author of *Changing Lenses: A New Focus for Crime and Justice,* is regarded by many as the founding father of restorative justice.

I introduce myself not as an academic or a practitioner, but simply as a mother with a story to tell. It is hard to contain my emotion as I explain that I am humbled to be in the presence of so many eminent figures from the restorative justice movement. I tell them that after I speak for one hour, it will be my privilege to listen and learn for the next three days.

The audience of two hundred graciously receives The Story of Bob, and I remain on the stage for another full hour, answering questions. For many at the conference, my presentation illustrates that the process they have dedicated their lives to constructing actually works. They hear from both victim and offender that this was the best outcome on the simplest, most human of levels. It sets a perfect tone for the specialized and technical work that will follow.

The following morning Margaret Thorsborne, an Australian expert in restorative practices in education, approaches me in the campus foyer. She is stylishly dressed and radiates charisma and warmth. As she thanks me for my presentation, she unclasps a beautiful pearl and leather bracelet from her wrist and does it up around mine. I am overwhelmed by her generous gesture. To even be here, in the presence of these people, is an honor, but to have them accept me and be willing to teach me is indescribable.

For three days I move from workshop to workshop, hearing about the successful implementation of restorative practice and the resulting challenges in countless contexts. I am particularly drawn to the work done at schools in both Australia and New Zealand, where conflict resolution is successfully handled in a reconciliatory manner. It makes perfect sense, for example, not to expel kids who bully others, but to bring them and their family together in a circle with the victims and their families, along with teachers and administrators, in order to remedy the harm.

This education model and the process Ryan and I have engaged in are all about inclusion. They are about bringing the people who cause harm into the heart of their community, not pushing them away into isolation. How can we possibly expect people to behave peacefully and respectfully if we isolate them rather than teaching them what it means to be humane?

In the case of criminal behavior, I understand that incarceration is about public safety, punishment, and the opportunity to provide essential rehabilitative programming. But as in economics, where we observe the law of diminishing returns, at what point is enough enough?

I've lost track of the number of people who have asked me why Ryan only got five years. I'll say it over and over: it's not the time served that matters, but what is done with that time. I know there are criminals who suffer from varying degrees of mental incapacitation that will affect their ability to rehabilitate. And I also know there are offenders who choose to immerse themselves in the negative subculture of prison and make no effort to deal with the problems that brought them into the system. They remain a risk to society. But what about the Ryans? We need the justice and corrections systems to clear a safe space for offenders who have chosen to step up and participate in the reconciliation process. We must acknowledge the work they've done with their victims and encourage them to speak of that work so restorative practice can take the place it deserves in punishment and rehabilitation. We do not need to look as far away as New Zealand for encouraging statistics about restorative justice's positive effect on recidivism. The research done by Community Justice Initiatives in British Columbia shows that 95 percent of offenders who meet with their victims do not reoffend.

I am presented with another gift while in New Zealand. The chief of the New Zealand Police gives me a jade koru on a thin leather thong. *Koru* is the Maori name for the young fern frond that, unfurled, symbolizes the beginning of a new life, growth, peace, and tranquility. The chief's six-foot-four frame towers over me, and I am moved by his quiet, almost shy, manner as he describes the impact my story has had on him. After I finish my trip to Whangarei, he asks, would I consider visiting some of his colleagues in South Auckland? I accept his invitation. It will be a fitting conclusion to my Pacific adventure.

First, however, I travel to Whangarei, where I meet Samu Tribe, a former police officer who now works with youth in this northern community. He has arranged for me to speak at a local outreach center. I also witness the preparation of a traditional

Hangi feast that will follow my storytelling. Chicken and vegetables, such as the sweet potato–like kumara, are wrapped in large leaves and then cooked underground amongst hot rocks. After about seven hours, the feast is unearthed and shared. I stay with Samu, his Dutch wife, and their children in their house on the beach before returning for my final days in Auckland.

Sharing The Story of Bob with the Maori liaison officers at the South Auckland Police Department leads into a discussion of contrasts and comparisons to the culture of Canadian First Nations. We speak about indigenous peoples' contributions of peacemaking and healing ritual, and the roles they play within our individual policing and justice systems. I see that we in Canada can learn a lot from the way Maori traditions and values have been entrenched in New Zealand's conflict resolution philosophy and practice.

Ten days after I left Victoria, I am back on a plane, heading home. I have traveled halfway around the world and found community with the restorative justice practitioners. I am thankful for these peacemakers, a global community tightly connected by a shared vision. I feel just as close, just as much a part of them, when I find myself back with my family in Victoria. I meet Michael, Emma, and Sam at the airport with the Maori greeting *Kia ora*.

It is several months before Ryan and I work together again. In the interim, he spends his third Christmas in jail, and my family makes it through another New Year's Eve. We have an unspoken agreement to keep the day low-key. We do not stay up until midnight, but have a quiet and close evening together and then tuck ourselves into bed early.

A friend involved in a motivational speaking team known as Extreme Kindness asks me if I have heard about the Forgiveness Project. I locate the organization on the Internet and am in awe of what I find. This British-based nonprofit organization has chronicled stories of forgiveness from all over the world. A photograph accompanies each story. In some cases it is the picture of a victim. Others show perpetrators, and there are some unforgettable images of both victims and perpetrators together. Names like Archbishop Desmond Tutu and Jo Berry, daughter of the British MP killed in the Brighton bombing in 1984, appear alongside lesser-known, but equally moving, stories of loss and healing from places like Africa, Ireland, and the Middle East.

I send an e-mail and receive an immediate reply from Marina Cantacuzino, the project's director. With the serendipity I'm becoming accustomed to, it turns out that her organization has just received funding to come to North America to collect stories. She asks if Ryan and I would consider being interviewed. He agrees, and within a month we hear that Marina and her photographer will be in Vancouver at the same time we are scheduled to make our first joint presentation to a public school. With Sue Ridout and her documentary film crew also covering the event, the complexity increases exponentially. I spend hours each day fielding calls and e-mails to confirm logistics and arrangements. I know that once we get there, the work is all about the kids we are speaking to. This knowledge gets me over the hurdles in making it all come together.

Someone tips off the Vancouver media that Ryan will be working with me at the school, so in the days before the presentation I also have to deal with inquiries from reporters. While I have had almost seven years' experience with the media, nearly all of it positive, the same has not been true for Ryan. His face has been splashed on the front pages under negative headlines, and his family has been followed out of the courthouse by aggressive TV camera operators. For every time he and his parents endured one of those frantic and sensationalistic encounters, I have been able to control a calm, rational interview about my experiences surrounding Bob's death.

Now our goal is to share the story with young people. I understand the public's interest, but I also fear that if a media frenzy takes place each time Ryan is escorted from jail to work with me, we won't be working together for long. I'm also sure that schools will not be interested in dealing with the media attention. So I muster my most courteous and direct demeanor and explain that news media will not be permitted in our presentation at the schools and that I hope they will honor my request.

It all comes together in a large gymnasium. The audience of more than three hundred students is in shock when Ryan, who looks like he is barely out of high school himself, joins me on the stage. He is received with respect and admiration. The only disappointment is that it took much longer than anticipated to seat all the students in the gym, so there is not enough time for them to ask questions. Ryan admits he had been looking forward to that more than anything. However, it doesn't stop the students from forming a long line so they can come up to shake his hand and personally thank him for being there.

A counselor kindly gives up his office after the presentation so Marina from the Forgiveness Project can interview Ryan and me privately. Her questions are thoughtful, and she includes generous amounts of silence that create a safe space for us both. The issues she raises reflect both enlightenment and support for what has become our improbable but powerful alliance.

Groups of students stare in disbelief as they watch us do a photo session together on the school field. The Forgiveness Project will feature a picture of us standing side by side, and the photographer works for a long time to capture just the right shot. I am pleased that we will have a visual record to commemorate Ryan's first in-person contribution to The Story of Bob in a school setting.

My friend Julie Czerwinski, at the youth custody center, is thrilled to hear that Ryan will be able to join my next booking with her young offender group. Ryan sits on the periphery, and the small group assumes he is an observer until it is time for him to participate in the presentation. Some of the kids are barely able to hold back their anger when he moves forward and begins to speak. Others seem to look on him as a hero, a bigger and better version of themselves. There is plenty of time for questions and answers, and we move ourselves into a circle so everyone feels included whether they have anything to say or not.

It astounds me how quickly Ryan gets the full attention of these kids. He sets them straight, challenging them for admiring him because he is doing time in a federal prison. I sit back and listen while he talks to them about the importance of salvaging family relationships if they have them. If they do not, he urges them to go out and find supportive relationships with other adults who can help them move forward in a more positive direction with their lives.

I speak about how I have chosen not to define myself or Ryan by Bob's death, and I encourage them not to define themselves by whatever brought them into custody.

Before speaking to another group that same afternoon, Ryan and I share a picnic lunch on the grounds of the custody center. Emma teased me the night before as I was packing food to bring. "How many people do you think bake cookies to share with the person who killed their husband?" Maybe no one. And I am sure it does look odd from the outside looking in. But I didn't get the choice to be on the outside. I am here in the middle, and Ryan is here too. I would prefer where we are to feel comfortable, and sometimes it's hard to find words to create that comfort. Simple, kind gestures, like the sharing of a meal, take over from the words, making where we are a place where we feel we belong. So much hope and possibility can radiate from the pleasing environment we consciously create.

Our next presentation is to an alternative school in the Fraser Valley. Carefully selected inmates visit the school each week to work with high-risk kids in a literacy program. I had heard about this program, Partners in Learning, just before Ryan moved from Matsqui to Ferndale, and based on Ryan's willingness to talk about the poor choices he had made around substance abuse and violence, I had hoped he would become involved in it. Now, a year later, Ryan is spending two days a week in this school, making a big difference in the lives of some young people.

While these students know that Ryan is serving time in federal prison, they do not know the details of Bob's death. One of the many unspoken rules of the prison subculture is that it is inappropriate to ask why someone is doing time. In this classroom setting, it is generally one of the first things the kids want to talk about, but the staff respond by explaining that it is a personal question and it takes time for people to build up trust before they are willing to confide such information. Ryan has been at the school for several months and has developed a good rapport with both staff and students. He and the program coordinator think it would be good for the kids to hear The Story of Bob. Even though it will expose more of his personal information than the students currently know, Ryan decides there is great potential for the benefits to outweigh the costs.

As we have done with other small groups, we move into a circle to handle questions after our presentation. The experience of watching someone "come clean" in this environment has a powerful impact on the students, and the outpouring of respect for Ryan's courage and honesty is phenomenal. The questions bounce back and forth between us, and what seemed at first to be an impossible alliance begins to make some sense to our audience.

"Take it out there into your own lives," I urge them. "Imagine the possibilities."

When I check in with Ryan in the weeks following the day at his school, he tells me his fears about being treated differently by the students after the presentation have not been realized, and he continues to bank some well-deserved self-respect.

For our next speaking engagement, we have another challenging audience. Ryan's mother, Marina, and his stepfather, Michael, will be hearing us speak for the first time at a community restorative justice forum. My periodic correspondence with Marina, which began with her letter passed to me by the lawyer after sentencing, is a cherished link, and while I have seen her at numerous court appearances and the parole hearing, we have never actually been introduced.

There is an added layer of tension at tonight's forum because the media will be in attendance. Even though Ryan and I are both interested in furthering the acceptance of the reconciliatory model within our communities, we fear the news coverage will simply feed on the public's prurient curiosity about the fact that he and I are sharing the stage. The media have been given strict instructions about filming only in the lobby prior to the event and not during our presentation.

Ryan arrives with his escort, and we find a private place away from the camera lenses to greet one another. I take a deep breath as he leads me into the auditorium to where his family is seated. We try to judge one another's comfort zone as we meet. An awkward handshake quickly becomes a hug.

I tell them how sorry I am for all they've been through. Having them here this evening means so much. I hope it will not be too hard for them to see the story presented on a screen. I am so proud of Ryan's contribution to this work.

It all comes out in big chunks. Messy. True. And grateful.

Ryan's stepfather holds me in a strong embrace. Grateful for the support he has been to Ryan and his mother throughout this ordeal, I thank him. I try not to let the warm smell of his leather jacket remind me of Bob. But it does. He tells me simply that I have completed the circle. What more could we ask for?

Before we take the stage, a local high school presents an original play called *Kryptonite*. Ryan saw the production at Ferndale and has been asked to introduce the young actors. I am not prepared for what is coming. The play is a relentless and graphic depiction of the issues that our youth face: bullying, drugs, violence, family breakdown, silence. It is all there. The actors never leave the stage; they simply turn their back when their lines have been delivered and then face the audience again on cue as they morph into their next character. Nothing has ever come this close to depicting what I know to be true of the world my children are living in. Many educators have told me every young person should hear my story. I think every young person should see *Kryptonite*.

I am shaking badly as I take the stage, and I ask for the audience's understanding as I try to compose myself. Ryan and I go to work. Afterward we discover that news cameras were taping us from the doorway during the presentation and we confront the reporters about not respecting the boundaries we set. I explain my fear that Ryan might not continue to do this work with me if the media intrudes. I implore them to look beyond tonight's sound bite at the bigger picture. There are so many kids who need to hear our message. Their apology seems insincere, and they appear more concerned about getting the tape to the studio for the eleven o'clock news than debating with me or the event organizers.

Ryan's parents make it through the evening and are visibly proud of their son. We say our goodbyes quickly, since the media are still present, and go our separate ways. My best friend Shauna has traveled to be with me for support and a much-needed mums-only sleepover in a hotel following the event. Curled up in our beds with glasses of wine, we watch the TV news segment. The coverage is fairly balanced and not as sensationalistic as I feared it would be. I hope the exposure won't discourage Ryan from continuing this important work.

In a telephone debriefing with the forum's organizer the next day, I review the positive impact of the presentation and discuss damage control for the media coverage. She tells me she has already talked to managers at the station that filmed the event. They have apologized that their coverage went beyond what we had agreed to. She also spoke to staff at Ferndale. They told her that Ryan and the fellows had watched the segment. Ryan was distressed and disappointed at the time, but his peers' support for the work he is doing with me overshadowed the fact that it had been made public. We decide the best course of action is to let it go. Tomorrow it will be old news.

I take the summer off and enjoy a much-needed vacation to England with Michael and our children, including his daughter Carlie, who has moved into our house. Her mother's work requires frequent travel, and Carlie feels she will have a more solid base for finishing high school if she lives with us.

Summer is a family-centered, precious, and rejuvenating time for me. It is anything but for Ryan. Once school is back in session and I'm able to communicate with him through one of our mutual contacts, I come to realize this. Ryan has had few opportunities to be out in the community, because his volunteer work at the alternative school does not continue through the summer. His family, busy with young grandchildren and work schedules, hasn't been able to visit frequently. A time of year we usually associate with warmth and freedom has been much different for Ryan. It's not something I can change, though I feel bad for him just the same.

I look forward to our first speaking engagement in the fall. Ryan is back working with the Partners in Learning program, and we actually have to sit down with our calendars to synchronize our schedules. The image of us sitting with our heads together, planning our presentation dates, amuses me. We are a most unlikely partnership doing such valuable work.

At the next engagement, I observe that the notes Ryan once clutched, for security more than anything else, are gone. He stands confidently at the podium and lets his story roll. He adds more details as he works on understanding how his past choices influenced his actions. He speaks now of being bullied because of a speech impediment and because he did not wear the right clothes. He refers to his parents' divorce. He admits that the young men who beat him badly when he was in his early teens are the very people he turned to when looking for new friends. I find it difficult to listen to his candid description of the suicidal thoughts that plagued him during his five years of silence. Ryan continues to refuse to blame his actions on alcohol and reminds our audiences that many people manage to enjoy alcohol in moderation and do not go out and kill people. He has dug deep in an alternatives-to-violence program and understands that it was bravado and a need for power and control that fueled him on New Year's Eve in 1997. He explains that what he thought at the time was a demonstration of power to gain respect was in reality a cowardly act that instilled fear in those around him.

One evening when we address a community services program, a woman stands to speak to Ryan. Through her tears she expresses her admiration for the choices he has made since he began serving his sentence. She calls him brave and courageous. She is right.

As I gather my computer equipment together after the presentation, I notice Ryan off to one side. He is speaking to a local reporter. This will be the first interview he has done on his own. I chuckle to myself as I hear him ask the reporter to be nice to him. She'd better be, or it will be the last interview he does.

Later the same reporter asks me a few questions, ones I have answered a hundred times. And then she asks us both if we would consider ourselves to be friends. We are silent for a moment. Ryan casts his gaze downward and shuffles his feet nervously. I am not going to rush this one. But if Ryan can be brave and courageous, so can I.

"Yes, I suppose we are," I respond, and then I continue by explaining, "If a friend is someone you have learned to respect, someone you trust, someone whom you have been through things with and come out the other side together with, then yes, we are. The world may not be ready to hear that, but I can only offer what is true for me. Friends do not let friends get away with anything. Friends will hold up the mirror when we need to take a long hard look at ourselves. Friends will hold the light when we are moving in the dark. And friends will be there if the ground gives way."

I expect ours will always be a friendship with a respectful distance. It will accommodate family who are not as sure as we are, friends who just don't get it, and the need for solitude. We cannot change the fact that our lives came crashing together on New Year's Eve in 1997. Ryan and I came at this journey from opposite directions. We met somewhere in the middle and chose to walk forward side by side. It is simply the best we can do. And for that I am very proud.

chapter 17

yes, we have no bananas

As most of us mortals struggle along with one wing,
attempting to somehow make a difference and grow
spiritually in the process, we on occasion have an encouraging
visit from a mortal with two wings. I have no doubt that I
met with one of these mortals when I was speaking with you.
You are making a difference, and I thank you.
—C. Beveridge, Westlock, Alberta

I am often asked how I did it. People hear my story and say, "I could never have done what you did."

"Don't be so sure" is my usual response. Ten years ago, if someone had described to me the circumstances that have been my life for the last eight years, I am certain I would have reacted as many do and exclaimed, "I could not make it through." I wouldn't have been able to imagine how I could handle it.

But I learned that you do what you need to do when faced with a life challenge. There is an eerie calm in the eye of the storm. It is a place where, if you listen to the whispers of your own heart, you are able to gather together your courage, and you cope. What come into play are the hidden life skills that you possess and may not even be aware of. In the future, I want to help people identify those skills and encourage their resiliency.

My father gave me some great gifts over the years. On my ninth birthday, my hands trembled over a dress box from the Stork Shop. I knew as I lifted the lid that I wouldn't find a piece of clothing from the store where my mother bought my clothes. My father was using this box to conceal something *he* chose for me. Out of the layers of tissue paper emerged an assortment of items from the stationery store. One after the other I pulled them from the box: my own tape dispenser, a tiny stapler, a hole punch, ballpoint pens in every color. There were pads of paper and envelopes, and an alphabetical accordion file.

It was the best gift I ever received. It was the best because what I knew about my father, I learned to be true of me as well. We both loved to keep things organized. Everything neatly in its place. This need goes far beyond the sorting and filing of physical things; it includes feelings and relationships too. My father's gift was not so much the contents of the box as the recognition of that shared trait. To this day I store precious letters in an old Dad's Cookie box that my father fashioned into a filing box.

I was sixteen when I moved away from home. My father's housewarming gift to me in my first apartment was a small toolbox. It contained a hammer, a screwdriver (Phillips *and* Robertson heads), pliers, a wrench, nails, screws, and a huge roll of duct tape. I am still using those tools, and each time I do I think about how my father quietly went about equipping me for life.

At eighteen the gift was *The Joy of Cooking*. The spine has fallen off that book, I use it so often. I still can't cook a roast without checking the section on proper meat temperatures. And each time I do, moving past the pages stuck together with remnants of hollandaise sauce and cake batter, I think of my father.

I had a love-hate relationship with another book he gave me some years later. It was a home medical dictionary, a perfect resource for late-night hypochondria. The real problem was the middle section of color photographs that were included to aid in self-diagnosis. I was never able to look at the graphic images of injuries or festering skin conditions or, God forbid, rare medical conditions—like one I saw by mistake when the book fell open to the middle, where black hair was actually growing from someone's tongue. This section of the book scared me so much I secured all the pages together with paper clips so I would never again accidentally see those images as I was poring over the other sections of the book. I just couldn't look.

After Bob's death my biggest decision was whether or not to look. Not just at the horrific reality of his corpse, but at all of it. I looked at things most people would turn away from. No matter how tightly I closed my eyes, I knew this was not going to go away. I could have delayed the looking by taking the tranquilizers offered to me, but I chose not to.

Looking meant feeling, as painful as it was. Feeling led to accepting the reality of losing Bob, dealing with the way in which he died, and learning to live after that loss. And accepting those realities was the beginning of the healing. Looking, feeling, dealing, healing. If I had avoided any part of that process, I believe I would not be where I am today. In looking I found strength. I found my voice, my heart, a future.

I wish I had had the opportunity to ask my father what there was in *his* life that he just couldn't look at.

I am working now with a larger-than-life woman named Sally Glover. She is a personal coach I engaged to help me keep my life in balance while I continue on my journey. Her philosophy is that we have all we need within us. Sally has helped me understand transformation—the digging down to, and mining of, our inner resources to carry us through conflict, crisis, celebration, and growth. She calls it "living a life of mastery."

Sometimes I get stuck, and we talk about it. Usually the barrier is an old way of seeing things or reacting to things that emerge from the past. Sally refers to these patterns as "old bananas." The imagery is helpful. It lets me understand that these things have no place in this time of my life, and I now consciously try to throw "old bananas" behind me.

My biggest old banana would be the need to please people. Only now am I starting to understand that worrying what other people think muddies the natural clarity that exists when you act from your heart. When I am my most authentic self, those around me *are* pleased. Following my gut instincts when I faced the enormous crisis of Bob's death moved me and my children forward in a positive way. There was no time to worry how others were going to interpret my decisions.

Eliminating old bananas helps me clarify what qualities of my character helped me through the ordeal. It shows me what to nurture and celebrate: my need for order, the ability to repair things, a desire to learn and be creative, and, finally, having the courage to look. All these are symbolized by the gifts my father gave me.

Many people hearing my story also assume that I must have come from a strongly religious background. How else could I have found the ability to forgive? My parents were both Catholic; my siblings were educated in Catholic schools and attended Mass and catechism every Sunday. But by the time I came along, seven years later, my mother and father had relaxed their views of formal religion considerably. I went to public school and attended church sometimes. I recall enjoying the reverence, the ritual, and the tradition of my limited exposure to church, but I always struggled with the God part.

Ironically, it wasn't until the year before Bob was killed that I revisited the idea of religion. I wanted Sam and Emma to enjoy the same routine I had experienced as a young child attending church. I looked for my own sense of community on those Sunday mornings while Bob was running the mountain trails with his friends. I still struggled with the God part that had confused me during my youth, and I had difficulty explaining it to Emma and Sam. After Bob's death I had no interest in trying to rationalize the existence of a God. I parted company with the whole idea.

Once I abandoned that inner conflict, I was able to see I was a spiritual person if not a religious one. The peace I derived from quietly drawing into myself and tapping my own strength is what led me to forgive. First I forgave myself for moving past Bob's death and not being the living memorial to him some thought I should be. Then I forgave Ryan. I wanted him to have a life beyond all this. He is not his crime.

I have so much gratitude for all that has come my way on this sacred journey. I am constantly seeking ways to more fully understand and better explain why I chose this path away from all the brokenness. I continue my exploration with a circle.

———————————

There are twenty-five of us seated on hard backed chairs in a circle. We are in a chapel, but there are no overtly religious symbols. The roof comes together with four peaks at the top, each fitted with a stained glass window. The glass panels depict the four seasons. I sit facing fall. The warm September sun is shining through the image of a tree; amber leaves gently move toward the earth. We have come together for a four-day workshop about peacemaking circles. I have already made peace, but now I am curious to understand how I did it.

I imagine what story is behind each person in the circle, twenty women and four men. Some look uncomfortable, pulled from behind their desks, their client loads, and the heaviness of the bureaucracies within which they work. Others are searching. Their eyes move eagerly about the room, looking for answers to questions that are going to change. I see burnout. I see sorrow. We are vulnerable and waiting to see what will happen.

The idea of peacemaking circles is rooted in the medicine wheel of some First Nations' cultures. Its four quadrants balance the emotional, mental, spiritual, and physical. A circle is a safe place created to speak, to listen, and ultimately to resolve conflict. Circles have no hierarchy, no beginning or end. Members sit face to face, shoulder to shoulder, and work toward getting well rather than getting even, as our facilitator Kay Pranis describes in her book *Peacemaking Circles: From Crime to Community*.

Kay is a minute woman with an enormous spirit that fills the room with gentleness and possibility. She reminds me of a feather. Her waist-length hair, a rich palette of brown, gold, and gray, spills over her tiny shoulders like a cape. Spending time with her is like being in a constant state of meditation: calm, focused, and fully present.

Assisting Kay with facilitating, or "keeping," is Jane Miller Ashton, formerly the head of Corrections Canada's Restorative Justice and Dispute Resolution Branch and currently teaching restorative justice and victimology at Simon Fraser University's School of Criminology. Both women have worked with the peacemaking-circle process in prisons, schools, and communities in the United States and Canada.

Our first exercise in the circle involves a canvas bag filled with driftwood. In silence we are given the opportunity, in turn, to do what we please with the contents of the bag. We are permitted to pass if we do not wish to do anything. One person builds a small houselike structure with the pieces; the next person gently changes the structure of the roof, and the next carefully lays the wood out in a series of rows. I pick up a smooth, gray piece and hand it to a woman I think needs to receive it. The next person hides a piece under the bag. Someone gathers all the wood together in the bag, and the next person roughly throws the contents back onto the ground. Distressed, the next person passes. And so we go, building, rebuilding, offering, taking, destroying, and passing. The circle does not stop until everyone passes. It takes more than an hour. I find myself on the verge of tears through most of the exercise and cannot understand why.

The metaphor, which we discover through sharing our feelings one by one around the circle, speaks to us of community. The struggles, the destruction, the beauty, the sharing, the indifference—all layered upon each other. We learn to speak in turn and only when in possession of the talking piece. This object can be anything, but is often a treasure from nature: a feather, a rock, or a stick. I am struck by the way the talking piece is handled with care and reverence as it moves around the circle, drawing wisdom toward our center.

As we work through a series of experiential exercises, all using this same circle pattern, our stories begin to emerge. I have told my story many hundreds of times. I have shared it with audiences of over a thousand people and with small, intimate groups. Nothing prepares me for sharing it in the circle. It is as though I am telling it for the first time. The words hurt as they are formed, and as they are spoken my chest aches, the tears flow. I gag on the loss and sadness. Afterward, the collective stillness soothes the wound left behind, and I understand why I have come. I understand we never stop healing.

At the end of the first day, we are all fraught with heaviness and fatigue. I respond to Michael's inquiry about my day by taking the dog for a long walk on the beach. Feeling rejuvenated, I serve a meal to Michael, Carlie, and three of her friends. Since Carlie came to live with us, she has not been eager to invite her friends over, finding Michael and me collectively to be too much parent for one home. But tonight I find myself caught up in listening to the smug nonsense and laughter fifteen-year-olds conjure so well. I let my guard down and share. They see it is real and listen too. Suddenly I realize we are in a circle. It works.

The second day takes us deeper into the sharing and receiving of stories. My patience is tested by a street-smart advocate for the homeless and drug addicted who goes past the sharing of her own lived experience and seems to begin promoting the work that she does. It is here I learn a lesson about the power of the circle. The discipline of the talking piece ceremony reminds me that when this woman has said all she needs to say, which will be all I need to hear, the piece will be passed on. I listen fully and move past being judgmental in a way that would not have happened in a different type of forum. There is a rhythm to the circle that is both seductive and healing. Above me, the warmth of the image in the summer window is comforting.

On the third day, I sit regarding the spring window as a member of the circle alludes to an elephant in the room. There is a feeling of tension and some fear in our midst. People speak of feeling unsafe. The synergy we have been building appears to be on shaky ground. The woman asks our keepers how we deal with it. Kay and Jane turn the question back to the circle, and one long, shaky round later, the elephant is released from hiding. The previous day's story about our community's homeless has upset someone, and not for a reason we would have readily identified. The advocate member of our group distributed pamphlets about hepatitis C, as well as handing out condoms, vials of clean water, and syringes. It was the syringes that paralyzed the other woman. She has just finished treatment for a serious illness, and the sight of syringes was a too-graphic reminder of her treatments. She was indeed no longer safe in the circle, and the elephant had to be named. Once again, the magic of the circle prevails. There is clarification and new understandings all around. We learn a vivid lesson: what sometimes feels like conflict may not in fact be conflict. We must remain aware that our stories and experience may trigger unintended upset in others, and we must be open to respectful sharing with each other so misunderstandings can be resolved. In our circle, gentle healing touches are exchanged. Harmony is restored, and the elephant quietly leaves the room.

I test myself on the morning of the last day. I have been avoiding a seat that would place me facing the winter window. It is my own elephant. Living in coastal British Columbia, I can largely keep the fear at bay. But when the trees lose their leaves and the sky lies flat and gray, I have to concentrate on pulling warmth from within as I look up at the window's spare, cool image.

Those who think I have simply grazed over the surface of grief have no idea of the anguish that is triggered for me when I find myself in the snow. The way it smells and the sound of it under my feet takes me back to a horrible moment that will always be open, raw, and unspeakably painful.

As we move through the circle on this day, we are asked to identify a mentor and explain what makes us see them as such. Emma is in my mind immediately. She has an innate sense of justice. Not in legal terms but in the sense of simple humanity. I am inspired to follow her quiet and thoughtful lead to seek harmony in our home and community. I believe in my heart that Emma will nurture her gift and give it back to the world in a remarkable way. Today she is my mentor.

When we finish speaking of our mentor, we tie the end of a piece of ribbon we hold to the ribbon held by the person next to us. When all the mentors are named, we are left holding a large ring of ribbon. We place it in the middle of our circle as a reminder of the people we admire and aspire to emulate.

Our homework was to bring in an item that represents something important in our lives. I bring a small, heart-shaped stone. It is pink, gray, and beige, perhaps quartz. The rock has a story.

While cleaning my mother's basement some months earlier with my siblings, I found a rock polisher my father had given her some thirty years before. I do not believe she ever plugged it in. I asked if I could take it home, thinking it was something my children would enjoy. As I unpacked the box, I found a bag of small stones. My father had collected them on the beach of a favorite getaway spot where my parents spent the weekends in the years leading up to his death in 1985. Holding those rocks in my hand before I placed them in the drum of the polisher, I savored the connection to the father who had left my life far too soon. The polisher turned day and night for weeks. I waited, noting patience was a trait I inherited from my father. Finally I emptied the tumbler, rinsed the chalky silt from the stones, and placed the smooth, shiny treasures in a low, wide bowl. They sit on my kitchen counter as a constant reminder of my father's grace, wisdom, and unfailingly kind heart.

Within the protective shelter of the group, I discover a deeper connection to my father that I have never allowed myself to explore before. I begin to understand he has been living in my heart all along and he has helped me navigate a safe path for myself and my family. Gradually I let myself get lost in memories that in the past I have pushed away. I find myself not burdened with grief, but lifted with faith and certainty. Not surprisingly, my father's rock in the center of the circle brings joy to everyone.

We ride waves of emotion as we hear the stories that accompany each person's object. In the end we sit quietly and contemplate the shrine filling our center. The talismans grace us with the strength to move forward.

Our final round includes music and song. It's not easy to leave—straggling around the doorway, exchanging hugs, we delay the inevitable, promising to stay in contact. It's unlikely we'll ever sit in such a place together again. The peacemaking circle has taken us each to a different place, but we've all been changed by our experience and part with confidence in knowing that we can use the circle to bring peace to those we touch.

Meagan O'Shea is not accustomed to stories of violent crimes and their emotional aftermath. She is the artist commissioned by the Church Council on Justice and Corrections to create a multimedia art installation that will challenge society's perception of justice. Meagan is traveling across the country, recording interviews with victims and offenders about their experiences of crime. The people she interviews are then asked to sew a quilt square using materials Meagan provides. The squares will be assembled into a "talking quilt." When someone touches a square, a computer mounted behind the quilt will play a short audio clip of the square's creator reflecting on his or her crime experience.

Meagan tries to remain composed as I tell the story I have told a thousand times. Her emotion touches me. It cannot be easy to hear all these stories. When she brings out the materials for me to create my quilt square, Emma appears in the room. If there is going to be any art created in our home, she will be involved. At twelve she has already had a piece of her artwork chosen to be blown up to billboard size for an outdoor art gallery built by, and in support of, an antiviolence organization called Rock Solid.

Meagan is delighted when we ask if we can use our own fabric. We disappear, scissors in hand, to collect our materials.

The square comes together quickly, with little conversation. A swatch of the McIntosh tartan from Bob's wedding kilt lies at the base of a snow-capped fleece mountain representing Squamish. Orange flames, symbolizing his death, rise from the red plaid. On the other side of the square is fabric cut to resemble waves on the beach we live near in Victoria. A moon made from the soft fabric taken from inside the hem of Michael's dressing gown looks over the water. In between the past and the present stretches a piece of silver mesh. Emma explains as she sews that this is the chain-link fence of a prison. Woven through the mesh is the quill of a single white feather—Ryan. The process of creating the square with Emma astonishes me.

After her cross-country tour, Meagan hands the squares over to two Mennonite quilters in Ontario for assembly. In Toronto, a computer artist prepares the wiring. The quilt is to be unveiled in Ottawa to mark the launch of Restorative Justice Week in November 2005, and Emma and I are invited to take part in the event. Sue Ridout's coproducer, Helen Slinger, and their cameraman, Steve Rendall, travel with us to document the week's events.

The atrium of the Ottawa courthouse fills up as the reception begins. Lorraine Berzins, the community chair of the

Church Council, welcomes the people gathered and gives an overview of the Justice Quilt Project. Taking the podium, I give a brief background of our story and describe my experience participating in the project. Emma joins me at the podium. Her old soul peers out from young eyes. She confidently holds her speaking notes, neatly written on index cards. I am honored Emma is speaking with me.

> *I have been taking art classes since I was six and have painted even longer. Even before my father's death I was creative. I never have been or will be angry at Ryan. It never occurred to me that I needed to hate him. Unfortunately that is how people expect victims to react. They expect it to ruin our lives, they expect us to hate others far beyond reason, they expect us not to forgive. But I did. I never hated him, ever. Now, eight years later, the main thing I feel for Ryan is respect. He is as human as you and me. Growing up, my peers never quite understood the way I felt about Ryan. So I painted, because I couldn't explain my feelings. My pictures depict birds flying from cages and people sitting alone. And it turns out that Ryan paints as well. I've seen his work; it's symbolic in a way that words won't describe, as is mine. So we have something in common. That was the biggest breakthrough I've made in my almost thirteen years on this planet. Sharing an interest with Ryan made him human. He's not just the man who made a fatal mistake, but a painter, a soccer player, and a poet who uses paint as his pen. He has equal rights and responsibilities. Someone who does not define himself by a mistake, but learns from his past and defines himself by today.*

There is little more that needs to be said. I am having difficulty keeping swells of emotion in check. I am so fiercely proud and moved by her courage. I manage to wrap up our address by saying:

Sharing stories, even the most painful stories,
illuminates the path of our humanity. This justice quilt
brings our stories of death to life, the fabric imagery
taking over where words have failed us. The caring way
in which our experiences—those of us affected by crime,
and those responsible for those crimes—have been sewn
together represents for me the fabric of healthy
community and the hope of a safer world for our
children. The experience of victims and offenders is often
painfully lonely, often silent. To see our stories stitched
together into a community with a voice gives me a true
sense of safety, peace, and connection. And that, for me,
is real justice.

There is a letter from Ryan in the mailbox. He writes about his artwork to Emma and shares his pregame soccer ritual with Sam, who plays the same position. Later in the letter, Ryan lets me know that he is feeling burnt-out from all the outside work he is doing. The Partners in Learning program and our speaking is taking up much of his time. As his second parole hearing approaches, he wants to focus his energies inward and concentrate on preparing for the process. I have so much respect for the self-awareness he has developed.

Ryan's letter concludes with the description of a design he has created for a tattoo he will get following his release from prison. There is to be a koi fish, which represents good fortune; a dragon to signify what he has faced and conquered; the face of his dog, which he was forced give up when he was incarcerated; and his lucky number, thirteen—not because he believes in luck, but because he believes in fate. Everything happens for a reason. Ryan says he also believes in karma. The tattoo will also contain a ribbon inscribed with the date of his sentencing because he believes it was the date he was truly set free. A winding path will connect all the images to symbolize the path he has now chosen and will continue to take. The empty space will be filled in with different sizes and shapes of snowflakes because Ryan loves the snow and winter.

Ryan's parole hearing is scheduled for December 21, 2005. Too close to Christmas for so many reasons. I worry that if he does not get parole, he will be more distressed because of the time of year. If parole is granted, I worry that it will be difficult to do all the paperwork in time to make a release possible by the twenty-fifth. No matter what the decision is, it will cause emotional overload as everyone scrambles to cope with the anxiety over the holidays.

Sally, my life coach, helps me to position myself through this stressful time. The holidays are always difficult for me as we approach the anniversary of Bob's death. With Sally's coaching, I determine my greatest need is to be sure the people I care about are safe. This applies to Ryan as well—especially given his potential release to a halfway house. I know there is little more I can do to influence the way things go for him. I have done enough. It is not up to me to determine if he is ready. Sally and I choose the image of a caring and detached witness to help me get through the process.

The National Parole Board agrees to my request to address Ryan directly at the hearing. I read my letter facing Ryan and both the board members who will decide upon his fate. It is much the same letter I read at his first hearing in September 2004, only now I am able to describe the growth I have seen in Ryan through the work we have done together. Ryan understands why he killed Bob. He grasps the distinction between what he thought was power and respect and what was really cowardice and fear. If the professionals who were charged with his rehabilitation are confident he is ready for day parole release, then I give my blessing.

I wait with two parole board representatives in Ferndale's chapel during the deliberations. I can only imagine the anxiety Ryan and his family must be experiencing as they wait in another area of the institution. Less than two hours later, we are summoned back to the hearing room.

The parole board spokesperson moves immediately to the ruling to relieve the tension in the room. They have granted Ryan day parole. The spokesperson says a five-page written decision will be available for review by the end of the day, and Ryan will be released to a halfway house in Vancouver as soon as the paperwork can be completed. He must reside at the house until his statutory release date in April 2006, after which he will be on full parole until his warrant expires in December 2007. According to the conditions of his release, he must continue with counseling, abstain from alcohol and other drugs, and commit to staying away from people who are involved in crime or substance use.

The emotional weight is lifted for me in a torrent of tears. The parole board bends protocol and allows Ryan's family to meet with me briefly in the chapel foyer. We embrace like old friends and simply repeat the words "It's over" again and again.

By the time I return to Victoria on the evening of December 22, an e-mail message is waiting for me. Ryan was released from Ferndale earlier that day. His father picked him up and took him to the halfway house.

It is December 31, 2005. Our kitchen is crowded with friends and kids. The aroma of delicious food fills the air. Michael's son Adam, visiting for the holidays, strums on his guitar beside the Christmas tree. It is the first time since Bob was killed that I have kept the decorations up past Boxing Day. Busy having fun, we forget to look at the clock for hours. Before we know it, it is ten minutes to midnight. I have not stayed awake to this time, on this date, for many years.

Hurrying into our warm coats, we stop to gather the sparklers we will light and set in the wet winter ground. Counting down the seconds at the top of our lungs, we erupt into cheers as the clock strikes midnight.

Michael holds me in his arms while Emma and Sam dance in the dark, illuminated by the jagged beauty of the sparklers' white light. Happy New Year.

recommended readings

The following books, organizations and websites have been helpful to me, and/or are referred to in *Walking after Midnight*.

BOOKS

Ban Breathnach, Sarah. 1995. *Simple Abundance: A Daybook of Comfort and Joy*. New York: Warner Books.

Cameron, Julia. 1992. *The Artist's Way: A Spiritual Path to Higher Creativity*. New York: G.P. Putnam's Sons.

Coloroso, Barbara. 2002. *The Bully, the Bullied, and the Bystander*. Toronto: HarperCollins Publishers Ltd.

Derksen, Wilma L. 2002. *Confronting the Horror: The Victim's Journey Through the 15 Elements of Serious Crime*. Winnipeg: Amity.

Frankl, Victor. 1985. *Man's Search for Meaning*. New York: Washington Square Press.

Gordon, Mary. 2005. *Roots of Empathy: Changing the World Child by Child*. Toronto: Thomas Allen Publishers.

Hanh,Thich Nhat. 1993. *For a Future to be Possible: Commentaries on the FiveWonderful Precepts*. Berkeley: Parallax Press.

Kavelin Popov, Linda. 2004. *A Pace of Grace: The Virtues of a Sustainable Life*. New York: Plume.

King, Stephen P. 2004. *Rapid Recovery: Accelerated Information Processing and Healing*. Victoria: Trafford Publishing.

Litwin, Val, Brad Stokes, Erik Hanson and Chris Bratseth. 2004. *Cool to be Kind: Random Acts and How to Commit Them*.Toronto: ECW Press.

Neufeld, Gordon and Gabor Maté. 2004. *Hold on to Your Kids: Why Parents Matter*. Toronto: Knopf Canada.

Pranis, Kaye, Barry Stuart and Mark Wedge. 2003. *Peacemaking Circles*. St. Paul: Living Justice Press.

Reeves, Nancy. 2001. A *Path through Loss: a Guide to Writing Your Healing and Growth*. Kelowna: Northstone.

Roberts, Julian V. and Michelle G. Grossman. 2004. *Criminal Justice in Canada*. Scarborough: Nelson.

Ryan Hyde, Catherine. 2000. *Pay it Forward*. New York: Simon and Schuster.

Zehr, Howard. 2001. *Transcending: Reflections of Crime Victims*. Intercourse: Good Books.

Zehr, Howard. 1990. *Changing Lenses: A New Focus for Crime and Justice*. Scottdale: Herald Press.

WEB SITES

Centre for Restorative Justice, Simon Fraser University:
 www.sfu.ca/crj

Childrens' International Summer Villages: **www.cisv.org**

Church Council on Justice and Corrections: **www.ccjc.ca**

Deep Humanity Institute: **www.deephumanity.org**

Extreme Kindness: **www.extremekindness.com**

Forgiveness Project: **www.theforgivenessproject.com**

Fraser Region Community Justice Initiatives Association:
 www.cjibc.org

Leave Out ViolencE (LOVE): **www.leaveoutviolence.com**

Lighten up for Results with Sally Glover:
 www.lightenup4results.com

Parent Action on Drugs: **www.parentactionondrugs.org**

Parents Together: **www.parentstogether.ca**

Rock Solid: **www.rocksolid.ca**

Search Institute – Asset Building Model:
 www.search-institute.org

Virtual Party: **www.virtual-party.org**

permissions

Bob with his parents, North Vancouver, 1962.

University of British Columbia Law School, class of 1986.

Dancing to "Walking After Midnight" at our wedding, 1988.
(David Nicholson)

Bob at our wedding with old friends from North Vancouver.
(David Nicholson)

Bob ski racing at Whistler, British Columbia, during the 1990s.

Bob at the Escape from Alcatraz Triathlon, San Francisco, 1993.

Our road trip to California, 1993.

Emma and Sam's first visit to Victoria, 1993.

Bob and the twins: story time at home in Squaminsh, 1994.

Bob and his Vancouver friends, 1996.

Bob and Emma at the Father and Daughter Dance, 1996.

Bob and Sam at Rathtrevor Beach, 1997.

Sam saying goodbye at Bob's funeral, 1998.
(Ward Perrin/*Vancouver Sun*)

Town's grim silence broken after four years

It was a tragedy that stunned a community and baffled police. A Squamish lawyer was beaten to death at a New Year's Eve house party in 1997. Now, a suspect has been charged with manslaughter
A3

Artist's sketch of accused Ryan Aldridge, 25, in Squamish court yesterday.
— BCTV News on Global

The media reacted quickly to Ryan Aldridge's arrest.
(© *The Province*)

'I was drunk. It was an angry moment'

Lawyer kicked 4 times in the head

By BRIAN MORTON

A man who admitted killing prominent Squamish lawyer Robert McIntosh five years ago kicked him four times in the head while McIntosh lay helpless on the ground, according to a videotaped confession played in North Vancouver provincial court on Thursday.

Ryan Aldridge, 25, who has pleaded guilty to manslaughter, also said in his confession that the incident haunted him for years and that he never intended to kill McIntosh, who died on Dec. 31, 1997.

"I was drunk," Aldridge told Vancouver RCMP major crimes unit Sergeant Kevin Hackett in a three-hour interview, which culminated in the confession with Aldridge's mother present. "Then I kicked him. I kicked him.

"It was an angry moment."

A second videotape was also played showing Aldridge breaking down and apologizing to McIntosh's widow, Katy Hutchinson, who was brought in by RCMP to talk to him.

"I'm so sorry," said Aldridge to Hutchinson, who at one point offered him a handkerchief and said that he would be all right. "I've had nightmare after nightmare."

The video showed Aldridge handing two letters to Hutchinson, one for her and one for her two children, Emma and Sam, who were five years old at the time of their father's death.

"You're so young and you have so much ahead of you," said Hutchison to Aldridge: "I needed you to know about us. There's so much you can do for yourself."

After the death, Hutchison and her two children moved to Victoria, where she remarried.

The five-year-old mystery of who killed McIntosh ended this year when Aldridge pleaded guilty after admitting to the crime.

Crown counsel Trevor Cockfield told Judge William Diebolt on Thursday that the confession followed an undercover RCMP operation in which Aldridge told an undercover officer that he had kicked McIntosh four times in the head.

A second man, facing a charge of assault causing bodily harm in the same case, is scheduled to appear in court today. Ryan Neil MacMillan, 25, has not yet entered a plea. Diebolt was also told that Josh

See **BLOW SEVERED** 36

Ryan Aldridge will be sentenced Monday for his role in the death of Squamish lawyer Bob McIntosh.

'I am so sorry,' killer tells widow

Five years after Squamish lawyer Bob McIntosh was kicked to death at a house party, the man who confessed to delivering the fatal blows to McIntosh's head is sentenced to five years in prison. And Ryan Aldridge apologizes to the victim's family, along with the whole community, for his crime **A3**

Wayne Leidenfrost — The Province
Ryan Aldridge arrives at court for his sentencing.

Katy and Michael's wedding day, 1998.
(Rob d'Estrube)

The Hutchison family, 1998.
(Rob d'Estrube)

Michael with Emma and Sam on their first day of school, 2000.

Leaving the sentencing hearing, December 2002.
(John Lehman/*The Globe and Mail*)

Katy and friends taking flowers to Alice Lake trail, 1998.

(Left): Emma and Sam on Bob's Trail in Alice Lake Provincial Park, 2002.
(Right): Sam firing the starting pistol at the Squamish Triathlon, 2004.

Sam and Olympian Simon Whitfield, 2000.

Emma and the Justice Quilt on Parliament Hill, Ottawa, 2005.

Best friends Katy and Shauna, 2004.

Katy at Rock Solid's Trackside Art Gallery, Victoria, 2005.
(Emma Hutchison)

Katy and friends at Leave Out ViolencE (LOVE) Camp,
Haliburton, Ontario, 2004.

Katy and Twinkle Rudberg at LOVE camp, 2004.

Telling "The Story of Bob," Huntsville, Ontario, 2004.
(Rachek Sa/*Huntsville Forester*)

Katy and Ryan Aldridge, 2005.
(Sylver McLaren)

(Left): Katy's family, Christmas, 2003.
(Right): Katy, Emma, and Sam on Galiano Island, 2005.

Katy and Michael with Carlie, Adam, Sam, Emma, and Michael's parents,
2004.